THE
DESIGN
OF EVERYDAY
THINGS

Donald A. Norman

CURRENCY DOUBLEDAY

New York London Toronto Sydney Auckland

PUBLISHED BY DOUBLEDAY
a division of Bantam Doubleday Dell
Publishing Group, Inc.
666 Fifth Avenue, New York, New York 10103

DOUBLEDAY/CURRENCY and the portrayal of an anchor
with a dolphin are trademarks of
Doubleday, a division of Bantam Doubleday Dell
Publishing Group, Inc.

This book was originally published in hardcover by Basic
Books in 1988. This Doubleday/Currency edition
reprinted by special arrangement with Basic Books Inc.,
Publishers, New York.

Library of Congress Cataloging-in-Publication Data
Norman, Donald A.
    [Psychology of everyday things]
    The design of everyday things / Donald A. Norman.
       p. cm.
    Reprint. Originally published: The psychology of everyday things.
    New York : Basic Books, c1988.
    Includes bibliographical references.
    1. Design, Industrial—Psychological aspects. 2. Human
    engineering. I. Title.
    [TS171.4.N67   1990]
    620.8'2—dc20   89-48989
                                                         CIP

ISBN 0-385-26774-6

CONTENTS

PREFACE TO THE
PAPERBACK EDITION

The Hidden Frustrations of Everyday Things

We are surrounded by large numbers of manufactured items, most intended to make our lives easier and more pleasant. In the office we have computers, copying machines, telephone systems, voice mail, and fax machines. In the home we have television sets, VCRs, automated kitchen appliances, answering machines, and home computers.

All these wonderful devices are supposed to help us save time and produce faster, superior results. But wait a minute—if these new devices are so wonderful, why do we need special dedicated staff members to make them work—"power users" or "key operators"? Why do we need manuals or special instructions to use the typical business telephone? Why do so many features go unused? And why do these devices add to the stresses of life rather than reduce them?

This book is intended to make you aware of the problems of design and interested in improving things. Many readers have told me that it has changed their lives, making them more sensitive to the problems of life and to the needs of people.

The examples in this book come mostly from Europe and the United States, but the same problems exist all over the world. Modern industry and manufacturing techniques have made high technology available to large numbers of nations and industries. Modern technology knows no national boundaries, and a company's services, design teams, and manufacturing plants may span the world.

Business and Industry

Business exists to serve people, a point that successful businesses understand and practice. But so too must the products of business be designed and manufactured to serve the needs and capabilities of the people who are its clients and customers.

Since the original publication of the book, I have found considerable interest in the business and industrial community. Companies have ordered copies for their staffs. I have been asked to speak at conferences, to business executives, and to research and development organizations in the United States, Europe, and Japan, along with innumerable radio talk shows. Hurrah! Not for me, but for the positive signs of increased concern for the customer-user.

The problems illustrated in this book result from a lack of concern and knowledge about how design affects the users of products. Moreover, in this day of increased legal liability for the way products are used, it is in everyone's best interest to make designs simple to use, simple to understand, yet still powerful enough for the job. Bad design cannot be patched up with labels, instruction manuals, or training courses.

Business and industry have learned that their products ought to be aesthetically pleasing. A large community of designers exists to help improve appearances. But appearances are only part of the story: usability and understandability are more important, for if a product can't be used easily and safely, how valuable is its attractiveness? Usable design and aesthetics should go hand in hand: aesthetics need not be sacrificed for usability, which can be designed in from the first conceptualization of the product.

Usable Design: The Next Competitive Frontier

Modern industry must distinguish itself through its consideration of the needs of its customers. This message has already been stated—and heard—in regard to interaction with the customer, service, and quality. Industry has learned that quality has to be designed into a product: insisting on proper design and manufacturing techniques from the very beginning is far more effective than attempts to discover and repair ill-made goods on the production line.

The same story applies to the usability and understandability of products. Human error is the leading cause of industrial accident and a major cost factor in the office. Humans do make mistakes, but with proper design, the incidence of error and its effects can be minimized. Warning labels and large instruction manuals are signs of failures, attempts to patch up problems that should have been avoided by proper design in the first place.

As companies design more for usability and understanding, they will discover a competitive edge, for these principles save customers time and money while increasing morale. As this message spreads, more and more customers will reject the products that are unusable or that lead to frequent error and frustration.

The Book Title: A Lesson in Design

In this book I urge designers to study people, to take their needs and interests into account. I also examine the failures of design and show why even the best-trained and best-motivated designers can go wrong when they listen to their instincts instead of testing their ideas on actual users. Designers know too much about their product to be objective judges: the features they have come to love and prefer may not be understood or preferred by the future customers.

The title of this book is a case history of design. A writer is also a designer, a designer of words rather than of things. I liked the original title, *The Psychology of Everyday Things*, both for the cleverness with which it suggested that inanimate objects had a psychology and for the clever acronym created by the first letters of the words: POET. Rule of thumb: if you think something is clever and sophisticated, beware—it is probably self-indulgence.

When Doubleday/Currency approached me about publishing the paperback version of this book, the editors also said, "But of course the title will have to be changed." Title changed? I was horrified. But I decided to follow my own advice and do some research on readers. I discovered that while the academic community liked the title and its cleverness, the business community did not. In fact, business often ignored the book because the title sent the wrong message. Bookstores placed the book in their psychology sections (along with books on sex, love, and self-help). The final nail in the title's coffin came when I was asked to talk to a group of senior executives of a leading manufacturing company. The person who introduced me to the audience praised the book, damned the title, and asked his colleagues to read the book *despite* the title.

Clearly the title had to be redone. Alas, the so-called "installed base problem" raised its head: the new title had to have some relation to the old. In Japan, things were easier, for the phrase "everyday things" is not easily translated, and "psychology" is not a popular subject: The Japanese title became *Design for Usability: The Psychology of Everyday Tools*. In English we had to keep compatibility with the original title. So here it is, the paperback edition, newly entitled *The Design of Everyday Things*.

—Donald A. Norman
Del Mar, California
September 1989

PREFACE

This is the book I have always wanted to write, but I didn't know it. Over the years I have fumbled my way through life, walking into doors, failing to figure out water faucets, incompetent at working the simple things of everyday life. "Just me," I would mumble. "Just my mechanical ineptitude." But as I studied psychology and watched the behavior of other people, I began to realize that I was not alone. My difficulties were mirrored by the problems of others. And we all seemed to blame ourselves. Could the whole world be mechanically incompetent?

The truth emerged slowly. My research activities led me to the study of human error and industrial accidents. Humans, I discovered, do not always behave clumsily. Humans do not always err. But they do when the things they use are badly conceived and designed. Nonetheless, we still see human error blamed for all that befalls society. Does a commercial airliner crash? "Pilot error," say the reports. Does a Soviet nuclear power plant have a serious problem? "Human error," says the newspaper. Do two ships at sea collide? "Human error" is the official cause. But careful analysis of these kinds of incidents usually gives the lie to such a story. At the famous American nuclear power plant disaster at Three Mile Island, the blame was placed on plant operators who misdiagnosed the problems. But was it human error? Consider the phrase "operators who misdiagnosed the problems." The phrase reveals that first there were problems—in fact, a series of mechanical failures. Then why wasn't equipment failure the real cause? What about the misdiagnoses? Why didn't the operators correctly determine the cause? Well, how about the fact that the proper instruments were not available, that the plant operators acted in ways that in the past had always been reasonable and proper? How about the pressure relief valve that failed to close, even though the operator pushed the proper button and even though a light came on stating it was closed? Why was the operator blamed for not checking two more instruments (one on the rear of the control panel) and determining that the light was faulty? (Actually, the operator did check one of them.) Human error? To me it sounds like equipment failure coupled with serious design error.

And, yes, what about my inability to use the simple things of everyday life? I can use complicated things. I am quite expert at computers, and electronics, and complex laboratory equipment. Why do I have trouble with doors, light switches, and water faucets? How come I can work a multimillion-dollar computer installation, but not my home refrigerator? While we all blame ourselves, the real culprit—faulty design—goes undetected. And millions of people feel themselves to be mechanically inept. It is time for a change.

Hence this book: POET, *The Psychology of Everyday Things.* POET is an outgrowth of my repeated frustrations with the operation of everyday things and my growing knowledge of how to apply experimental psychology and cognitive science. The combination of experience and knowledge has made POET necessary, at least for me and for my own feeling of ease.

So here it is: part polemic, part science. Part serious, part fun: POET.

Acknowledgments

POET was conceived and the first few drafts written while I was in Cambridge, England, on a sabbatical leave from the University of California, San Diego. In Cambridge, I worked at the Applied Psychology Unit (the APU), a laboratory of the British Medical Research Council.

Special thanks are due to the people at the APU for their hospitality. They are a special group of people, with special expertise in applied and theoretical psychology, especially in the topics of this book. World-famous experts in the design of instruction manuals, warning signals, computer systems, working in an environment filled with design flaws—doors that are difficult to open (or that bash the hands when they do), signs that are illegible (and nonintelligible), stovetops that confuse, light switches that defy even the original installer to figure them out. A striking example of all that is wrong with design, lodged in the home of the most knowledgeable of users. A perfect combination to set me off. Of course, my own university and my own laboratory have horrors of their own, as will become all too apparent later in this book.

A major argument in POET is that much of our everyday knowledge resides in the world, not in the head. This is an interesting argument and, for cognitive psychologists, a difficult one. What could it possibly mean for knowledge to be in the world? Knowledge is interpreted, the stuff that can be only in minds. Information, yes, that could be in the world, but knowledge, never. Well, yeah, the distinction between knowledge and information is not clear. If we are sloppy with terms, then perhaps you can see the issues better. People certainly do rely upon the placement and location of objects, upon written texts, upon the information contained within other people, upon the artifacts of society, and upon the information transmitted within and by a culture. There certainly is a lot of information out there in the world, not in the head. My understanding of this point has been strengthened by years of debate and interaction with a very powerful team of people at La Jolla, the Cognitive Social Science Group at the University of California, San Diego. This was a small group of faculty from the departments of psychology, anthropology, and sociology, organized by Mike Cole, who met informally once a week for several years. The primary members were Roy d'Andrade, Aaron Cicourel, Mike Cole, Bud Mehan, George Mandler, Jean Mandler, Dave Rumelhart, and me. Given the peculiar (although typically academic) nature of this group's interaction, they may not wish to acknowledge anything to do with the ideas as they are presented in POET.

And, finally, at the Applied Psychology Unit in England, I met another visiting American professor, David Rubin of Duke University, who was analyzing the recall of epic poetry—those long, huge feats of prodigious memory in which an itinerant poet sings from memory hours of material. Rubin showed me that it wasn't all in memory: much of the information was in the world, or at least in the structure of the tale, the poetics, and the life styles of the people.

My previous research project was on the difficulties of using computers and the methods that might be used to make things easier. But the more I looked at computers (and other demons of our society, such as aircraft systems and nuclear power), the more I realized that there was nothing special about them: they had the same problems as did the simpler, everyday things. And the everyday things were more pervasive, more of a problem. Especially as people feel guilt when they are unable to use simple things, guilt that should be not theirs but rather the designers and manufacturers of the objects.

So it all came together. These ideas, the respite of the sabbatical. My experiences over the years fighting the difficulties of poor design, of equipment that could not be used, of everyday things that seemed foreign to human functioning. The fact that I was asked to give a talk on my work at the APU, which caused me to start writing down my ideas. And finally, Roger Schank's Paris birthday party, where I discovered the works of the artist Carelman and decided it was time to write the book.

Formal Research Support

The actual writing was done at three locations. The work began while I was on sabbatical leave from San Diego. I spent the first half of my sabbatical year at the Applied Psychology Unit in Cambridge, England, and the last half at MCC (the Microelectronics and Computer Technology Corporation) in Austin, Texas. MCC is America's research consortium dedicated to the task of developing computer systems of the future. Officially I was "visiting scientist"; unofficially I was a sort of "minister without portfolio," free to wander and interact with the numerous research programs under way, especially those in the area called "human interface." England is chilly in the winter, Texas hot in the summer. But both provided exactly the proper friendly, supportive environments that I required to do the work. Finally, when I returned to UCSD, I revised the book several more times. I used it in classes and sent copies to a variety of colleagues for suggestions. The comments of my students and readers were invaluable, causing radical revision from the original structure.

The research was partially supported by contract N00014-85-C-0133 NR 667-547 with the Personnel and Training Research Program of the Office of Naval Research and by a grant from the System Development Foundation.

People

There is a big difference between early drafts of POET and the final version. Many of my colleagues took the time to read various drafts and give me critical reviews. In particular, I wish to thank Judy Greissman of Basic Books for her patient critique through several revisions. My hosts at the APU in Britain were most gracious, especially Alan Baddeley, Phil Barnard, Thomas Green, Phil Johnson-Laird, Tony Marcel, Karalyn and Roy Patterson, Tim Shallice, and Richard Young. The scientific staff at MCC gave useful suggestions, especially Peter Cook, Jonathan Grudin, and Dave Wroblewski. At UCSD, I especially wish to thank the students in Psychology 135 and 205: my undergraduate and graduate courses at UCSD entitled "Cognitive Engineering."

My colleagues in the design community were most helpful with their comments: Mike King, Mihai Nadin, Dan Rosenberg, and Bill Verplank. Special thanks must be given to Phil Agre, Sherman DeForest, and Jef Raskin, all of whom read the manuscript with care and provided numerous and valuable suggestions.

Collecting the illustrations became part of the fun as I traveled the world with camera in hand. Eileen Conway and Michael Norman helped collect and organize the figures and illustrations. Julie Norman helped as she does on all my books, proofing, editing, commenting, and encouraging. Eric Norman provided valuable advice, support, and photogenic feet and hands.

Finally, my colleagues at the Institute for Cognitive Science at the University of California, San Diego, helped throughout—in part through the wizardry of international computer mail, in part through their personal assistance to the details of the process. I single out Bill Gaver, Mike Mozer, and Dave Owen for their detailed comments, but many helped out at one time or another during the research that preceded the book and the several years of writing.

CHAPTER ONE

THE PSYCHOPATHOLOGY OF EVERYDAY THINGS

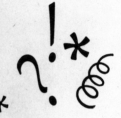

"Kenneth Olsen, the engineer who founded and still runs Digital Equipment Corp., confessed at the annual meeting that he can't figure out how to heat a cup of coffee in the company's microwave oven."[1]

You Would Need an Engineering Degree to Figure This Out

"You would need an engineering degree from MIT to work this," someone once told me, shaking his head in puzzlement over his brand new digital watch. Well, I have an engineering degree from MIT. (Kenneth Olsen has two of them, and he can't figure out a microwave oven.) Give me a few hours and I can figure out the watch. But why should it take hours? I have talked with many people who can't use all the features of their washing machines or cameras, who can't figure out how to work a sewing machine or a video cassette recorder, who habitually turn on the wrong stove burner.

Why do we put up with the frustrations of everyday objects, with objects that we can't figure out how to use, with those neat plastic-wrapped packages that seem impossible to open, with doors that trap people, with washing machines and dryers that have become too con-

1.1 Carelman's Coffeepot for Masochists. The French artist Jacques Carelman in his series of books *Catalogue d'objets introuvables (Catalog of unfindable objects)* provides delightful examples of everyday things that are deliberately unworkable, outrageous, or otherwise ill-formed. Jacques Carelman: "Coffeepot for Masochists." Copyright © 1969–76–80 by Jacques Carelman and A. D. A. G. P. Paris. From Jacques Carelman, *Catalog of Unfindable Objects,* Balland, éditeur, Paris-France. Used by permission of the artist.

fusing to use, with audio-stereo-television-video-cassette-recorders that claim in their advertisements to do everything, but that make it almost impossible to do anything?

The human mind is exquisitely tailored to make sense of the world. Give it the slightest clue and off it goes, providing explanation, rationalization, understanding. Consider the objects—books, radios, kitchen appliances, office machines, and light switches—that make up our everyday lives. Well-designed objects are easy to interpret and understand. They contain visible clues to their operation. Poorly designed objects can be difficult and frustrating to use. They provide no clues— or sometimes false clues. They trap the user and thwart the normal process of interpretation and understanding. Alas, poor design predominates. The result is a world filled with frustration, with objects that cannot be understood, with devices that lead to error. This book is an attempt to change things.

The Frustrations of Everyday Life

If I were placed in the cockpit of a modern jet airliner, my inability to perform gracefully and smoothly would neither surprise nor bother me. But I shouldn't have trouble with doors and switches, water faucets and stoves. "Doors?" I can hear the reader saying, "you have trouble opening doors?" Yes. I push doors that are meant to be pulled, pull doors that should be pushed, and walk into doors that should be slid. Moreover, I see others having the same troubles—unnecessary troubles. There are psychological principles that can be followed to make these things understandable and usable.

Consider the door. There is not much you can do to a door: you can open it or shut it. Suppose you are in an office building, walking down a corridor. You come to a door. In which direction does it open? Should you pull or push, on the left or the right? Maybe the door slides. If so, in which direction? I have seen doors that slide up into the ceiling. A door poses only two essential questions: In which direction does it move? On which side should one work it? The answers should be given by the design, without any need for words or symbols, certainly without any need for trial and error.

A friend told me of the time he got trapped in the doorway of a post office in a European city. The entrance was an imposing row of perhaps six glass swinging doors, followed immediately by a second, identical row. That's a standard design: it helps reduce the airflow and thus maintain the indoor temperature of the building.

My friend pushed on the side of one of the leftmost pair of outer doors. It swung inward, and he entered the building. Then, before he could get to the next row of doors, he was distracted and turned around for an instant. He didn't realize it at the time, but he had moved slightly to the right. So when he came to the next door and pushed it, nothing happened. "Hmm," he thought, "must be locked." So he pushed the side of the adjacent door. Nothing. Puzzled, my friend decided to go outside again. He turned around and pushed against the side of a door. Nothing. He pushed the adjacent door. Nothing. The door he had just entered no longer worked. He turned around once more and tried the inside doors again. Nothing. Concern, then mild panic. He was trapped! Just then, a group of people on the other side of the entranceway (to my friend's right) passed easily through both sets of doors. My friend hurried over to follow their path.

How could such a thing happen? A swinging door has two sides. One contains the supporting pillar and the hinge, the other is unsupported. To open the door, you must push on the unsupported edge. If you push on the hinge side, nothing happens. In this case, the designer aimed for beauty, not utility. No distracting lines, no visible pillars, no visible hinges. So how can the ordinary user know which side to push

1.2 A Row of Swinging Glass Doors in a Boston Hotel. A similar problem to the doors from that European post office. On which side of the door should you push? When I asked people who had just used the doors, most couldn't say. Yet only a few of the people I watched had trouble with the doors. The designers had incorporated a subtle clue into the design. Note that the horizontal bars are not centered: they are a bit closer together on the sides you should push on. The design almost works—but not entirely, for not everyone used the doors right on the first try.

on? While distracted, my friend had moved toward the (invisible) supporting pillar, so he was pushing the doors on the hinged side. No wonder nothing happened. Pretty doors. Elegant. Probably won a design prize.

The door story illustrates one of the most important principles of design: *visibility.* The correct parts must be visible, and they must convey the correct message. With doors that push, the designer must provide signals that naturally indicate where to push. These need not destroy the aesthetics. Put a vertical plate on the side to be pushed, nothing on the other. Or make the supporting pillars visible. The vertical plate and supporting pillars are *natural* signals, *naturally* interpreted, without any need to be conscious of them. I call the use of natural signals *natural design* and elaborate on the approach throughout this book.

Visibility problems come in many forms. My friend, trapped between the glass doors, suffered from a lack of clues that would indicate what part of a door should be operated. Other problems concern the *mappings* between what you want to do and what appears to be possible, another topic that will be expanded upon throughout the book. Consider one type of slide projector. This projector has a single button to control whether the slide tray moves forward or backward. One button to do two things? What is the mapping? How can you figure out how to control the slides? You can't. Nothing is visible to give the slightest hint. Here is what happened to me in one of the many unfamiliar places I've lectured in during my travels as a professor:

The Leitz slide projector illustrated in figure 1.3 has shown up several times in my travels. The first time, it led to a rather dramatic incident. A conscientious student was in charge of showing my slides. I started my talk and showed the first slide. When I finished with the first slide and asked for the next, the student carefully pushed the control button and watched in dismay as the tray backed up, slid out of the projector and plopped off the table onto the floor, spilling its entire contents. We had to delay the lecture fifteen minutes while I struggled to reorganize the slides. It wasn't the student's fault. It was the fault of the elegant projector. With only one button to control the slide advance, how could one switch from forward to reverse? Neither of us could figure out how to make the control work.

All during the lecture the slides would sometimes go forward, sometimes backward. Afterward, we found the local technician, who explained it to us. A brief push of the button and the slide would go

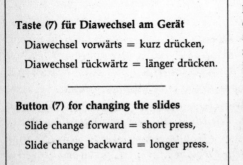

Taste (7) für Diawechsel am Gerät

Diawechsel vorwärts = kurz drücken,

Diawechsel rückwärtz = länger drücken.

———————————

Button (7) for changing the slides

Slide change forward = short press,

Slide change backward = longer press.

1.3 Leitz Pravodit Slide Projector. I finally tracked down the instruction manual for that projector. A photograph of the projector has its parts numbered. The button for changing slides is number 7. The button itself has no labels. Who could discover this operation without the aid of the manual? Here is the entire text related to the button, in the original German and in my English translation:

forward, a long push and it would reverse. (Pity the conscientious student who kept pushing it hard—and long—to make sure that the switch was making contact.) What an elegant design. Why, it managed to do two functions with only one button! But how was a first-time user of the projector to know this?

As another example, consider the beautiful Amphithéâtre Louis-Laird in the Paris Sorbonne, which is filled with magnificent paintings of great figures in French intellectual history. (The mural on the ceiling shows lots of naked women floating about a man who is valiantly trying to read a book. The painting is right side up only for the lecturer—it is upside down for all the people in the audience.) The room is a delight to lecture in, at least until you ask for the projection screen to be lowered. "Ah," says the professor in charge, who gestures to the technician, who runs out of the room, up a short flight of stairs, and out of sight behind a solid wall. The screen comes down and stops. "No, no," shouts the professor, "a little bit more." The screen comes down again, this time too much. "No, no, no!" the professor jumps up and down and gestures wildly. It's a lovely room, with lovely paintings. But why can't the person who is trying to lower or raise the screen see what he is doing?

New telephone systems have proven to be another excellent example of incomprehensible design. No matter where I travel, I can count upon finding a particularly bad example.

When I visited Basic Books, the publishers of this book, I noticed a new telephone system. I asked people how they liked it. The question unleashed a torrent of abuse. "It doesn't have a hold function," one woman complained bitterly—the same complaint people at my university made about their rather different system. In older days, business phones always had a button labeled "hold." You could push the button and hang up the phone without losing the call on your line. Then you could talk to a colleague, or pick up another telephone call, or even pick up the call at another phone with the same telephone number. A light on the hold button indicated when the function was in use. It was an invaluable tool for business. Why didn't the new phones at Basic Books or in my university have a hold function, if it is so essential? Well, they did, even the very instrument the woman was complaining about. But there was no easy way to discover the fact, nor to learn how to use it.

I was visiting the University of Michigan and I asked about the new

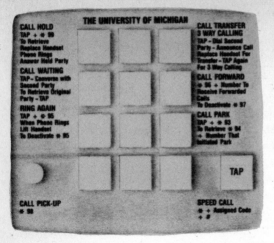

THE UNIVERSITY OF MICHIGAN

CALL HOLD
TAP + *98
To Retrieve
Replace Handset
Phone Rings
Answer Hold Party

CALL WAITING
TAP – Converse with
Second Party
To Retrieve Original
Party – TAP

RING AGAIN
TAP + *95
When Phone Rings
Lift Handset
To Deactivate # *95

CALL PICK-UP
#*98

CALL TRANSFER
3 WAY CALLING
TAP – Dial Second
Party – Announce Call
Replace Handset For
Transfer – TAP Again
For 3 Way Calling

CALL FORWARD
+ *96 + Number To
Receive Forwarded
Calls
To Deactivate # *97

CALL PARK
TAP + *93
To Retrieve + *94
+ Number That
Initiated Park

TAP

SPEED CALL
* + Assigned Code
* #

1.4 **Plate Mounted Over the Dial of the Telephones at the University of Michigan.** These inadequate instructions are all that most users see. (The button labeled "TAP" at the lower right is used to transfer or pick up calls—it is pressed whenever the instruction plate says "TAP." The light on the lower left comes on whenever the telephone rings.)

system there. "Yech!" was the response, "and it doesn't even have a hold function!" Here we go again. What is going on? The answer is simple: first, look at the instructions for hold. At the University of Michigan the phone company provided a little plate that fits over the keypad and reminds users of the functions and how to use them. I carefully unhooked one of the plates from the telephone and made a photocopy (figure 1.4). Can you understand how to use it? I can't. There is a "call hold" operation, but it doesn't make sense to me, not for the application that I just described.

The telephone hold situation illustrates a number of different problems. One of them is simply poor instructions, especially a failure to relate the new functions to the similarly named functions that people already know about. Second, and more serious, is the lack of visibility of the operation of the system. The new telephones, for all their added sophistication, lack both the hold button and the flashing light of the old ones. The hold is signified by an arbitrary action: dialing an arbitrary sequence of digits (*8, or *99, or what have you: it varies from one phone system to another). Third, there is no visible outcome of the operation.

Devices in the home have developed some related problems: functions and more functions, controls and more controls. I do not think that simple home appliances—stoves, washing machines, audio and television sets—should look like Hollywood's idea of a spaceship control room. They already do, much to the consternation of the consumer who, often as not, has lost (or cannot understand) the instruction manual, so—faced with the bewildering array of controls and displays—simply memorizes one or two fixed settings to approximate what is desired. The whole purpose of the design is lost.

In England I visited a home with a fancy new Italian washer-drier combination, with super-duper multi-symbol controls, all to do everything you ever wanted to do with the washing and drying of clothes. The husband (an engineering psychologist) said he refused to go near it. The wife (a physician) said she had simply memorized one setting and tried to ignore the rest.

Someone went to a lot of trouble to create that design. I read the instruction manual. That machine took into account everything about today's wide variety of synthetic and natural fabrics. The designers worked hard; they really cared. But obviously they had never thought of trying it out, or of watching anyone use it.

If the design was so bad, if the controls were so unusable, why did the couple purchase it? If people keep buying poorly designed products, manufacturers and designers will think they are doing the right thing and continue as usual.

The user needs help. Just the right things have to be visible: to indicate what parts operate and how, to indicate how the user is to interact with the device. Visibility indicates the mapping between intended actions and actual operations. Visibility indicates crucial distinctions—so that you can tell salt and pepper shakers apart, for example. And visibility of the effects of the operations tells you if the lights have turned on properly, if the projection screen has lowered to the correct height, or if the refrigerator temperature is adjusted correctly. It is lack of visibility that makes so many computer-controlled devices so difficult to operate. And it is an excess of visibility that makes the gadget-ridden, feature-laden modern audio set or video cassette recorder (VCR) so intimidating.

The Psychology of Everyday Things

This book is about the psychology of everyday things. POET emphasizes the understanding of everyday things, things with knobs and dials, controls and switches, lights and meters. The instances we have just examined demonstrate several principles, including the importance of visibility, appropriate clues, and feedback of one's actions. These principles constitute a form of psychology—the psychology of how people interact with things. A British designer once noted that the kinds of materials used in the construction of passenger shelters affected the way vandals responded. He suggested that there might be a psychology of materials.

AFFORDANCES

"In one case, the reinforced glass used to panel shelters (for railroad passengers) erected by British Rail was smashed by vandals as fast as it was renewed. When the reinforced glass was replaced by plywood boarding, however, little further damage occurred, although no extra force would have been required to produce it. Thus British Rail managed to elevate the desire for defacement to those who could write, albeit in somewhat limited terms. Nobody has, as yet, considered whether there is a kind of psychology of materials. But on the evidence, there could well be!"[2]

There already exists the start of a psychology of materials and of things, the study of affordances of objects. When used in this sense, the term *affordance* refers to the perceived and actual properties of the thing, primarily those fundamental properties that determine just how the thing could possibly be used (see figures 1.5 and 1.6). A chair affords ("is for") support and, therefore, affords sitting. A chair can also be carried. Glass is for seeing through, and for breaking. Wood is normally used for solidity, opacity, support, or carving. Flat, porous, smooth surfaces are for writing on. So wood is also for writing on. Hence the problem for British Rail: when the shelters had glass, vandals smashed it; when they had plywood, vandals wrote on and carved it. The planners were trapped by the affordances of their materials.[3]

Affordances provide strong clues to the operations of things. Plates are for pushing. Knobs are for turning. Slots are for inserting things into. Balls are for throwing or bouncing. When affordances are taken advantage of, the user knows what to do just by looking: no picture, label, or instruction is required. Complex things may require explanation, but simple things should not. When simple things need pictures, labels, or instructions, the design has failed.

A psychology of causality is also at work as we use everyday things.

1.5 Affordances of Doors. Door hardware can signal whether to push or pull without signs. The flat horizontal bar of *A* (above left) affords no operations except pushing: it is excellent hardware for a door that must be pushed to be opened. The door in *B* (above right) has a different kind of bar on each side, one relatively small and vertical to signify a pull, the other relatively large and horizontal to signify a push. Both bars support the affordance of grasping: size and position specify whether the grasp is used to push or pull—though ambiguously.

1.6 When Affordances Fail. I had to tie a string around my cabinet door to afford pulling.

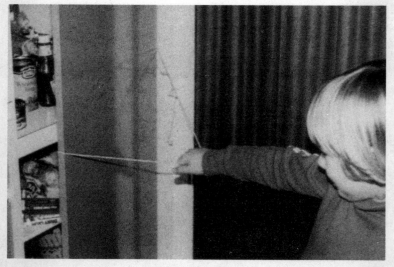

Something that happens right after an action appears to be caused by that action. Touch a computer terminal just when it fails, and you are apt to believe that you caused the failure, even though the failure and your action were related only by coincidence. Such false causality is the basis for much superstition. Many of the peculiar behaviors of people using computer systems or complex household appliances result from such false coincidences. When an action has no apparent result, you may conclude that the action was ineffective. So you repeat it. In earlier days, when computer word processors did not always show the results of their operations, people would sometimes attempt to change their manuscript, but the lack of visible effect from each action would make them think that their commands had not been executed, so they would repeat the commands, sometimes over and over, to their later astonishment and regret. It is a poor design that allows either kind of false causality to occur.

TWENTY THOUSAND EVERYDAY THINGS

There are an amazing number of everyday things, perhaps twenty thousand of them. Are there really that many? Start by looking about you. There are light fixtures, bulbs, and sockets; wall plates and screws; clocks, watches, and watchbands. There are writing devices (I count twelve in front of me, each different in function, color, or style). There are clothes, with different functions, openings, and flaps. Notice the variety of materials and pieces. Notice the variety of fasteners—buttons, zippers, snaps, laces. Look at all the furniture and food utensils: all those details, each serving some function for manufacturability, usage, or appearance. Consider the work area: paper clips, scissors, pads of paper, magazines, books, bookmarks. In the room I'm working in, I counted more than a hundred specialized objects before I tired. Each is simple, but each requires its own method of operation, each has to be learned, each does its own specialized task, and each has to be designed separately. Furthermore, many of the objects are made of many parts. A desk stapler has sixteen parts, a household iron fifteen, the simple bathtub-shower combination twenty-three. You can't believe these simple objects have so many parts? Here are the eleven basic parts to a sink: drain, flange (around the drain), pop-up stopper, basin, soap dish, overflow vent, spout, lift rod, fittings, hot-water handle, and cold-water handle. We can count even more if we start taking the faucets, fittings, and lift rods apart.

The book *What's What: A Visual Glossary of the Physical World* has more than fifteen hundred drawings and pictures and illustrates twenty-three thousand items or parts of items.[4] Irving Biederman, a psychologist who studies visual perception, estimates that there are probably "30,000 readily discriminable objects for the adult."[5] Whatever the exact number, it is clear that the difficulties of everyday life are amplified by the sheer profusion of items. Suppose that each everyday thing takes only one minute to learn; learning 20,000 of them occupies 20,000 minutes—333 hours or about 8 forty-hour work weeks. Furthermore, we often encounter new objects unexpectedly, when we are really concerned with something else. We are confused and distracted, and what ought to be a simple, effortless, everyday thing interferes with the important task of the moment.

How do people cope? Part of the answer lies in the way the mind works—in the psychology of human thought and cognition. Part lies in the information available from the appearance of the objects—the psychology of everyday things. And part comes from the ability of the designer to make the operation clear, to project a good image of the operation, and to take advantage of other things people might be expected to know. Here is where the designer's knowledge of the psychology of people coupled with knowledge of how things work becomes crucial.

CONCEPTUAL MODELS

Consider the rather strange bicycle illustrated in figure 1.7. You know it won't work because you form a *conceptual model* of the device and mentally simulate its operation. You can do the simulation because the parts are visible and the implications clear.

Other clues to how things work come from their visible structure—in particular from *affordances, constraints,* and *mappings.* Consider a pair of scissors: even if you have never seen or used them before, you can see that the number of possible actions is limited. The holes are clearly there to put something into, and the only logical things that will fit are fingers. The holes are affordances: they allow the the fingers to be inserted. The sizes of the holes provide *constraints* to limit the possible fingers: the big hole suggests several fingers, the small hole only one. The mapping between holes and fingers—the set of possible operations—is suggested and constrained by the holes. Moreover, the operation is not sensitive to finger placement: if you use the wrong fingers,

1.7 Carelman's Tandem "Convergent Bicycle (Model for Fiancés)." Jacques Carelman: "Convergent Bicycle" Copyright © 1969–76–80 by Jacques Carelman and A. D. A. G. P. Paris. From Jacques Carelman, *Catalog of Unfindable Objects,* Balland, éditeur, Paris-France. Used by permission of the artist.

the scissors still work. You can figure out the scissors because their operating parts are visible and the implications clear. The conceptual model is made obvious, and there is effective use of affordances and constraints.

As a counterexample, consider the digital watch, one with two to four push buttons on the front or side. What are those push buttons for? How would you set the time? There is no way to tell—no evident relationship between the operating controls and the functions, no constraints, no apparent mappings. With the scissors, moving the handle makes the blades move. The watch and the Leitz slide projector provide no visible relationship between the buttons and the possible actions, no discernible relationship between the actions and the end result.

Principles of Design for Understandability and Usability

We have now encountered the fundamental principles of designing for people: (1) provide a good conceptual model and (2) make things visible.

PROVIDE A GOOD CONCEPTUAL MODEL

A good conceptual model allows us to predict the effects of our actions. Without a good model we operate by rote, blindly; we do operations as we were told to do them; we can't fully appreciate why, what effects to expect, or what to do if things go wrong. As long as things work properly, we can manage. When things go wrong, however, or when we come upon a novel situation, then we need a deeper understanding, a good model.

For everyday things, conceptual models need not be very complex. After all, scissors, pens, and light switches are pretty simple devices. There is no need to understand the underlying physics or chemistry of each device we own, simply the relationship between the controls and the outcomes. When the model presented to us is inadequate or wrong (or, worse, nonexistent), we can have difficulties. Let me tell you about my refrigerator.

My house has an ordinary, two-compartment refrigerator—nothing very fancy about it. The problem is that I can't set the temperature properly. There are only two things to do: adjust the temperature of the freezer compartment and adjust the temperature of the fresh food compartment. And there are two controls, one labeled "freezer," the other "fresh food." What's the problem?

You try it. Figure 1.8 shows the instruction plate from inside the refrigerator. Now, suppose the freezer is too cold, the fresh food section just right. You want to make the freezer warmer, keeping the fresh food constant. Go on, read the instructions, figure them out.

1.8 My Refrigerator. Two compartments—fresh food and freezer—and two controls (in the fresh food unit). The illustration shows the controls and instructions. Your task: Suppose the freezer is too cold, the fresh food section just right. How would you adjust the controls so as to make the freezer warmer and keep the fresh food the same? (From Norman, 1986.)

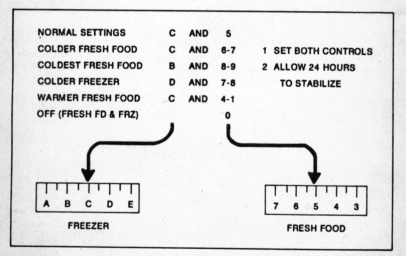

NORMAL SETTINGS	C	AND	5	
COLDER FRESH FOOD	C	AND	6-7	1 SET BOTH CONTROLS
COLDEST FRESH FOOD	B	AND	8-9	2 ALLOW 24 HOURS
COLDER FREEZER	D	AND	7-8	TO STABILIZE
WARMER FRESH FOOD	C	AND	4-1	
OFF (FRESH FD & FRZ)			0	

A B C D E
FREEZER

7 6 5 4 3
FRESH FOOD

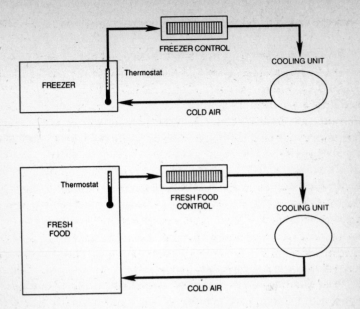

1.9 Two Conceptual Models for My Refrigerator. The model *A* (above) is provided by the system image of the refrigerator as gleaned from the controls and instructions; *B* (below) is the correct conceptual model. The problem is that it is impossible to tell in which compartment the thermostat is located and whether the two controls are in the freezer and fresh food compartment, or vice versa.

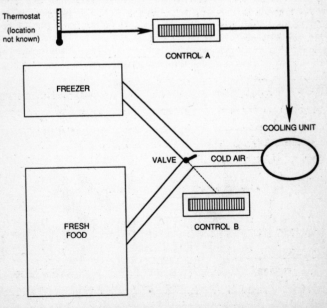

Oh, perhaps I'd better warn you. The two controls are not independent. The freezer control affects the fresh food temperature, and the fresh food control affects the freezer. And don't forget to wait twenty-four hours to check on whether you made the right adjustment, if you can remember what you did.

Control of the refrigerator is made difficult because the manufacturer provides a false conceptual model. There are two compartments and two controls. The setup clearly and unambiguously provides a simple model for the user: each control is responsible for the temperature of the compartment that carries its name. Wrong. In fact, there is only one thermostat and only one cooling mechanism. One control adjusts the thermostat setting, the other the relative proportion of cold air sent to each of the two compartments of the refrigerator. This is why the two controls interact. With the conceptual model provided by the manufacturer, adjusting the temperatures is almost impossible and always frustrating. Given the correct model, life would be much easier (figure 1.9).

Why did the manufacturer present the wrong conceptual model?

1.10 **Conceptual Models.** The *design model* is the designer's conceptual model. The *user's model* is the mental model developed through interaction with the system. The *system image* results from the physical structure that has been built (including documentation, instructions, and labels). The designer expects the user's model to be identical to the design model. But the designer doesn't talk directly with the user—all communication takes place through the system image. If the system image does not make the design model clear and consistent, then the user will end up with the wrong mental model. (From Norman, 1986.)

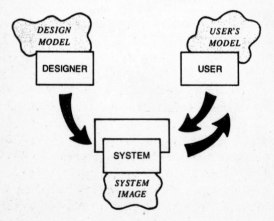

Perhaps the designers thought the correct model was too complex, that the model they were giving was easier to understand. But with the wrong conceptual model, it is impossible to set the controls. And even though I am convinced I now know the correct model, I still cannot accurately adjust the temperatures because the refrigerator design makes it impossible for me to discover which control is for the thermostat, which control is for the relative proportion of cold air, and in which compartment the thermostat is located. The lack of immediate feedback for the actions does not help: with a delay of twenty-four hours, who can remember what was tried?

The topic of conceptual models will reappear in the book. They are part of an important concept in design: *mental models,* the models people have of themselves, others, the environment, and the things with which they interact. People form mental models through experience, training, and instruction. The mental model of a device is formed largely by interpreting its perceived actions and its visible structure. I call the visible part of the device the *system image* (figure 1.10). When the system image is incoherent or inappropriate, as in the case of the refrigerator, then the user cannot easily use the device. If it is incomplete or contradictory, there will be trouble.

MAKE THINGS VISIBLE

The problems caused by inadequate attention to visibility are all neatly demonstrated with one simple appliance: the modern telephone.

I stand at the blackboard in my office, talking with a student, when my telephone rings. Once, twice it rings. I pause, trying to complete my sentence before answering. The ringing stops. "I'm sorry," says the student. "Not your fault," I say. "But it's no problem, the call now transfers to my secretary's phone. She'll answer it." As we listen we hear her phone start to ring. Once, twice. I look at my watch. Six o'clock: it's late, the office staff has left for the day. I rush out of my office to my secretary's phone, but as I get there, it stops ringing. "Ah," I think, "it's being transferred to another phone." Sure enough, the phone in the adjacent office now starts ringing. I rush to that office, but it is locked. Back to my office to get the key, out to the locked door, fumble with the lock, into the office, and to the now quiet phone. I hear a telephone down the hall start to ring. Could that still be my call, making its way mysteriously, with a predetermined lurching path, through the phones of the building? Or is it just another telephone call coincidentally arriving at this time?

In fact, I could have retrieved the call from my office, had I acted quickly enough. The manual states: "Within your pre-programmed pick-up group, dial 14 to connect to incoming call. Otherwise, to answer any ringing extension, dial ringing extension number, listen for busy tone. Dial 8 to connect to incoming call." Huh? What do those instructions mean? What is a "pre-programmed pick-up group," and why do I even want to know? What is the extension number of the ringing phone? Can I remember all those instructions when I need them? No.

Telephone chase is the new game in the modern office, as the automatic features of telephones go awry—features designed without proper thought, and certainly without testing them with their intended users. There are several other games, too. One game is announced by the plea, "How do I answer this call?" The question is properly whined in front of a ringing, flashing telephone, receiver in hand. Then there is the paradoxical game entitled "This telephone doesn't have a hold function." The accusation is directed at a telephone that actually *does* have a hold function. And, finally, there is "What do you mean I called you, you called me!"

Many of the modern telephone systems have a new feature that automatically keeps trying to dial a number for you. This feature resides under names such as automatic redialing or automatic callback. I am supposed to use this feature whenever I call someone who doesn't answer or whose line is busy. When the person next hangs up the phone, my phone will dial it again. Several automatic callbacks can be active at a time. Here's how it works. I place a phone call. There's no answer, so I activate the automatic callback feature. Several hours later my telephone rings. I pick it up and say "Hello," only to hear a ringing sound and then someone else saying "Hello."

"Hello," I answer, "who is this?"

"Who is this?" I hear in reply, "you called me."

"No," I say, "you called me, my phone just rang."

Slowly I realize that perhaps this is my delayed call. Now, let me see, who was I trying to call several hours ago? Did I have several callbacks in place? Why was I making the call?

The modern telephone did not happen by accident: it was carefully designed. Someone—more likely a team of people—invented a list of features thought desirable, invented what seemed to them to be plausible ways of controlling the features, and then put it all together. My university, focusing on cost and perhaps dazzled by the features, bought the system, spending millions of dollars on a telephone installation that has proved vastly unpopular and even unworkable. Why did the university buy the system? The purchase took several years of committee work and studies and presentations by competing telephone companies, and piles of documentation and specification. I myself took part, looking at the interaction between the telephone system and the computer networks, ensuring that the two would be compatible and reasonable in price. To my knowledge, nobody ever thought of trying out the telephones in advance. Nobody suggested installing them in a sample office to see whether users' needs would be met or whether users could understand how to operate the phone. The result: disaster. The main culprit—lack of visibility—was coupled with a secondary culprit—a poor conceptual model. Any money saved on the installation and purchase is quickly disappearing in training costs, missed calls, and frustration. Yet from what I have seen, the competing phone systems would not have been any better.

I recently spent six months at the Applied Psychology Unit in Cambridge, England. Just before I arrived the British Telecom Company had installed a new telephone system. It had lots and lots of features. The telephone instrument itself was unremarkable (figure 1.11). It was the standard twelve-button, push-button phone, except that it had an extra key labeled "R" off on the side. (I never did find out what that key did.)

The telephone system was a standing joke. Nobody could use all the features. One person even started a small research project to record people's confusions. Another person wrote a small "expert systems" computer program, one of the new toys of the field of artificial intelligence; the program can reason through complex situations. If you wanted to use the phone system, perhaps to make a conference call among three people, you asked the expert system and it would explain how to do it. So, you're on the line with someone and you need to add a third person to the call. First turn on your computer. Then load the expert system. After three or four minutes (needed for loading the program), type in what you want to accomplish. Eventually the computer will tell you what to do—if you can remember why you want to

1.11 British Telecom Telephone. This was in my office at the Applied Psychology Unit in Cambridge, England. It certainly looks simple, doesn't it?

1.12 Two Ways to Use Hold on Modern Telephones. Illustration *A* (below left) is the instruction manual page for British Telecom. The procedure seems especially complicated, with three 3-digit codes to be learned: 681, 682, and 683. Illustration *B* (below right) shows the equivalent instructions for the Ericsson Single Line Analog Telephone installed at the University of California, San Diego. I find the second set of instructions easier to understand, but one must still dial an arbitrary digit: 8 in this case.

HOLD

This feature allows you to hold an existing call, then to replace the handset or to make another call. The held call may be retrieved from the holding extension or from any other extension within the system.

TO HOLD THE CALL

RECALL   CODE   DIAL   REPLACE   MAKE
          681   TONE   HANDSET   ANOTHER CALL
                                OR

You may use your extension normally.

TO RETRIEVE THE CALL AT YOUR PHONE

LIFT   CODE   YOU ARE CONNECTED
HANDSET   682   TO THE HELD CALL

TO RETRIEVE THE CALL AT SOMEONE ELSE'S PHONE

LIFT   CODE   YOU ARE CONNECTED
HANDSET   683   TO THE HELD CALL
                       YOUR EXTENSION
                       NUMBER

CALL HOLD/CALL PARK

With party on line
● Press **R** key
● Listen for recall dial tone (three beeps and dial tone)
● Hang up handset

TO RETRIEVE FROM SAME PHONE
● Lift handset; you are connected to the call

TO RETRIEVE FROM ANOTHER PHONE
● Lift handset
● Dial extension where call was parked; listen for busy tone
● Dial **8**; you are connected to the call

NOTE: Call will remain parked for 3 minutes before re-ringing

do it, and if the person on the other end of the line is still around. But, as it happens, using the expert system is a lot easier than reading and understanding the manual provided with the telephone (figure 1.12).

Why is that telephone system so hard to understand? Nothing in it is conceptually difficult. Each of the operations is actually quite simple. A few digits to dial, that's all. The telephone doesn't even look complicated. There are only fifteen controls: the usual twelve buttons—ten labeled o through 9, #, and *—plus the handset itself, the handset button, and the mysterious "R" button. All except the "R" are the everyday parts of a normal modern telephone. Why was the system so difficult?

A designer who works for a telephone company told me the following story:

"I was involved in designing the faceplate of some of those new multifunction phones, some of which have buttons labeled "R." The "R" button is kind of a vestigial feature. It is very hard to remove features of a newly designed product that had existed in an earlier version. It's kind of like physical evolution. If a feature is in the genome, and if that feature is not associated with any negativity (i.e., no customers gripe about it), then the feature hangs on for generations.

"It is interesting that things like the "R" button are largely determined through examples. Somebody asks, 'What is the "R" button used for?' and the answer is to give an example: 'You can push "R" to access loudspeaker paging.' If nobody can think of an example, the feature is dropped. Designers are pretty bright people, however. They can come up with a plausible-sounding example for almost anything. Hence, you get features, many many features, and these features hang on for a long time. The end result is complex interfaces for essentially simple things."[6]

As I pondered this problem, I decided it would make sense to compare the phone system with something that was of equal or greater complexity but easier to use. So let us temporarily leave the difficult telephone system and take a look at my automobile. I bought a car in Europe. When I picked up the new car at the factory, a man from the company sat in the car with me and went over each control, explaining its function. When he had gone through the controls once, I said fine, thanked him, and drove away. That was all the instruction it took. There are 112 controls inside the car. This isn't quite as bad as it sounds. Twenty-five of them are on the radio. Another 7 are the temperature control system, and 11 work the windows and sunroof. The trip computer has 14 buttons, each matched with a specific function. So four devices—the radio, temperature controls, windows, and trip computer—have together 57 controls, or just over 50 percent of the ones available.

Why is the automobile, with all its varied functions and numerous controls, so much easier to learn and to use than the telephone system, with its much smaller set of functions and controls? What is good about the design of the car? Things are visible. There are good mappings, natural relationships, between the controls and the things controlled. Single controls often have single functions. There is good feedback. The system is understandable. In general, the relationships among the user's intentions, the required actions, and the results are sensible, nonarbitrary, and meaningful.

What is bad about the design of the telephone? There is no visible structure. Mappings are arbitrary: there is no rhyme or reason to the relationship between the actions the user must perform and the results to be accomplished. The controls have multiple functions. There isn't good feedback, so the user is never sure whether the desired result has been obtained. The system, in general, is not understandable; its capabilities aren't apparent. In general, the relationships among the user's intentions, the required actions, and the results are completely arbitrary.

Whenever the number of possible actions exceeds the number of controls, there is apt to be difficulty. The telephone system has twenty-four functions, yet only fifteen controls—none of them labeled for specific action. In contrast, the trip computer for the car performs seventeen functions with fourteen controls. With minor exceptions, there is one control for each function. In fact, the controls with more than one function are indeed harder to remember and use. When the number of controls equals the number of functions, each control can be specialized, each can be labeled. The possible functions are visible, for each corresponds with a control. If the user forgets the functions, the controls serve as reminders. When, as on the telephone, there are more functions than controls, labeling becomes difficult or impossible. There is nothing to remind the user. Functions are invisible, hidden from sight. No wonder the operation becomes mysterious and difficult. The controls for the car are visible and, through their location and mode of operation, bear an intelligent relationship to their action. Visibility acts as a good reminder of what can be done and allows the control to specify how the action is to be performed. The good relationship between the placement of the control and what it does makes it easy to find the appropriate control for a task. As a result, there is little to remember.

THE PRINCIPLE OF MAPPING

Mapping is a technical term meaning the relationship between two things, in this case between the controls and their movements and the results in the world. Consider the mapping relationships involved in steering a car. To turn the car to the right, one turns the steering wheel clockwise (so that its top moves to the right). The user must identify two mappings here: one of the 112 controls affects the steering, and the steering wheel must be turned in one of two directions. Both are somewhat arbitrary. But the wheel and the clockwise direction are natural choices: visible, closely related to the desired outcome, and providing immediate feedback. The mapping is easily learned and always remembered.

Natural mapping, by which I mean taking advantage of physical analogies and cultural standards, leads to immediate understanding. For example, a designer can use spatial analogy: to move an object up, move the control up. To control an array of lights, arrange the controls in the same pattern as the lights. Some natural mappings are cultural or biological, as in the universal standard that a rising level represents more, a diminishing level, less. Similarly, a louder sound can mean a greater amount. Amount and loudness (and weight, line length, and brightness) are additive dimensions: add more to show incremental increases. Note that the logically plausible relationship between musical pitch and amount does not work: Would a higher pitch mean less or more of something? Pitch (and taste, color, and location) are substitutive dimensions: substitute one value for another to make a change. There is no natural concept of more or less in the comparison of different pitches, or hues, or taste qualities. Other natural mappings follow from the principles of perception and allow for the natural grouping or patterning of controls and feedback (see figure 1.13).

Mapping problems are abundant, one of the fundamental causes of difficulties. Consider the telephone. Suppose you wish to activate the callback on "no reply" function. To initiate this feature on one tele-

1.13 Seat Adjustment Control from a Mercedes-Benz Automobile. This is an excellent example of natural mapping. The control is in the shape of the seat itself: the mapping is straightforward. To move the front edge of the seat higher, lift up on the front part of the button. To make the seat back recline, move the button back. Mercedes-Benz automobiles are obviously not everyday things for most people, but the principle doesn't require great expense or wealth. The same principle could be applied to much more common objects.

phone system, press and release the "recall" button (the button on the handset), then dial 60, then dial the number you called.

There are several problems here. First, the description of the function is relatively complex—yet incomplete: What if two people set up callback at the same time? What if the person does not come back until a week later? What if you have meanwhile set up three or four other functions? What if you want to cancel it? Second, the action to be performed is arbitrary. (Dial 60. Why 60? Why not 73 or 27? How does one remember an arbitrary number?) Third, the sequence ends with what appears to be a redundant, unnecessary action: dialing the number of the person to be called. If the phone system is smart enough to do all these other things, why can't it remember the number that was just attempted; why must it be told all over again? And finally, consider the lack of feedback. How do I know I did the right action? Maybe I disconnected the phone. Maybe I set up some other special feature. There is no visible or audible way to know immediately.

A device is easy to use when there is visibility to the set of possible actions, where the controls and displays exploit natural mappings. The principles are simple but rarely incorporated into design. Good design takes care, planning, thought. It takes conscious attention to the needs of the user. And sometimes the designer gets it right:

Once, when I was at a conference at Gmunden, Austria, a group of us went off to see the sights. I sat directly behind the driver of the brand new, sleek, high-technology German tour bus. I gazed in wonder at the hundreds of controls scattered all over the front of the bus.

"How can you ever learn all those controls?" I asked the driver (with the aid of a German-speaking colleague). The driver was clearly puzzled by the question.

"What do you mean?" he replied. "Each control is just where it ought to be. There is no difficulty."

A good principle, that. Controls are where they ought to be. One function, one control. Harder to do, of course, than to say, but essentially this is the principle of natural mappings: the relationship between controls and actions should be apparent to the user. I return to this topic later in the book, for the problem of determining the "naturalness" of mappings is difficult, but crucial.

I've already described how my car's controls are generally easy to use. Actually, the car has lots of problems. The approach to usability used in the car seems to be to make sure that you can reach everything and see everything. That's good, but not nearly good enough.

Here is a simple example: the controls for the loudspeakers—a simple control that determines whether the sound comes out of the front speakers, the rear, or a combination (figure 1.14). Rotate the wheel from left to right or right to left. Simple, except how do you know which way to rotate the control? Which direction moves the sound to the rear, which to the front? If you want sound to come out of the front speaker, you should be able to move the control to the front. To get it out of the back, move the control to the back. Then the form of the motion would mimic the function and make a natural mapping. But the way the control is actually mounted in the car, forward and backward get translated into left and right. Which direction is which? There is no natural relationship. What's worse, the control isn't even labeled. Even the instruction manual does not say how to use it.

1.14 The Front/Rear Speaker Selector of an Automobile Radio. Rotating the knob with the pictures of the speaker at either side makes the sound come entirely out of the front speakers (when the knob is all the way over to one side), entirely out of the rear speakers (when the knob is all the way the other way), or equally out of both (when the knob is midway). Which way is front, which rear? You can't tell by looking. While you're at it, imagine trying to manipulate the radio controls while keeping your eyes on the road.

The control should be mounted so that it moves forward and backward. If that can't be done, rotate the control 90° on the panel so that it moves vertically. Moving something up to represent forward is not as natural as moving it forward, but at least it follows a standard convention.

In fact, we see that both the car and the telephone have easy functions and difficult ones. The car seems to have more of the easy ones, the telephone more of the difficult ones. Moreover, with the car, enough of the controls are easy that I can do almost everything I need to. Not so with the telephone: it is very difficult to use even a single one of the special features.

The easy things on both telephone and car have a lot in common, as do the difficult things. When things are visible, they tend to be easier than when they are not. In addition, there must be a close, *natural* relationship between the control and its function: a *natural mapping*.

THE PRINCIPLE OF FEEDBACK

Feedback—sending back to the user information about what action has actually been done, what result has been accomplished—is a well-known concept in the science of control and information theory. Imagine trying to talk to someone when you cannot even hear your own voice, or trying to draw a picture with a pencil that leaves no mark: there would be no feedback.

In the good old days of the telephone, before the American telephone system was divided among competing companies, before telephones were fancy and had so many features, telephones were designed with much more care and concern for the user. Designers at the Bell Telephone Laboratories worried a lot about feedback. The push buttons were designed to give an appropriate feel—tactile feedback. When a button was pushed, a tone was fed back into the earpiece so the user could tell that the button had been properly pushed. When the phone call was being connected, clicks, tones, and other noises gave the user feedback about the progress of the call. And the speaker's voice was always fed back to the earpiece in a carefully controlled amount, because the auditory feedback (called "sidetone") helped the person regulate how loudly to talk. All this has changed. We now have telephones that are much more powerful and often cheaper than those that existed just a few years ago—more function for less money. To be fair, these new designs are pushing hard on the paradox of technology: added functionality generally comes along at the price of added complexity. But that does not justify backward progress.

Why are the modern telephone systems so difficult to learn and to use? Basically, the problem is that the systems have more features and less feedback. Suppose all telephones had a small display screen, not unlike the ones on small, inexpensive calculators. The display could be used to present, upon the push of a button, a brief menu of all the features of the telephone, one by one. When the desired one was encountered, the user would push another button to indicate that it should be invoked. If further action was required, the display could tell the person what to do. The display could even be auditory, with speech instead of a visual display. Only two buttons need be added to the telephone: one to change the display, one to accept the option on display. Of course, the telephone would be slightly more expensive. The tradeoff is cost versus usability.[7]

Pity the Poor Designer

Designing well is not easy. The manufacturer wants something that can be produced economically. The store wants something that will be attractive to its customers. The purchaser has several demands. In the store, the purchaser focuses on price and appearance, and perhaps on prestige value. At home, the same person will pay more attention to functionality and usability. The repair service cares about maintainability: how easy is the device to take apart, diagnose, and service? The needs of those concerned are different and often conflict. Nonetheless, the designer may be able to satisfy everyone.

A simple example of good design is the $3\frac{1}{2}$-inch magnetic diskette for computers, a small circle of "floppy" magnetic material encased in hard plastic. Earlier types of floppy disks did not have this plastic case, which protects the magnetic material from abuse and damage. A sliding metal cover protects the delicate magnetic surface when the diskette is not in use and automatically opens when the diskette is inserted into the computer. The diskette has a square shape: there are apparently eight possible ways to insert it into the machine, only one of which is correct. What happens if I do it wrong? I try inserting the disk sideways. Ah, the designer thought of that. A little study shows that the case really isn't square: it's rectangular, so you can't insert a longer side. I try backward. The diskette goes in only part of the way. Small protrusions, indentations, and cutouts prevent the diskette from being inserted backward or upside down: of the eight ways one might try to insert the diskette, only one is correct, and only that one will fit. An excellent design.

Take another example of good design. My felt-tipped marking pen has ribs along only one of its sides; otherwise all sides look identical. Careful examination shows that the tip of the marker is angled and makes the best line if the marker is held with the ribbed side up, a natural result if the forefinger rests upon the ribs. No harm results if I hold the marker another way, but the marker writes less well. The ribs are a subtle design cue—functional, yet visibly and aesthetically unobtrusive.

The world is permeated with small examples of good design, with the amazing details that make important differences in our lives. Each detail was added by some person, a designer, carefully thinking through the uses of the device, the ways that people abuse things, the kinds of errors that can get made, and the functions that people wish to have performed.

Then why is it that so many good design ideas don't find their way into products in the marketplace? Or something good shows up for a short time, only to fall into oblivion? I once spoke with a designer about the frustrations of trying to get the best product out:

It usually takes five or six attempts to get a product right. This may be acceptable in an established product, but consider what it means in a new one. Suppose a company wants to make a product that will perhaps make a real difference. The problem is that if the product is truly revolutionary, it is unlikely that anyone will quite know how to design it right the first time; it will take several tries. But if a product is introduced into the marketplace and fails, well that is it. Perhaps it could be introduced a second time, or maybe even a third time, but after that it is dead: everyone believes it to be a failure.

I asked him to explain. "You mean," I said, "that it takes five or six tries to get an idea right?"

"Yes," he said, "at least that."

"But," I replied, "you also said that if a newly introduced product doesn't catch on in the first two or three times, then it is dead?"

"Yup," he said.

"Then new products are almost guaranteed to fail, no matter how good the idea."

"Now you understand," said the designer. "Consider the use of voice messages on complex devices such as cameras, soft-drink machines, and copiers. A failure. No longer even tried. Too bad. It really is a good idea, for it can be very useful when the hands or eyes are busy elsewhere. But those first few attempts were very badly done and the public scoffed—properly. Now, nobody dares try it again, even in those places where it is needed."

The Paradox of Technology

Technology offers the potential to make life easier and more enjoyable; each new technology provides increased benefits. At the same time, added complexities arise to increase our difficulty and frustration. The development of a technology tends to follow a U-shaped curve of complexity: starting high; dropping to a low, comfortable level; then climbing again. New kinds of devices are complex and difficult to use. As technicians become more competent and an industry matures, devices become simpler, more reliable, and more powerful. But then, after the industry has stabilized, newcomers figure out how to add increased power and capability, but always at the expense of added complexity and sometimes decreased reliability. We can see the curve of complexity in the history of the watch, radio, telephone, and television set. Take the radio. In the early days, radios were quite complex. To tune in a station required several adjustments, including one for the antenna, one for the radio frequency, one for intermediate frequencies, and controls for both sensitivity and loudness. Later radios were simpler and had controls only to turn it on, tune the station, and adjust the loudness. But the latest radios are again very complex, perhaps even more so than early ones. Now the radio is called a tuner, and it is littered with numerous controls, switches, slide bars, lights, displays, and meters. The modern sets are technologically superior, offering higher quality sound, better reception, and enhanced capability. But what good is the technology if it is too complex to use?

The design problem posed by technological advances is enormous. Consider the watch. A few decades ago, watches were simple. All you had to do was set the time and keep them wound. The standard control was the stem: a knob at the side of the watch. Turning the knob wound the spring that worked the watch. Pulling the knob out and turning it made the hands move. The operations were easy to learn and easy to do. There was a reasonable relation between the turning of the knob and the resulting turning of the hands. The design even took into account human error: the normal position of the stem was for winding the spring, so that an accidental turn would not reset the time.

In the modern digital watch the spring is gone, replaced by a motor run by long-lasting batteries. All that remains is the task of setting the watch. The stem is still a sensible solution, for you can go fast or slow, forward or backward, until the exact desired time is reached. But the stem is more complex (and therefore more expensive) than simple push-button switches. If the only change in the transition from the spring-wound analog watch to the battery-run digital watch were in how the time was set, there would be little difficulty. The problem is that new technology has allowed us to add more functions to the watch: the watch can give the day of the week, the month, and the year; it can act as a stop watch (which itself has several functions), a countdown timer, and an alarm clock (or two); it has the ability to show the time for different time zones; it can act as a counter and even as a calculator. But the added functions cause problems: How do you design a watch that has so many functions while trying to limit the size, cost, and complexity of the device? How many buttons does it take to make the watch workable and learnable, yet not too expensive? There are no easy answers. Whenever the number of functions and required operations exceeds the number of controls, the design becomes arbitrary, unnatural, and complicated. The same technology that simplifies life by providing more functions in each device also complicates life by making the device harder to learn, harder to use. This is the paradox of technology.

The paradox of technology should never be used as an excuse for poor design. It is true that as the number of options and capabilities of any device increases, so too must the number and complexity of the controls. But the principles of good design can make complexity manageable.

In one of my courses I gave as homework the assignment to design a multiple-function clock radio:

You have been employed by a manufacturing company to design their new product. The company is considering combining the following into one item:

- *AM-FM radio*
- *Cassette player*
- *CD player*
- *Telephone*
- *Telephone answering machine*
- *Clock*
- *Alarm clock (the alarm can turn on a tone, radio, cassette, or CD)*
- *Desk or bed lamp*

The company is trying to decide whether to include a small (two-inch screen) TV set and a switched electric outlet that can turn on a coffee maker or toaster.

Your job is (A) to recommend what to build, then (B) to design the control panel, and finally (C) to certify that it is actually both what customers want and easy to use.

State what you would do for the three parts of your job: A, B, and C. Explain how you would go about validating and justifying your recommendations.

Draw a rough sketch of a control panel for the items in the indented list, with a brief *justification and analysis of the factors that went into the choice of design.*

There are several things I looked for in the answer. (Figure 1.15 is an unacceptable solution.) First, how well did the answer address the

1.15 Possible Solution to My Homework Assignment. Completely unacceptable. (Thanks to Bill Gaver for devising and drawing this sample.)

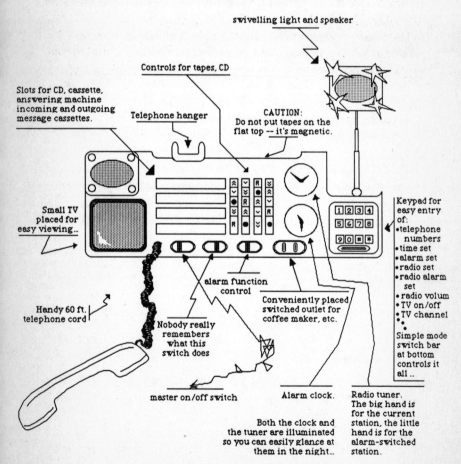

real needs of the user? I expected my students to visit the homes of potential users to see how their current devices were being used and to determine how the combined multipurpose device would be used. Next, I evaluated whether all the controls were usable and understandable, allowing all the desired functions to be operated with minimum confusion or error. Clock radios are often used in the dark, with the user in bed and reaching overhead to grope for the desired control. Therefore the unit had to be usable in the dark by feel only. It was not supposed to be possible to make a serious mistake by accidentally hitting the wrong control. (Alas, many existing clock radios do not tolerate serious errors—for example, the user may reset the time by hitting the wrong button accidentally.) Finally, the design was expected to take into account real issues in cost, manufacturability, and aesthetics. The finished design had to pass muster with users. The point of the exercise was for the student to realize the paradox of technology: added complexity and difficulty cannot be avoided when functions are added, but with clever design, they can be minimized.

CHAPTER TWO

THE PSYCHOLOGY
OF EVERYDAY
ACTIONS

During my family's stay in England, we rented a furnished house while the owners were away. One day, our landlady returned to the house to get some personal papers. She walked over to her filing cabinet and attempted to open the top drawer. It wouldn't open. She pushed it forward and backward, right and left, up and down, without success. I offered to help. I wiggled the drawer. Then I twisted the front panel, pushed down hard, and banged the front with the palm of one hand. The cabinet drawer slid open. "Oh," she said, "I'm sorry. I am so bad at mechanical things."

**Falsely Blaming
Yourself**

I have studied people making errors—sometimes serious ones—with mechanical devices, light switches and fuses, computer operating systems and word processors, even airplanes and nuclear power plants. Invariably people feel guilty and either try to hide the error or blame themselves for "stupidity" or "clumsiness." I often have difficulty getting permission to watch: nobody likes to be observed performing badly. I point out that the design is faulty and that others make the same errors. Still, if the task *appears* simple or trivial, then people blame themselves.[1] It is as if they take perverse pride in thinking of themselves as mechanically incompetent.

I once was asked by a large computer company to evaluate a brand new product. I spent a day learning to use it and trying it out on various problems. In using the keyboard to enter data, it was necessary to differentiate between the the "return" key and the "enter" key. If the wrong key was typed, the last few minutes' work was irrevocably lost.

I pointed this problem out to the designer, explaining that I myself had made the error frequently and that my analyses indicated that this was very likely to be a frequent error among users. The designer's first response was: "Why did you make that error? Didn't you read the manual?" He proceeded to explain the different functions of the two keys.

"Yes, yes," I explained, "I understand the two keys, I simply confuse them. They have similar functions, are located in similar locations on the keyboard, and as a skilled typist, I often hit "return" automatically, without thought. Certainly others have had similar problems."

"Nope," said the designer. He claimed that I was the only person who had ever complained, and the company's secretaries had been using the system for many months. I was skeptical, so we went together to some of the secretaries and asked them whether they had ever hit the "return" key when they should have hit "enter." And did they ever lose their work as a result?

"Oh, yes," said the secretaries, "we do that a lot."

"Well, how come nobody ever said anything about it?" we asked the secretaries. After all, they were encouraged to report all problems with the system.

The reason was simple: when the system stopped working or did something strange, the secretaries dutifully reported it as a problem. But when they made the "return" versus "enter" error, they blamed themselves. After all, they had been told what to do. They had simply erred.

Of course, people do make errors. Complex devices will always require some instruction, and someone using them without instruction should expect to make errors and to be confused. But designers should take special pains to make errors as cost-free as possible. Here is my credo about errors:

If an error is possible, someone will make it. The designer must assume that all possible errors will occur and design so as to minimize the chance of the error in the first place, or its effects once it gets made. Errors should be easy to detect, they should have minimal consequences, and, if possible, their effects should be reversible.

Misconceptions of Everyday Life

Our lives are filled with misconceptions. This should not be surprising: we must frequently deal with unfamiliar situations. Psychologists love errors and misconceptions, for they give important clues about the organization and operation of our minds. Many everyday misunderstandings are classified as "naive" or "folk" understandings. And not just plain folk hold these misconceptions: Aristotle developed an entire theory of physics that physicists find quaint and amusing. Yet Aristotle's theories correspond much better to common-sense, everyday observations than do the highly refined and abstract theories we are taught in school. Aristotle developed what we might call naive physics. It is only when you study the esoteric world of physics that you learn what is "correct" and are able to understand why the "naive" view is wrong.

ARISTOTLE'S NAIVE PHYSICS

For example, Aristotle thought that moving objects kept moving only if something kept pushing them. Today's physicist says nonsense: a moving object continues to move unless some force is exerted to stop it. This is Newton's first law of motion, and it contributed to the development of modern physics. Yet anyone who has ever pushed a heavy box along a street or, for that matter, hiked for miles into the wilderness, knows that Aristotle was right: if you don't keep on pushing, the movement stops. Of course, Newton and his successors assume the absence of friction and air. Aristotle lived in a world where there was always friction and air resistance. Once friction is involved, then objects in motion tend to stop unless you keep pushing. Aristotle's theory may be bad physics, but it describes reasonably well what we can see in the real world. Think about how you might answer the following questions.

1. I take a pistol and, carefully aiming it on a level, horizontal line, I fire a bullet. With my other hand, I hold a bullet so that the bullet in the pistol and the one in my hand are exactly the same distance from the ground. I drop the bullet at the same instant as I fire the pistol. Which bullet hits the ground first?

2. Imagine someone running across a field carrying a ball. As you watch, the runner drops the ball. Which path (a, b, or c in figure 2.1) does the ball take as it falls to the ground?²

The physicist says the answer to the bullet problem is trivial: both bullets hit the ground at the same time. The fact that one bullet is traveling horizontally very rapidly has absolutely no effect on how fast it falls downward. Why should we accept that answer? Shouldn't the speeding bullet develop some lift—sort of like an airplane—so that it will stay up a bit longer because it is kept up by the air? Who knows? The theory of physics is based upon a situation where there is no air. The popular misconception is that the pistol bullet will hit the ground long after the dropped bullet; yet this naive view doesn't seem so strange.

2.1 A Running Man Drops a Ball. Which path does the ball take as it falls to the ground, path A, B, or C? When this question was asked of sixth-grade students in Boston schools, only 3 percent answered A, the right answer; the others were evenly divided between B and C. Even high school students did not do well: of forty-one students who had just studied Newtonian mechanics for a month and a half, only 20 percent got the right answer; the others were almost equally divided between B and C. (The study was performed by White & Horwitz, 1987. The figure is reprinted from *Intuitive Physics* by McCloskey. Copyright © 1983 by *Scientific American,* Inc. All rights reserved.)

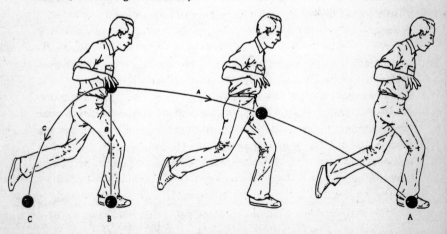

In the case of the falling ball, our prediction is that the ball will drop straight down. In fact, the falling ball follows trajectory A (figure 2.1). As it is carried by the runner, it is set into horizontal motion. It then maintains the same forward speed upon being released, even as it also falls to the ground.[3]

Naive physics—and naive views of psychology and other fields—are often sensible, even if wrong. But at times they can get us into trouble. Yet we must have a way to digest the unfamiliar, for people are explanatory creatures.

PEOPLE AS EXPLANATORY CREATURES

Mental models, our conceptual models of the way objects work, events take place, or people behave, result from our tendency to form explanations of things. These models are essential in helping us understand our experiences, predict the outcomes of our actions, and handle unexpected occurrences. We base our models on whatever knowledge we have, real or imaginary, naive or sophisticated.

Mental models are often constructed from fragmentary evidence, with but a poor understanding of what is happening, and with a kind of naive psychology that postulates causes, mechanisms, and relationships even where there are none. Some faulty models lead to the frustrations of everyday life, as in the case of my unsettable refrigerator, where my mental model of its operation (figure 1.9 A) did not correspond to reality (figure 1.9 B). Far more serious are faulty models of such complex systems as an industrial plant or passenger airplane. Misunderstanding there can lead to devastating accidents.

Consider the room thermostat. How does it work? Here is a device that offers almost no evidence of its operation except in a highly roundabout manner. We walk into a room and feel too cold: so we walk over to the thermostat and set it higher. Eventually we feel warmer. Note that the same thing applies to the temperature control for a cooking oven (or a pottery kiln, or an air conditioner, or almost any device whose temperature is to be regulated). Want to bake a cake, but the oven is off? Set the oven thermostat and the oven gets to the desired temperature. Is the room too hot? Set the thermostat on the air conditioner. Fine, but how does the thermostat work?

If you are in a cold room, in a hurry to get warm, will the room heat more quickly if you turn the thermostat all the way up? Or if you want the oven to reach its working temperature faster, should you turn the temperature dial all the way to maximum, then turn it down once the desired temperature is reached? Or to cool a room most quickly, should you set the air conditioner thermostat to its lowest temperature setting?

If you think that the room or oven will heat (or cool) faster if the thermostat is turned all the way to the maximum setting, you are wrong. You hold a folk theory of thermostats. There are two commonly held folk theories about thermostats: the timer theory and the valve theory. The timer theory proposes that the thermostat simply controls the relative proportion of time that the device stays on. Set the thermostat midway, and the device is on about half the time; set it all the way up and the device is on all the time. Hence, to heat or cool something most quickly, set the thermostat so that the device is on all the time. The valve theory proposes that the thermostat controls how much heat (or cold) comes out of the device. Turn the thermostat all the way up, and you get maximum heating or cooling.[4]

The correct story is that the thermostat is just an on-off switch. It treats the heater, oven, and air conditioner as all-or-nothing devices that can be either fully on or fully off, with no in-between states. The thermostat turns the heater, oven, or air conditioner completely on—at full power—until the temperature setting on the thermostat is reached. Then it turns the unit completely off. Setting the thermostat at one extreme cannot affect how long it takes to reach the desired temperature.[5]

The real point of the example is not that some people have erroneous theories; it is that everyone forms theories (mental models) to explain what they have observed. In the case of the thermostat, the design gives absolutely no hint as to the correct answer. In the absence of external information, people are free to let their imaginations run free as long as the mental models they develop account for the facts as they perceive them.

Blaming the Wrong Cause

"Look at this!" my colleague exclaimed to me, "My computer terminal is broken. The library did it! Every time I connect it to the library catalog I have trouble. Now I can't even use the terminal to read my computer mail anymore."

"That doesn't make sense," I replied. "You can't even turn on the

power to the terminal. How could a computer program possibly do that kind of damage?"

"All I know," he said, "is that everything was working fine until I tried to look up an author in the library catalog using that new library program, and then my terminal stopped working. I always have trouble with that program. And this is simply too much of a coincidence to be anything else."

Well, it was a coincidence. It turns out that the power supply to the terminal had burned out, a fact that had nothing to do with the computer program. Coincidence is enough to set the causal wheels rolling.

Earlier I suggested that people have a tendency to blame themselves for difficulties with technology. Actually, the point is a bit more complicated. People do tend to find causes for events, and just what they assign as the cause varies. In part people tend to assign a causal relation whenever two things occur in succession. If I do some action A just prior to some result R, then I conclude that A must have caused R, even if, as in the example above, there really was no relationship between the two. The story is more complex when we intend an action to produce a desired result and fail, and there are problems when we have done the action through some intermediate mechanism.

Just where do we put the blame for failure? The answer is not clear. The psychology of blame (or, to be more accurate, of attribution) is complex and not fully understood. In part, there seems to have to be some perceived causal relationship between the thing being blamed and the result. The word *perceived* is critical: the causal relationship does not have to exist; the person simply has to think it is there. Sometimes we attribute the cause to things that had nothing to do with the action. And sometimes we ignore the real culprit.

One major aspect of the assignment of blame is that we frequently have little information on which to make the judgment, and what little we have may be wrong. As a result, blame or credit can be assessed almost independently of reality. Here is where the apparent simplicity of everyday objects causes problems. Suppose I try to use an everyday thing, but I can't: Where is the fault, in my action or in the thing? We are apt to blame ourselves. If we believe that others are able to use the device and if we believe that it is not very complex, then we conclude that any difficulties must be our own fault. Suppose the fault really lies in the device, so that lots of people have the same problems. Because everyone perceives the fault to be his or her own, nobody wants to admit to having trouble. This creates a conspiracy of silence, maintaining the feelings of guilt and helplessness among users.

Interestingly enough, the common tendency to blame ourselves for failures with everyday objects goes against the normal attributions people make. In general, it has been found that people attribute their own problems to the environment, those of other people to their personalities.

Here is a made-up example. Consider Tom, the office terror. Today Tom got to work late, slammed the door to his office, and yelled at his colleagues. "Ah," his colleagues and staff said, "there he goes again. He's so excitable—always gets mad at the slightest thing."

Now consider Tom's point of view. "I really had a hard day," Tom explains. "I woke up late because when my clock radio turned on, I tried to hit the snooze bar to give me five minutes' more sleep; instead I reset the time so that I overslept for a whole hour. That wasn't my fault—the radio's badly designed. I didn't even have time for my morning coffee. I couldn't find a close parking spot because I was late. And then because I was in such a rush I dropped my papers all over the street and got them dirty. Then when I went to get a cup of coffee from the office machine, it was all out. None of this was my fault—I had a run of really bad events. Yes, I was a bit curt with my colleagues, but who wouldn't be under the same circumstances? Surely they understand."

But Tom's colleagues see a different picture. They don't have access to his inner thoughts or even to his morning's activities. All they see is that Tom yelled at them simply because the office coffee machine was empty. And this reminds them of another time when the same thing happened. "He does that all the time," they conclude, "always blowing up over the most minor events." The events are the same events, but there are two different points of view and two different interpretations. The protagonist, Tom, views his actions as sensible responses to the trials of life. The onlooker views Tom's actions as a result of his explosive, irascible personality.

It seems natural for people to blame their own misfortunes on the environment. It seems equally natural to blame other people's misfortunes on their personalities. Just the opposite attribution, by the way, is made when things go well. When things go right, people credit their own forceful personalities and intelligence: "I really did a good job today; no wonder we finished the project so well." The onlookers do the reverse. When they see things go well for someone else, they credit the environment: "Joan really was lucky today; she just happened to be standing there when the boss came by, so she got all the credit for the project work. Some people have all the luck."

In all cases, whether a person is inappropriately accepting blame for the inability to work simple objects or attributing behavior to environment or personality, a faulty mental model is at work.

LEARNED HELPLESSNESS

The phenomenon called *learned helplessness* may help explain the self-blame. It refers to the situation in which people experience failure at a task, often numerous times. As a result, they decide that the task cannot be done, at least not by them: they are helpless. They stop trying. If this feeling covers a group of tasks, the result can be severe difficulties coping with life. In the extreme case, such learned helplessness leads to depression and to a belief that the person cannot cope with everyday life at all. Sometimes all that it takes to get such a feeling of helplessness is a few experiences that accidentally turn out bad. The phenomenon has been most frequently studied as a precursor to the clinical problem of depression, but it might easily arise with a few bad experiences with everyday objects.

TAUGHT HELPLESSNESS

Do the common technology and mathematics phobias result from a kind of learned helplessness? Could a few instances of failure in what appear to be straightforward situations generalize to every technological object, every mathematics problem? Perhaps. In fact, the design of everyday things (and the design of mathematics courses) seems almost guaranteed to cause this. We could call this phenomenon *taught helplessness*.

With badly designed objects—constructed so as to lead to misunderstanding—faulty mental models, and poor feedback, no wonder people feel guilty when they have trouble using objects, especially when they perceive (even if incorrectly) that nobody else is having the same problems. Or consider the normal mathematics curriculum, which continues relentlessly on its way, each new lesson assuming full knowledge and understanding of all that has passed before. Even though each point may be simple, once you fall behind it is hard to catch up. The result: mathematics phobia. Not because the material is difficult, but because it is taught so that difficulty in one stage hinders further progress. The problem is that once failure starts, it soon generalizes by self-blame to all of mathematics. Similar processes are at work with technology. The vicious cycle starts: if you fail at something, you think it is your fault. Therefore you think you can't do that task. As a result, next time you have to do the task, you believe you can't so you don't even try. The result is that you can't, just as you thought. You're trapped in a self-fulfilling prophecy.

The Nature of Human Thought and Explanation

It isn't always easy to tell just where the blame for a problem should be placed. A number of dramatic accidents have come about, in part, from the false assessment of blame in a situation. Highly skilled, well-trained people are using complex equipment when suddenly something goes wrong. They have to figure out what the problem is. Most industrial equipment is pretty reliable. When the instruments indicate that something is wrong, one has to consider the possibility that the instruments themselves are wrong. Often this is the correct assessment. But when operators mistakenly blame the instruments for an actual equipment failure, the situation is ripe for a major accident.

It is spectacularly easy to find examples of false assessment in industrial accidents. Analysts come in well after the fact, knowing what actually did happen; with hindsight, it is almost impossible to understand how the people involved could have made the mistake. But from the point of view of the person making decisions at the time, the sequence of events is quite natural.

At the Three Mile Island nuclear power plant, operators pushed a button to close a valve; the valve had been opened (properly) to allow excess water to escape from the nuclear core. In fact, the valve was deficient, so it didn't close. But a light on the control panel indicated that the valve position was closed. The light actually didn't monitor the valve, only the electrical signal to the valve, a fact known by the operators. Still, why suspect a problem? The operators did look at the temperature in the pipe leading from the valve: it was high, indicating that fluid was still flowing through the closed valve. Ah, but the operators knew that the valve had been leaky, so the leak would explain the high temperature; but the leak was known to be small, and operators assumed that it wouldn't affect the main operation. They were wrong, and the water that was able to escape from the core added significantly to the problems of that nuclear disaster. I think the operators' assessment was perfectly reasonable: the fault was in the design of the lights and in the equipment that gave false evidence of a closed valve.

Similar misinterpretations take place all the time. I have studied a number of airline accidents. Consider the flight crew of the Lockheed L-1011 flying from Miami, Florida, to Nassau, Bahamas. The plane was over the Atlantic Ocean, about 110 miles from Miami, when the low oil pressure light for one of the three engines went on. The crew turned off the engine and turned around to go back to Miami. Eight minutes later, the low pressure lights for the remaining two engines also went on, and the instruments showed zero oil pressure and quantity in all three engines. What did the crew do now? They didn't believe it! After all, the pilot correctly said later, the likelihood of simultaneous oil exhaustion in all three engines was "one in millions I would think." At the time, sitting in the airplane, simultaneous failure did seem most unlikely. Even the National Transportation Safety Board declared, "The analysis of the situation by the flightcrew was logical, and was what most pilots probably would have done if confronted by the same situation."[6]

What happened? The second and third engines were indeed out of oil, and they failed. So there were no operating engines: one had been turned off when its gauge registered low, the other two had failed. The pilots prepared the plane for an emergency landing on the water. The pilots were too busy to instruct the flight crew properly, so the passengers were not prepared. There was semi-hysteria in the passenger cabin. At the last minute, just as the plane was about to ditch in the ocean, the pilots managed to restart the first engine and to land safely at Miami. Then that engine failed at the end of the runway.

Why did all three engines fail? Three missing O-rings, one missing from each of three oil plugs, allowed all the oil to seep out. The O-rings were put in by two different people who worked on the three engines (one for the two plugs on the wings, the other for the plug on the tail). How did both workers make the same mistake? Because the normal method by which they got the oil plugs had been changed that day. The whole tale is very instructive, for there were four major failures of different sorts, from the omission of the O-rings, to the inadequacy of the maintenance procedures, to the false assessment of the problem, to the poor handling of the passengers. Fortunately, nobody was injured. The analysts of the National Transportation Safety Board got to write a fascinating report.

I've misinterpreted signals, as I'm sure most people have. My family was driving from San Diego to Mammoth, California, a ski area about 500 miles north: a ten- to twelve-hour drive. As we drove, we noticed more and more signs advertising the hotels and gambling casinos of Las Vegas, Nevada. "Strange," we said, "Las Vegas always did advertise a long way off—there is even a billboard in San Diego—but this seems excessive, advertising on the road to Mammoth." We stopped for gasoline and continued on our journey. Only later, when we tried to find a place to eat supper, did we discover that we had taken the wrong turn nearly two hours earlier, before we had stopped for gasoline, and that we were on the road to Las Vegas, not the road to Mammoth. We had to backtrack the entire two-hour segment, wasting four hours of driving. It's humorous now; it wasn't then.

Find an explanation, and we are happy. But our explanations are based on analogy with past experience, experience that may not apply in the current situation. In the Three Mile Island incident, past experience with the leaky valve explained away the discrepant temperature reading; on the flight from Miami to Nassau, the pilots' lack of experience with simultaneous oil pressure failure triggered their belief that the instruments must be faulty; in the driving story, the prevalence of billboards for Las Vegas seemed easily explained. Once we have an explanation—correct or incorrect—for otherwise discrepant or puzzling events, there is no more puzzle, no more discrepancy. As a result, we are complacent, at least for a while.

How People Do Things: The Seven Stages of Action

I am in Italy, at a conference. I watch the next speaker attempt to thread a film onto a projector that he has never used before. He puts the reel into place, then takes it off and reverses it. Another person comes to help. Jointly they thread the film through the projector and hold the free end, discussing how to put it on the takeup reel. Two more people come over to help, and then another. The voices grow louder, in three languages: Italian, German, and English. One person investigates the controls, manipulating each and announcing the result. Confusion mounts. I can no longer observe all that is happening. The conference organizer comes over. After a few moments he turns and faces the audience, which has been waiting patiently in the auditorium. "Ahem," he says, "is anybody expert in projectors?" Finally, fourteen minutes after the speaker had started to thread the film (and eight minutes after the scheduled start of the session) a blue-coated technician appears. He scowls, then promptly takes the entire film off the projector, rethreads it, and gets it working.

What makes something—like threading the projector—difficult to do? To answer this question, the central one of this book, we need to know what happens when someone does something. We need to examine the structure of an action.

The basic idea is simple. To get something done, you have to start with some notion of what is wanted—the goal that is to be achieved. Then, you have to do something to the world, that is, take action to move yourself or manipulate someone or something. Finally, you check to see that your goal was made. So there are four different things to consider: the goal, what is done to the world, the world itself, and the check of the world. The action itself has two major aspects: doing something and checking. Call these *execution* and *evaluation* (figure 2.2).

Real tasks are not quite so simple. The original goal may be imprecisely specified—perhaps "get something to eat," "get to work," "get dressed," "watch television." Goals do not state precisely what to do—where and how to move, what to pick up. To lead to actions goals must be transformed into specific statements of what is to be done, statements that I call *intentions*. A *goal* is something to be achieved, often vaguely stated. An *intention* is a specific action taken to get to the goal. Yet even intentions are not specific enough to control actions.

Suppose I am sitting in my armchair, reading a book. It is dusk, and the light has gotten dimmer and dimmer. I decide I need more light (that is the goal: get more light). My goal has to be translated into the intention that states the appropriate action in the world: push the switch button on the lamp. There's more: I need to specify how to move my body, how to stretch to reach the light switch, how to extend my finger to push the button (without knocking over the lamp). The goal

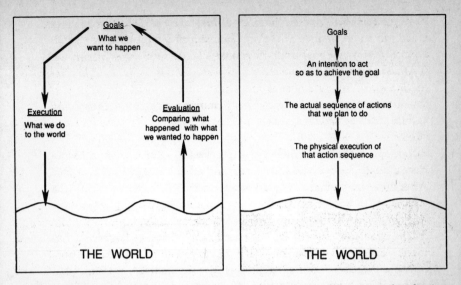

2.2 The Action Cycle (above left). Human action has two aspects, execution and evaluation. Execution involves doing something. Evaluation is the comparison of what happened in the world with what we wanted to happen (our goal).   **2.3 Stages of Execution** (above right). Start at the top with the *goal,* the state that is to be achieved. The goal is translated into an *intention* to do some action. The intention must be translated into a set of internal commands, an *action sequence* that can be performed to satisfy the intention. The action sequence is still a mental event: nothing happens until it is *executed,* performed upon the world.   **2.4 Stages of Evaluation** (below left). Evaluation starts with our *perception* of the world. This perception must then be *interpreted* according to our expectations and then compared *(evaluated)* with respect to both our intentions (from figure 2.3) and our goals.   **2.5 Seven Stages of Action** (below right).

The stages of execution from figure 2.3 (intentions, action sequence, and execution) are coupled with the stages of evaluation from figure 2.4 (perception, interpretation, and evaluation), with goals common to both stages.

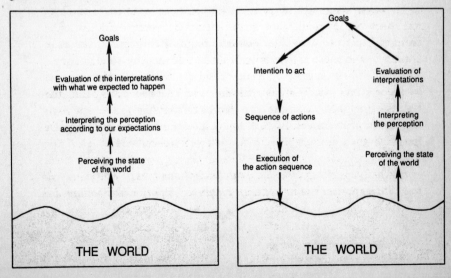

*has to be translated into an intention, which in turn has to be made into
a specific action sequence, one that can control my muscles. Note that
I could satisfy my goal with other action sequences, other intentions.
If someone walked into the room and passed by the lamp, I might alter
my intention from pushing the switch button to asking the other person to do it for me. The goal hasn't changed, but the intention and
resulting action sequence have.*

The specific actions bridge the gap between what we would like to
have done (our goals and intentions) and all possible physical actions.
After we specify what actions to make, we must actually do them—the
stage of execution. All in all, there are three stages that follow from the
goal: intention, action sequence, and execution (figure 2.3).

The evaluation side of things, checking up on what happened, has
three stages: first, perceiving what happened in the world; second,
trying to make sense of it (interpreting it); and, finally, comparing what
happened with what was wanted (figure 2.4).

There we have it. Seven stages of action: one for goals, three for
execution, and three for evaluation.

· Forming the goal
· Forming the intention
· Specifying an action
· Executing the action
· Perceiving the state of the world
· Interpreting the state of the world
· Evaluating the outcome

The seven stages form an *approximate model,* not a complete psychological theory. In particular, the stages are almost certainly not discrete
entities. Most behavior does not require going through all stages in
sequence, and most activities will not be satisfied by single actions.
There must be numerous sequences, and the whole activity may last
hours or even days. There is a continual feedback loop, in which the
results of one activity are used to direct further ones, in which goals
lead to subgoals, intentions lead to subintentions. There are activities
in which goals are forgotten, discarded, or reformulated.[7]

*For many everyday tasks, goals and intentions are not well specified:
they are* opportunistic *rather than planned. Opportunistic actions are*

those in which the behavior takes advantage of the circumstances. Rather than engage in extensive planning and analysis, the person goes about the day's activities and performs the intended actions if the relevant opportunity arises. Thus, we may not go out of our way to go to a shop, or to the library, or to ask a question of a friend. Rather, we go through the day's activities, and if we find ourselves at the shop, near the library, or encountering the friend, then we allow the opportunity to trigger the relevant activity. Otherwise, the task remains undone. Only in the case of crucial tasks do we make special efforts to ensure that they get done. Opportunistic actions are less precise and certain than specified goals and intentions, but they result in less mental effort, less inconvenience, and perhaps more interest.

The seven-stage process of action can be started at any point. People do not always behave as full, logical, reasoning organisms, starting with high-level goals and working to achieve them. Our goals are often ill-formed and vague. We may respond to the events of the world (in what is called data-driven behavior) rather than to think out plans and goals. An event in the world may trigger an interpretation and a resulting response. Actions may be executed before they are fully developed. In fact, some of us adjust our lives so that the environment can control our behavior. For example, sometimes when I must do an important task, I make a formal, public promise to get it done by a certain date. I make sure that I will be reminded of the promise. And then, hours before the deadline, I actually get to work and do the job. This kind of behavior is fully compatible with the seven-stage analysis.

The Gulfs of Execution and Evaluation

Remember the movie projector story? People's problems threading the projector did not come from a lack of understanding of the goal or the task. It did not come from deep, subtle complexity. The difficulty lay entirely in determining the relationship between the intended actions and the mechanisms of the projector, in determining the functions of each of the controls, in determining what specific manipulation of each control enabled each function, and in deciding by the sights, sounds, lights, and movements of the projector whether the intended actions were being done successfully. The users had a problem with mappings and feedback, as they would have with the projector in figure 2.6.

The projector story is only an extreme case of the difficulties faced in the conduct of many tasks. For a surprisingly large number of everyday tasks, the difficulty resides entirely in deriving the relationships between the mental intentions and interpretations and the physical actions and states. There are several *gulfs* that separate mental states from physical ones. Each gulf reflects one aspect of the distance between the mental representations of the person and the physical com-

2.6 Threading the Movie Projector. The dark line at the right shows the path of the film. This picture doesn't tell the whole story, for the several loops of film have to be threaded just right, neither too loose nor too taut. (From *Projectionist's manual,* Department of the Army and the Air Force, May 1966.)

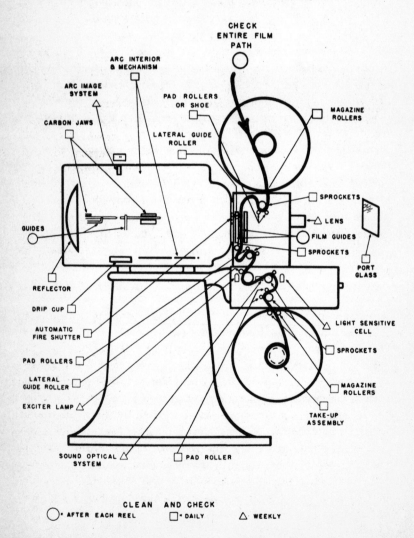

ponents and states of the environment. And these gulfs present major problems for users.[8]

THE GULF OF EXECUTION

Does the system provide actions that correspond to the intentions of the person? The difference between the intentions and the allowable actions is the Gulf of Execution. One measure of this gulf is how well the system allows the person to do the intended actions directly, without extra effort: Do the actions provided by the system match those intended by the person?

Consider the movie projector example: one problem resulted from the Gulf of Execution. The person wanted to set up the projector. Ideally, this would be a simple thing to do. But no, a long, complex sequence was required. It wasn't at all clear what actions had to be done to accomplish the intentions of setting up the projector and showing the film.

Self-threading projectors do exist. These nicely bridge the gulf. Or look at VCRs. They have the same mechanical problem as film projectors: the videotape has to be threaded through their mechanism. But the solution is to hide this part of the system, to put the task on the machine, not the person. So the machinery bridges the gulf. All the user has to do is to plop in the cartridge and push the start button. It's a pity the film companies are so far behind. Well, in a while it won't matter. There won't be any film, just videotape.

THE GULF OF EVALUATION

Does the system provide a physical representation that can be directly perceived and that is directly interpretable in terms of the intentions and expectations of the person? The Gulf of Evaluation reflects the amount of effort that the person must exert to interpret the physical state of the system and to determine how well the expectations and intentions have been met. The gulf is small when the system provides information about its state in a form that is easy to get, is easy to interpret, and matches the way the person thinks of the system.

In the movie projector example there was also a problem with the Gulf of Evaluation. Even when the film was in the projector, it was difficult to tell if it had been threaded correctly. With VCRs all you have to know is whether the cartridge is properly inserted into the machine. If it isn't, usually it won't fit right: it sticks out obviously, and you know that things are not right.

But VCRs aren't perfect, either. I remember a conference speaker who pushed the start button on the VCR and told the audience to watch the screen. No picture. She fiddled with the machine, then called for help. One, then two, then three technicians appeared on the scene. They carefully checked the power connections, the leads to the VCR, the circuits. The audience waited impatiently, giggling. Finally the problem was found: there wasn't any tape in the VCR. No tape, no picture. The problem was that once the cartridge door to that particular VCR was shut, there was no visible way to tell whether it contained a tape. Bad design. That Gulf of Evaluation sunk another user.

The gulfs are present to an amazing degree in a variety of devices. Usually the difficulties are unremarked and invisible. The users either take the blame themselves (in the case of things they believe they should be capable of using, such as water faucets, refrigerator temperature controls, stove tops, radio and television sets) or decide that they are incapable of operating the pesky devices (sewing machines, washing machines, digital watches, digital controls on household appliances, VCRs, audio sets). These are indeed the gadgets of everyday household use. None of them has a complex structure, yet many of them defeat the otherwise capable user.

The Seven Stages of Action as Design Aids

The seven-stage structure can be a valuable design aid, for it provides a basic checklist of questions to ask to ensure that the Gulfs of Evaluation and Execution are bridged (figure 2.7).

In general, each stage of action requires its own special design strategies and, in turn, provides its own opportunity for disaster. It would be fun, were it not also so frustrating, to look over the world and gleefully analyze each deficiency. On the whole, as you can see in figure 2.7, the questions for each stage are relatively simple. And these, in turn, boil down to the principles of good design introduced in chapter 1.

· *Visibility.* By looking, the user can tell the state of the device and the alternatives for action.

> **How Easily Can One:**
>
> Determine The Function
> of the Device?
>
> Tell What Actions   Tell if System is
> Are Possible?   in Desired State?
>
> Determine Mapping   Determine Mapping
> from Intention to   from System State
> Physical Movement?   to Interpretation?
>
> Perform the Action?   Tell What State
>   the System is In?

· *A good conceptual model.* The designer provides a good conceptual model for the user, with consistency in the presentation of operations and results and a coherent, consistent system image.

· *Good mappings.* It is possible to determine the relationships between actions and results, between the controls and their effects, and between the system state and what is visible.

· *Feedback.* The user receives full and continuous feedback about the results of actions.

Each point provides support for one or more of the seven stages of action. The next time you can't immediately figure out the shower control in a motel or work an unfamiliar television set or stove, remember that the problem is in the design. And the next time you pick up an unfamiliar object and use it smoothly and effortlessly on the first try, stop and examine it: the ease of use did not come about by accident. Someone designed the object carefully and well.

CHAPTER THREE

KNOWLEDGE IN
THE HEAD AND IN
THE WORLD

A friend kindly let me borrow his car. Just before I was about to leave, I found a note waiting for me: "I should have mentioned that to get the key out of the ignition the car needs to be in reverse." The car needs to be in reverse! If I hadn't seen the note, I never could have figured that out. There was no visible cue in the car: the knowledge needed for this trick had to reside in the head. If the driver lacks that knowledge, the key stays in the ignition forever.

It is easy to show the faulty nature of human knowledge and memory. A common classroom exercise in the United States demonstrates that students cannot recall the pairing of letters and numbers on their telephones. One of my graduate students found that when professional typists were given caps for typewriter keys, they could not arrange them in the proper configuration.[1] American students dial telephones properly, and all those typists could type rapidly and accurately. Why the apparent discrepancy between the precision of behavior and the imprecision of knowledge? Because not all of the knowledge required for precise behavior has to be in the head. It can be distributed—partly in the head, partly in the world, and partly in the constraints of the world. Precise behavior can emerge from imprecise knowledge for four reasons.

1. *Information is in the world.* Much of the information a person needs to do a task can reside in the world. Behavior is determined by combining the information in memory (in the head) with that in the world.

2. *Great precision is not required.* Precision, accuracy, and completeness of knowledge are seldom required. Perfect behavior will result if the knowledge describes the information or behavior sufficiently to distinguish the correct choice from all others.

3. *Natural constraints are present.* The world restricts the allowed behavior. The physical properties of objects constrain possible operations: the order in which parts can go together and the ways in which an object can be moved, picked up, or otherwise manipulated. Each object has physical features—projections, depressions, screwthreads, appendages—that limit its relationships to other objects, operations that can be performed to it, what can be attached to it, and so on.

4. *Cultural constraints are present.* In addition to natural, physical constraints, society has evolved numerous artificial conventions that govern acceptable social behavior. These cultural conventions have to be learned, but once learned they apply to a wide variety of circumstances.

Because of these natural and artificial constraints, the number of alternatives for any particular situation is reduced, as are the amount and specificity of knowledge required within human memory.

In everyday situations, behavior is determined by the combination of internal knowledge and external information and constraints. People routinely capitalize on this fact. They can minimize the amount of material they must learn or the completeness, precision, accuracy, or depth of the learning. People can deliberately organize the environment to support their behavior. Some people with brain damage can function so well that even their co-workers may not be aware of their handicap. Nonreaders have been known to fool others, even in situations where their job presumably requires reading skills. They know what is expected of them, follow the behavior of their co-workers, and set up situations so that they do not need to read or so that their co-workers do the reading for them.

What is true in these extreme cases must certainly also be true of ordinary people in ordinary situations: it is only the amount of reliance upon the external world that differs. There is a tradeoff between the amount of mental knowledge and the amount of external knowledge required in performing tasks. People are free to operate variously in allowing for this tradeoff.

Precise Behavior
from Imprecise Knowledge

INFORMATION IS IN THE WORLD

Whenever information needed to do a task is readily available in the world, the need for us to learn it diminishes. For example, we lack knowledge about common coins, even though we recognize them just fine (figure 3.1). Or consider typing. Many typists have not memorized the keyboard. Usually each letter is labeled, so nontypists can hunt and peck letter by letter, relying on knowledge in the world and minimizing the time required for learning. The problem is that such typing is slow and difficult. With experience, of course, hunt-and-peck typists learn the positions of many of the letters on the keyboard, even without instruction, and typing speed increases notably, quickly surpassing handwriting speeds and, for some, reaching quite respectable rates. Peripheral vision and the feel of the keyboard provide some information about key locations. Frequently used keys become completely learned, infrequently used keys are not learned well, and the other keys are partially learned. But as long as the typist needs to watch the keyboard, the speed is limited. The knowledge is still mostly in the world, not in the head.

If a person needs to type large amounts of material regularly, further investment is worthwhile: a course, a book, or an interactive computer program. The important thing is to learn the proper placement of fingers on the keyboard, to learn to type without looking, to get knowledge about the keyboard from the world into the head. It takes several hours to learn the system and several months to become expert. But the payoff of all this effort is increased typing speed, increased accuracy, and decreased mental load and effort at the time of typing.

There is a tradeoff between speed and quality of performance and mental effort. Thus, in finding your way through a city, locating items in a store or house, or working complex machinery, the tradeoff can determine what needs to be learned. Because you know that the infor-

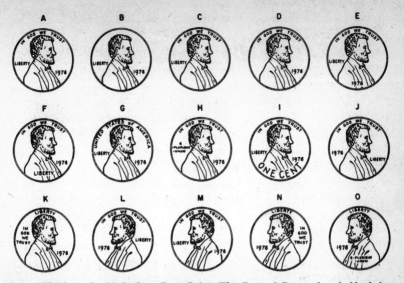

3.1 Which Is the U. S. One Cent Coin—The Penny? Fewer than half of the American college students who were given this set of drawings and asked to select the correct one could do so. Pretty bad performance, except that the students, of course, have no difficulty using the money: in normal life, we have to distinguish between the penny and other U.S. coins, not between several versions of one denomination. (From Nickerson & Adams, *Cognitive Psychology, 11,* © 1979. Reprinted by permission of Academic Press.)

mation is available in the environment, the information you internally code in memory need be precise enough only to sustain the quality of behavior you desire. This is one reason people can function well in their environment and still be unable to describe what they do. For example, a person can travel accurately through a city without being able to describe the route precisely.

People function through their use of two kinds of knowledge: knowledge *of* and knowledge *how.* Knowledge *of*—what psychologists call declarative knowledge—includes the knowledge of facts and rules. "Stop at red lights." "New York City lies on a parallel a bit south of Madrid, San Diego's longitude is east of Reno." "To get the key out of the ignition, the car must be in reverse." Declarative knowledge is easy to write down and to teach. Knowledge *how*—what psychologists call procedural knowledge—is the knowledge that enables a person to perform music, to stop a car smoothly with a flat tire on an icy road, to return a serve in tennis, or to move the tongue properly when saying the phrase "frightening witches." Procedural knowledge is difficult or impossible to write down and difficult to teach. It is best taught by demonstration and best learned through practice. Even the best teachers cannot usually describe what they are doing. Procedural knowledge is largely subconscious.

Knowledge from the world is usually easy to come by. Designers provide a large number of memory aids. The letters on the typewriter keyboard are one example. The lights and labels on controls act as external memory aids, reminding the user of the purpose and state of the control. Industrial equipment is replete with signal lights, indicators, and other reminders. We make extensive use of written notes. We place items in specific locations as reminders. In general, people structure the environment to provide a considerable amount of the information required for something to be remembered.

Many people organize their lives in the world, creating a pile here, a pile there, each indicating some activity to be done, some event in progress. Probably everybody uses such a strategy to some extent. Look around you at the variety of ways people structure their rooms and desks. Many styles of organization are possible, but the physical arrangement and visibility of the items frequently convey information about relative importance. Want to do your friends a nasty turn? Do them a favor—clean up their desks or rooms. Do this to some people and you can completely destroy their ability to function. [2]

GREAT PRECISION IS NOT REQUIRED

Normally, people do not need precise memory information. People can remember enough to distinguish one familiar coin from another although they may be unable to remember the faces, pictures, and words on the coins.[3] But make more precise memory necessary and you get havoc. Three countries have rediscovered this fact in recent years: the United States, when it introduced the Susan B. Anthony one-dollar coin; Great Britain, when it introduced the one-pound coin; and France, when it introduced a new ten-franc coin. The new U.S. dollar coin was confused with the existing twenty-five-cent piece (the quarter), and the British pound coin was confused with the existing five-pence piece. (The one-pound coin has the same diameter as the five-pence piece, but is considerably thicker and heavier.) Here is what happened in France:

"PARIS . . ." With a good deal of fanfare, the French government released the new 10-franc coin (worth a little more than $1.50) on Oct. 22 [1986]. The public looked at it, weighed it, and began confusing it so quickly with the half-franc coin (worth only 8 cents) that a crescendo of fury and ridicule fell on both the government and the coin.

"Five weeks later, Minister of Finance Edouard Balladur suspended circulation of the coin. Within another four weeks, he canceled it altogether.

"In retrospect, the French decision seems so foolish that it is hard to fathom how it could have been made. . . . After much study, designers came up with a silver-colored coin made of nickel and featuring a modernistic drawing by artist Joaquim Jimenez of a Gallic rooster on one side and of Marianne, the female symbol of the French republic, on the other. The coin was light, sported special ridges on its rim for easy reading by electronic vending machines and seemed tough to counterfeit.

"But the designers and bureaucrats were obviously so excited by their creation that they ignored or refused to accept the new coin's similarity to the hundreds of millions of silver-colored, nickel-based half-franc coins in circulation . . . [whose] size and weight were perilously similar."[4]

The confusions probably occurred because the users of coins formed representations in their memory systems that were sufficiently precise only to distinguish among the coins that they actually had to use. It is a general property of memory that we store only partial descriptions of the things to be remembered, descriptions that are sufficiently precise to work at the time something is learned, but that may not work later on, when new experiences have also been encountered and entered into memory. The descriptions formed to distinguish among the old coins were not precise enough to distinguish between the new one and at least one of the old ones.[5]

Suppose I keep all my notes in a small red notebook. If this is my only notebook, I can describe it simply as my notebook. If I buy several more notebooks, the earlier description will no longer work. Now I must call the first one small or red, or maybe both small and red, whichever allows me to distinguish it from the others. But what if I acquire several small, red notebooks? Now I must find some other means of describing the first book, adding to the richness of the de-

scription and thereby to its ability to discriminate among the several similar items. Descriptions need discriminate only among the choices in front of me, but what works for one purpose may not for another. [6]

THE POWER OF CONSTRAINTS

Back in the good old days of oral tradition (and even today for some cultures), performers traveled around reciting epic poems thousands of lines long. How did they do it? Do some people have huge amounts of knowledge in their heads? Not really. It turns out that external constraints exert powerful control over the permissible choice of words, thus dramatically reducing the memory load.

Consider the constraints of rhyming. If you wish to rhyme one word with another in English, there are usually ten to twenty alternatives. But if you must have a word with a particular meaning to rhyme with another, there are usually no candidates at all. And if there are any, in most cases there is only one. Combining the two constraints of rhyme and meaning can therefore reduce the information about the particular word that must be kept in memory to nothing; as long as the constraints are known, the choice of word can be completely determined. The learning of material like poetry is greatly aided by these kinds of constraints, which work on the general schema for the class of poem, meter, and topic.

Here is an example. I am thinking of three words: one means "a mythical being," the second is "the name of a building material," and the third is "a unit of time." What words do I have in mind? Although you can probably think of three words that fit the descriptions, you are not likely to get the same three that I have in mind. There simply are not enough constraints.

Now try a second task, this time looking for rhyming words. I am thinking of three words: one rhymes with "post," the second with "eel," and the third with "ear." What words am I thinking of?

Suppose I now tell you that the words I seek are the same in both tasks: What is a word that means a mythical being and rhymes with "post"? What word is the name of a building material and rhymes with "eel"? And what word is a unit of time and rhymes with "ear"? Now the task is easy: the joint specification of the words completely constrains the selection.

In the psychology laboratory, people almost never got the correct meanings or rhymes for the first two tasks, but they correctly answered "ghost," "steel," and "year" in the combined task almost always.[7]

The classic study of memory for epic poetry was done by Albert Bates Lord. He went to Yugoslavia and found people who still followed the oral tradition. He demonstrated that the "singer of tales," the person who learns epic poems and goes from village to village reciting them, is really recreating them, composing poetry on the fly in such a way that it obeys the rhythm, theme, story line, structure, and other characteristics of the poem. This is a prodigious feat, but it is not an example of rote memory. Rather, the practice illustrates the immense power of the multiple constraints that allow the singer to listen to another singer tell a lengthy tale once, and then (after a delay of a few hours or a day) apparently recite "the same song, word for word, and line for line."[8] In fact, as Lord points out, the original and new recitations are not the same word for word. But the listener would perceive them as the same, even if the second version were twice as long as the first. They are the same in the ways that matter to the listener: they tell the same story, express the same ideas, and follow the same rhyme and meter. They are the same in all senses that matter to the culture. Lord shows just how the combination of memory for poetics, theme, and style combine with cultural structures into what he calls a formula for producing an appropriate poem, perceived as identical to earlier recitations. The notion that someone should be able to recite word for word is relatively modern. Such a notion can be held only after printed texts become available; otherwise who could judge the accuracy of a recitation? Perhaps more important, who would care? All this is not to detract from the feat. Learning and reciting an epic poem such as Homer's *Odyssey* or *Iliad* is clearly difficult even if the singer is recreating it: there are 27,000 lines of verse in the written version.[9]

Most of us do not learn epic poems. But we do make use of strong constraints that serve to simplify what must be retained in memory. Consider an example from a completely different domain: taking apart and reassembling a mechanical device. Typical items in the home that an adventuresome person might attempt to repair include a door lock, toaster, and washing machine. The device is apt to have tens of parts. What has to be remembered in order to put the parts together again in proper order? Not as much as might appear from an initial analysis. In the extreme case, if there are ten parts, there are 10! (10 factorial: 10

$\times$ 9 $\times$ 8 . . .) different ways in which to reassemble them—a little over 3.5 million alternatives. But never can all possible orderings be produced: there will be a number of physical constraints on the ordering. Some pieces must be assembled before it is even possible to assemble the others. Some pieces are physically constrained from fitting into the spots reserved for others: bolts must fit into holes of an appropriate diameter and depth; nuts and washers must be paired with bolts and screws of appropriate sizes; and washers must always be put on before nuts. There are even cultural constraints: we turn screws clockwise to tighten, counterclockwise to loosen; the heads of screws tend to go on the visible part (front or top) of a piece, bolts on the less visible part (bottom, side, or interior) of a piece; wood screws and machine screws look different and are inserted into different kinds of materials. In the end, the apparently large number of decisions is reduced to only a few choices that should have been learned or otherwise noted during the disassembly. The constraints by themselves are often not sufficient to determine the proper reassembly of the device—mistakes do get made—but the constraints reduce the amount that must be learned to a reasonable quantity.

Memory Is Knowledge in the Head

Remember the story of 'Ali Baba and the forty thieves? 'Ali Baba discovered the secret words that opened the thieves' cave. His brother-in-law, Kasim, forced him to reveal the secret. Kasim then went to the cave.

"When he reached the entrance of the cavern, he pronounced the words, Open Simsim!

"The door immediately opened, and when he was in, closed on him. In examining the cave he was greatly astonished to find much more riches than he had expected from 'Ali Baba's relation. He quickly lade at the door of the cavern as many bags of gold as his ten mules could carry, but his thoughts were now so full of the great riches he should possess, that he could not think of the necessary words to make the door open. Instead of Open Simsim! he said Open Barley! and was much amazed to find that the door remained shut. He named several sorts of grain, but still the door would not open.

"Kasim never expected such an incident, and was so alarmed at the

danger he was in that the more he endeavoured to remember the word Simsim the more his memory was confounded, and he had as much forgotten it as if he had never heard it mentioned."

Kasim never got out. The thieves returned, cut off Kasim's head, and quartered his body.[10]

THE CONSPIRACY AGAINST MEMORY

Most of us will not get our heads cut off if we fail to remember a secret code, but it can still be very hard to do. It is one thing to have to memorize one or two secrets: a combination, or a password, or the secret to opening the door. But when the number of secret codes gets too large, memory fails. There seems to be a conspiracy, one calculated to destroy our sanity by overloading our memory. Consider what we are asked to remember in our "convenient" world. A simple search through my own wallet and papers reveals the following things.

· Postal codes ranging in the United States from the "short form" of five digits to the "long form" of nine. Human short-term memory can comfortably retain only a five- to seven-digit number, yet here I am asked to use nine. I need to know the code for where I live, the code for where I work, the codes for my parents and for my children, the codes for my friends, and the codes for anyone with whom I correspond regularly. American codes, such as 92014-6207; British codes, such as WC1N 3BG; Canadian codes, such as M6P2V8. All for the sake of the machinery, and despite the fact that addresses are perfectly sensible and normally unambiguous. But machines have trouble with addresses, whereas they can deal with simple postal codes.

· Telephone numbers, sometimes with area codes and extensions. A seven-digit number becomes ten when the area code is added, and then fourteen when there is a four-digit extension. International codes, with country code and city code, add more digits. How many telephone numbers must I know? More than I wish to contemplate. All my personal contacts. Numbers for information, time, and weather; the special number for emergencies. And I mustn't forget to dial 9 (or, in some cases, 8) so that the call will go outside the institution or company.

· Access numbers for telephone budget cards, so that when I make a long distance call from my university, I can cause the correct account to pay the bill: a five-digit number for each account (and I have four of them). Don't show these to anyone, I am warned. Keep them hidden in a secret place.

· Access numbers for telephone credit cards, so when I travel I can have the bill automatically put on my home telephone number. The codes consist of my home telephone number plus four secret digits. The secret digits aren't even printed on the card: memorize and destroy. But I have six of them (two home phone accounts and four different university phone accounts). If I want to dial a long distance number from a hotel using one of my telephone credit cards, I must dial as many as thirty-six digits.

· Passwords or numbers for bank automatic teller machines, those clever machines that let you put in a card, type in your secret password, and get money. Two bank accounts, two secret passwords. Don't write them down, a thief might see them. Memorize. Memorize.

· Secret passwords for my computer accounts: can't let people steal my valuable data, or perhaps change their course grades, or peek at the examination questions. Make the password at least six characters long, we are told. And no words—words are too easy for someone to discover—make it nonsense. (I cheat and make all my computer accounts use the same password.)

· Driver's license number. When I lived briefly in Texas I couldn't do anything without my driver's license number: not pay for food at the supermarket, not pay the telephone bill, not even open up a bank account. That was one letter, seven digits. Other states have longer numbers.

· Social security numbers for me, my wife, and my children. Nine digits each.

· Passport numbers, again for my whole family.

· My employee number.

· License plate numbers for our cars.

· Birthdays.

· Ages.

· Clothing sizes.

· Addresses.

- Credit card numbers.
- Bah and humbug.

So many of these numbers and codes must be kept secret. Apparently, thieves are everywhere, just waiting for me to write down my secret password or number, anxious to make that phone call on my account or to purchase items with my charge card. There is no way that I can learn all those numbers. And they keep changing, anyway, some of them annually. I even have trouble remembering how old I am: it changes every year too. (Quick: what magic phrase was Kasim trying to remember to open the cavern door?)

How can we remember all these things? Most of us can't, even with the use of mnemonics to make some sense of nonsensical material. Books and courses on improving memory can work, but the methods are laborious to learn and need continued practice to maintain. So we put the memory in the world, writing things down in books, on scraps of paper, even on the backs of our hands. But we disguise them to thwart would-be thieves. That creates another problem: How do we disguise the items, how do we hide them, and how do we remember what the disguise was or where we put them? Ah, the foibles of memory.

Where should you hide something so that nobody else will find it? In unlikely places, right? Money is hidden in the freezer, jewelry in the medicine cabinet or in shoes in the closet. The key to the front door is hidden under the mat or just below the window ledge. The car key is under the bumper. The love letters are in a flower vase. The problem is, there aren't that many unlikely places in the home. You may not remember where the love letters or keys are hidden, but your burglar will. Two psychologists who examined the issue described the problem this way:

"There is often a logic involved in the choice of unlikely places. For example, a friend of ours was required by her insurance company to acquire a safe if she wished to insure her valuable gems. Recognizing that she might forget the combination to the safe, she thought carefully about where to keep the combination. Her solution was to write it in her personal phone directory under the letter S next to 'Mr. and Mrs. Safe,' as if it were a telephone number. There is a clear logic here: Store numerical information with other numerical information. She was appalled, however, when she heard a reformed burglar on a daytime

television talk show say that upon encountering a safe, he always headed for the phone directory because many people keep the combination there."[11]

All these numbers to remember add up to unwitting tyranny. It is time for a revolt.

THE STRUCTURE OF MEMORY

"Say aloud the numbers 1, 7, 4, 2, 8. Next, without looking back, repeat them. Try again if you must, perhaps closing your eyes, the better to 'hear' the sound still echoing in mental activity. Have someone read a random sentence to you. What were the words? The memory of the just present is available immediately, clear and complete, without mental effort.

"What did you eat for dinner three days ago? Now the feeling is different. It takes time to recover the answer, which is neither as clear nor as complete a remembrance as that of the just present, and the recovery is likely to require considerable mental effort. Retrieval of the past differs from retrieval of the just present. More effort is required, less clarity results. Indeed, the 'past' need not be so long ago. Without looking back, what were those digits? For some people, this retrieval now takes time and effort."[12]

Psychologists distinguish between two major classes of memory: short-term memory and long-term memory (abbreviated STM and LTM, respectively). The two are quite different. Short-term memory is the memory of the just present. Information is retained in it automatically and retrieved without effort; but the amount of information that can be retained this way is severely limited. Something like five to seven items is the limit of STM, with the number going to ten or twelve if a person also rehearses, mentally repeating the items to be retained. Short-term memory is invaluable in the performance of everyday tasks, in letting us remember words, names, phrases, and parts of tasks. It acts as a working or temporary memory. But the memory is quite fragile. Get distracted by some other activity and, poof, the stuff in STM disappears. It is capable of holding a five-digit postal code or seven-digit telephone number from the time you look them up until the time they are used—as long as no distractions occur. Nine- or ten-digit numbers give trouble, and when the number starts to exceed that—don't bother. Write it down. Or divide the number into several shorter segments.

Long-term memory is memory for the past. As a rule, it takes time to put stuff away in LTM and time and effort to get it out again. This is how we maintain our experiences, not as an exact recording of the events, but as interpreted through our understanding of them, subject to all the distortions and changes that the human explanatory mechanism imposes upon life. How well we can ever recover experiences and knowledge from LTM is highly dependent upon how the material was interpreted in the first place. What is stored in LTM under one interpretation probably cannot be found later on when sought under some other interpretation. As for how large the memory is, nobody really knows: billions of items, probably. One informed scientist estimates the capacity as a billion (10^9) bits or about 100 million (10^8) items.[13] Whatever the size, it is so large as not to impose any practical limit. The difficulty with LTM is in organization—in getting material in and in figuring out how to retrieve it—not in capacity. Storage and retrieval are easier when the material makes sense, when it fits into what is already known. When the material makes no sense, it will have to be worked on, structured, and interpreted, until finally it can be retained.

Human memory is essentially knowledge in the head, or internal knowledge. If we examine how people use their memories and how they retrieve information, we discover a number of categories. Three are important for us now:

1. *Memory for arbitrary things.* The items to be retained seem arbitrary, with no meaning and no particular relationship to one other or to things already known.

2. *Memory for meaningful relationships.* The items to be retained form meaningful relationships with themselves or with other things already known.

3. *Memory through explanation.* The material does not have to be remembered, but rather can be derived from some explanatory mechanism.

MEMORY FOR ARBITRARY THINGS

Arbitrary knowledge can be classified as the simple remembering of what is to be done, without reliance on an understanding of why or on internal structure. This is how we learned the alphabet and how to tie a shoelace. It is even how we learned the multiplication tables, that 3 times 2 is 6, although for that we could refer to an external structure. This is how we are expected to learn arbitrary codes to operate the modern, misbegotten telephone system. It is also how we are forced to learn many procedures required of modern technology: "To load this program, put the floppy diskette into drive A and type ALT MODE, CONTROL-SHIFT-X, DELETE." This is rote learning, the bane of modern existence.

Rote learning creates problems. First, because what is being learned is arbitrary, the learning is difficult: it can take considerable time and effort. Second, when a problem arises, the memorized sequence of actions gives no hint of what has gone wrong, no suggestion of what might be done to fix the problem. Although some things are appropriate to learn by rote (the letters of the alphabet, for example), most are not. Alas, it is still the dominant method of instruction in many school systems, and even for much adult training. This is how some people are taught to use computers, or to cook. It is how we have to learn to use some of the new (poorly designed) gadgets of our technology.

Most psychologists would argue that it is not really possible to learn arbitrary associations or sequences. Even where there appears to be no structure, people manufacture some artificial and usually rather unsatisfactory one, which is why the learning is so bad. For our purposes it does not matter whether arbitrary learning is impossible or simply very difficult, the end result is the same: it is not the best way to go, not if there is any choice in the matter. Thus, in teaching the alphabet, we try to make it into a tune, using the natural constraints of rhyme and rhythm to simplify the memory load. People who have learned to use computers or cook by rote are probably not very good. Since they do not understand the reasons for their actions, they must find tasks arbitrary and strange. When something goes wrong, they don't know what to do (unless they've memorized solutions). Although rote learning is at times necessary or efficient—so that emergency procedures for things like high-speed military jet aircraft are handled quickly, automatically when the need arises—on the whole, it is most unsatisfactory.

MEMORY FOR MEANINGFUL RELATIONSHIPS

Most things in the world have a sensible structure, which tremendously simplifies the memory task. When things make sense, they correspond to knowledge that we already have, so the new material can be understood, interpreted, and integrated with previously acquired material. Now we can use rules and constraints to help understand what things go together. Meaningful structure can organize apparent chaos and arbitrariness.

Remember the discussion of mental models in chapter 2? Part of the power of a good mental model lies in its ability to provide meaning to things. Let's look at an example to show how a meaningful interpretation transforms an apparently arbitrary task into a natural one. Note that the appropriate interpretation may not at first be obvious; it, too, is knowledge and has to be discovered.

A Japanese colleague, call him Mr. Tanaka, had difficulty remembering how to use the turn-signal switch on his motorcycle's left handlebar. Moving the switch forward signaled a right turn, backward a left turn. The meaning of the switch was clear and unambiguous, but the direction in which it should be moved was not. Tanaka kept thinking that because the switch was on the left handlebar, pushing it forward should signal a left turn. That is, he was trying to map the action "push the left switch forward" to the intention "turn left," which was wrong. As a result, he had trouble remembering which switch direction should be used for which turning direction. Most motorcycles have the turn-signal switch mounted differently, rotated 90°, so that moving it left signals a left turn, moving it right a right turn. This mapping is easy to learn (it is a natural mapping). But the turn switch on Tanaka's motorcycle moved forward and back, not left and right. How could he learn it?

Mr. Tanaka solved the problem by reinterpreting the action. Consider the way the handlebars of the motorcycle turn. For a left turn, the left handlebar moves backward. For a right turn, the left handlebar moves forward. The required switch movements exactly paralleled the handlebar movements. If the task is reconceptualized as signaling the direction of motion of the handlebars rather than the direction of the motorcycle, the switch motion can be seen to mimic the desired motion; finally we have a natural mapping. At first, the motion of the switch seemed arbitrary, indirect, and difficult to remember. With the proper interpretation, the switch motion is direct and logical, and, as a result, easy to learn and to use. A meaningful relationship can be indispensable, but you have to have the right one. [14]

Without the proper interpretation, it was difficult to remember the switch directions. With it, both the remembering and the performance of the task became trivial. Note that Tanaka's interpretation of the switch movement did not *explain* anything. It simply let him relate the proper direction to move the switch with the direction in which he was turning the motorcycle. The interpretation is essential, but it should not be confused with understanding.

MEMORY THROUGH EXPLANATION

Now we come to a different, more powerful form of internal memory: understanding. People are explanatory creatures, as I showed in chapter 2. Explanations and interpretations of events are fundamental to human performance, both in understanding the world and in learning and remembering. Here mental models play a major role. Mental models simplify learning, in part because the details of the required behavior can be derived when needed. They can be invaluable in dealing with unexpected situations. Note that the use of mental models to remember (in this case, derive) behavior is not ideal for tasks that must be done rapidly and smoothly. The derivation takes time and requires mental resources, neither of which may be in great supply during critical incidents. Mental models let people derive appropriate behavior for situations that are not remembered (or never before encountered). People probably make up mental models for most of the things they do. This is why designers should provide users with appropriate models: when they are not supplied, people are likely to make up inappropriate ones.[15]

The sewing machine provides a good example of the power of a mental model. A sewing machine is a mysterious beast, managing to loop an upper thread through a lower thread, even though each thread is always connected to its spool or bobbin, respectively. The mental model has to explain how the upper thread goes through the material being sewn, dips under the surface plate, and then loops around the lower thread.

The proper model, it turns out, is something like this. Picture the lower bobbin held gently in the machine by a kind of cup with sloping sides. The cup keeps the bobbin stable, allowing it to rotate so its thread can be unwound. Yet the cup is loose enough so that the upper thread can go inside the cup and around the bobbin—and therefore around the bottom thread. When the upper needle goes through the material and under the plate, a rotating hook grabs its thread and guides it between the inner walls of the cup and the outer walls of the bobbin case. This helps explain why the machine won't work properly if the bobbin is bent, even if the bobbin still appears to fit and the bottom thread unrolls properly. It explains why dirt on the bobbin or in the cup will mess things up, and why certain kinds of upper thread might cause more trouble than others. (A thick upper thread, especially one that was rough or sticky, might not go smoothly around the bobbin.)

To be honest, I don't know if anything I just said about the failures of bobbins is true. I derived each example from my mental model of a sewing machine. I can't sew. But when Naomi Miyake did her research for her doctoral thesis in my laboratory, she studied people's understanding of sewing and of the machines. The result was twofold: a fine piece of research for her and a mental model for me. So now I can derive what would happen, even if it has never happened to me.

The power of mental models is that they let you figure out what would happen in novel situations. Or, if you are actually doing the task and there is a problem, they let you figure out what is happening. If the model is wrong, you will be wrong too. Am I right about the sewing machine? Decide for yourself: go look at one.

After word got out that I was collecting instances of design peculiarities, a friend reported the following about the sunroof of his new car, an Audi. Supposedly, if the ignition is not on, the sunroof cannot be operated. However, a mechanic explained that you could close the sunroof even without the ignition key if you turned on the headlights and then (1) pulled back on the turn-signal stalk (which normally switches the headlights to high beam), and (2) pushed the close control for the sunroof.

My friend said that it was thoughtful of Audi to provide this override of the ignition key in case the sunroof was open when it started raining. You could close it even if you didn't have your key. But we both wondered why the sequence was so peculiar.

Ever skeptical, I asked to see the manual for the car. The manual was explicit: "You cannot work the sunroof if the ignition is off." A similar statement appeared in the discussion of the electrically powered windows. My friend's mental model was functional: it explained why you would want such a feature, but not how it worked. If the feature was so desirable, why was it not mentioned in the manual?

We searched for another explanation. Perhaps it wasn't a design feature, after all. Perhaps it was an accident of design. Perhaps turning on the lights and pulling back on the stalk connected the electrical power to the car, overriding the fact that the ignition key was off. This would allow the sunroof to work, but only as a by-product of the way the lights were wired.

This model was more specific. It explained what was happening and allowed us to predict that all electrical items should work. So we checked. Turning on the light switch without engaging the ignition did not turn on the headlights; only the parking lights went on. But when we also pulled back on the turn-signal stalk, the headlights did turn on, even though the ignition was off. With the stalk pulled back, the sunroof would close and open. The windows would close and open. The fan on the heating system worked. So did the radio. This was an effective mental model. Now we could understand better what was happening, predict new results, and more easily remember the peculiar set of operations required for the task.

Memory Is Also Knowledge in the World

As we have seen, knowledge in the world, external knowledge, can be very valuable. But it, too, has drawbacks. For one, it is available only if you are there, in the appropriate situation. When you are somewhere else, or if the world has changed meanwhile, the knowledge is gone. The critical memory aids provided by the external information are absent, and so the task or item may not be remembered. A folk saying captures this situation well: *"Out of sight, out of mind."*

REMINDING

One of the most important and interesting aspects of the role of external memory is reminding, a good example of the interplay between knowledge in the head and in the world. Suppose a neighboring family asks you to take them to the airport. You agree to take them next Saturday at 3:30 P.M. Now the knowledge is in your head, but how are you going to remember it at the proper time? You will need to be reminded. There are many strategies for reminding. One is simply to keep the information in your head. If the event is important enough, you count on having it come repeatedly to mind—what psychologists call rehearsal—so that you can simply assume that there will be no difficulty at all remembering when to leave on Saturday. You can keep the information in your head especially when the event is of great personal importance: suppose you are catching the plane for your first trip to Paris. You won't have any problem remembering. But keeping the knowledge in your head is not ordinarily a good reminding technique.

Suppose the event is not personally important, it is several days away, and you are leading a very busy life. Now you'd better transfer some of the burden of remembering to the outside world. Here is where you use notes to yourself, or pocket and desk calendars or diaries, or electronic alarm clocks that can be set for time of day and date. Or you can ask a friend to remind you. Those of us with secretaries put the burden on them. They, in turn, write notes, enter events on calendars, or set an alarm on the computer system (if it is well enough designed that they can figure out how to work it).

A good reminding method is to put the burden on the thing itself. Do my neighbors want me to take them to the airport? Fine, but they have to call me up the night before and remind me. Do I want to remember to take a book to the university to give to a colleague? I put the book someplace where I cannot fail to see it when I leave the house. A good spot is against the front door of the house. I can't leave without tripping over the book. If I am at a friend's house and I borrow a paper or a book, I remember to take it by putting my car keys on it. Then when I leave, I am reminded. Even if I forget and go out to my car, I can't drive away without the keys.

There are two different aspects to a reminder: the signal and the message. Just as in doing an action we can distinguish between knowing what can be done and knowing how to do it, in reminding we must distinguish between knowing that something is to be remembered and remembering what it is. Most popular reminding devices provide only one of these two critical aspects. The famous "tie a string around your finger" reminder provides only the signal. It gives no hint of what is to be remembered. Writing a note to yourself provides only the message; it doesn't remind you ever to look at it. (Tying a knot in your handkerchief—Carelman's device in figure 3.2—provides neither signal nor message.) The ideal reminder has to have both components: the signal that something is to be remembered, the message of what it is.

3.2 Carelman's Preknotted Handkerchief. What an aid to the forgetful—except that the act of tying the knot is probably just as useful a memory cue as the knot itself. (Jacques Carelman: "Preknotted Handkerchief" Copyright © 1969–76–80 Jacques Carelman and A. D. A. G. P. Paris. From Jacques Carelman, *Catalog of Unfindable Objects.* Balland, éditeur, Paris-France. Used by permission of the artist.)

The need for timely reminders has created loads of products that make it easier to put the knowledge in the world—alarm clocks, diaries, calendars. A variety of sophisticated watches and small, calculator-sized reminding devices are starting to appear. So far they are limited in power and difficult to use. But I believe there is a need for them. They just need more work, better technology, and better design.

Would you like a pocket-size device that reminded you of each appointment and daily event? I would. I am waiting for the day when portable computers become small enough that I can keep one with me at all times. I will definitely put all my reminding burdens upon it. It has to be small. It has to be convenient to use. And it has to be relatively powerful, at least by today's standards. It has to have a full, standard typewriter keyboard and a reasonably large display. It needs good graphics, because that makes a tremendous difference in usability, and a lot of memory—a huge amount, actually. And it should be easy to hook up to the telephone; I need to connect it to my home and laboratory computers. Of course, it should be relatively inexpensive.

What I ask for is not unreasonable. The technology I need is available today. It's just that the full package has never been put together, partly because the cost in today's world would be prohibitive. But it will exist in imperfect form in five years, possibly in perfect form in ten.

NATURAL MAPPINGS

The arrangement of burners and controls on the kitchen stove provides a good example of the power of natural mappings to reduce the need for information in memory. Without a good mapping, the user cannot readily determine which burner goes with which control. Consider the standard stove with four burners, arranged in the traditional rectangle. If the four controls were truly arbitrary, as in figure 3.3, the user would have to learn each control separately: twenty-four possible arrangements. Why twenty-four? Start with the leftmost control: it could work any of the four burners. That leaves three possibilities for the next leftmost. So there are 12 (4×3) possible arrangements of the first two controls: four for the first, three for the second. The third control could work either of the two remaining burners, and then there is only one burner left for the last control. This makes twenty-four possible mappings between the controls and burners: $4 \times 3 \times 2 \times 1 = 24$. With the completely arbitrary arrangement, the stove is unworkable unless each control is fully labeled to indicate which burner it controls.

Most stoves have controls arranged in a line, even though the burners are arranged rectangularly. Controls are not mapped naturally to burners. As a result, you have to learn which control goes with which burner. Consider how the use of spatial analogies can relieve the memory burden. Start with a partial mapping that is in common use today: the controls are segregated into left and right halves, as in figure 3.4. Now we need know only which left burner each of the two left controls affects and which right burner each right control affects—two alternatives for each of the four burners. The number of possible arrangements is now only four—two possibilities for each side: quite a reduction from the twenty-four. But the controls must still be labeled, which indicates that the mapping is still imperfect. Since some of the information is now in the spatial arrangement, each control need only be labeled back or front; the left and right labels are no longer needed.

What about a proper, full, natural mapping, with the controls spatially arranged in the same pattern as the burners, as in figure 3.5? The organization of the controls now carries all the information required. We know immediately which control goes with which burner. Such is the power of natural mapping. We can see that the number of possible sequences has been reduced from twenty-four to one.[16] If all possible

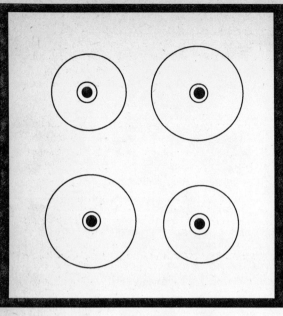

Back
Right

Front
Left

Back
Left

Front
Right

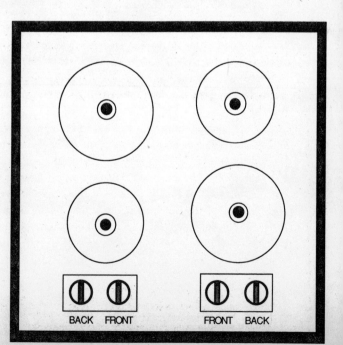

BACK   FRONT

FRONT   BACK

3.3 Arbitrary Arrangement of Stove Controls (top of opposite page). Couple the usual rectangular arrangement of burners with this arbitrary row of controls, and there is trouble: which control goes with which burner? You don't know unless the controls are labeled. The memory load for this arrangement is high: there are twenty-four possible arrangements, and you have to remember which of the twenty-four this one is. Fortunately, the controls are seldom arranged quite this arbitrarily.

3.4 Paired Stove Controls (bottom of opposite page). This is the type of partial mapping of controls to burners in common use today. The two controls on the left work the left burners, and the two controls on the right work the right burners. Now there are only four possible arrangements (two for each side). Even so, confusion is possible (and, I can assure you, it occurs often).

3.5 Full Natural Mapping of Controls and Burners (below). Two of the Possible Ways. There is no ambiguity, no need for learning or remembering, no need for labels. Why can't all stoves be like these?

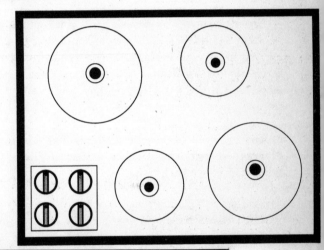

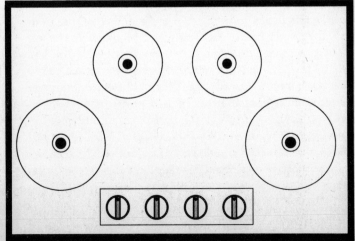

natural mappings were applied in our lives, the cumulative effect would be enormous.

The problem of the stove top may seem trivial, but in fact it is a cause of great frustration for many homeowners. Why do stove designers insist on arranging the burners in a rectangular pattern and the controls in a row? We have known for forty years just how bad such an arrangement is. Sometimes the stove comes with clever little diagrams to indicate which control works which burner. Sometimes there is a short label. But the proper natural mapping requires no diagrams, no labels, and no instructions. There is a simple design principle lurking here:

> If a design depends upon labels, it may be faulty. Labels are important and often necessary, but the appropriate use of natural mappings can minimize the need for them. Wherever labels seem necessary, consider another design.

The shame about stove design is that it isn't hard to do right. Textbooks of ergonomics, human factors, psychology, and industrial engineering all show various sensible solutions. And some stove manufacturers do use good designs. Oddly, some of the very best and the very worst are manufactured by the same companies and are illustrated side by side in the same catalogs.

Why do designers insist on frustrating users? Why do users still purchase stoves that cause so much trouble? Why not revolt and refuse to buy them unless the controls have an intelligent relationship to the burners? I bought a bad one myself.

Usability is not often thought of as a criterion during the purchasing process. Moreover, unless you actually test a number of units in a realistic environment doing typical tasks, you are not likely to notice the ease or difficulty of use. If you just look at something, it appears straightforward enough, and the array of wonderful features seems to be a virtue. You may not realize that you won't be able to figure out how to use those features. I urge you to test products before you buy them. Pretending to cook a meal, or setting the channels on a video set, or attempting to program a VCR will do. Do it right there in the store. Do not be afraid to make mistakes or ask stupid questions. Remember, any problems you have are probably the design's fault, not yours.

A major problem is that often the purchaser is not the user. Appliances may be in a home when people move in. In the office, the purchasing department orders equipment based upon such factors as price, personal relationships with the supplier, and perhaps reliability: usability is seldom considered. Finally, even when the purchaser is the end user, it is sometimes necessary to trade one desirable feature for an undesirable one. In the case of my family's stove, we did not like the arrangement of controls, but we bought the stove anyway: we traded off layout of the burner controls for another feature that was more important to us and available only from one manufacturer. (I return to these issues in chapter 6.)

The Tradeoff between Knowledge in the World and in the Head

Knowledge (or information) in the world and in the head are both essential in our daily functioning. But to some extent we can choose to lean more heavily on one or the other. That choice requires a trade-

3.6 Tradeoffs

PROPERTY	KNOWLEDGE IN THE WORLD	KNOWLEDGE IN THE HEAD
Retrievability	Retrievable whenever visible or audible.	Not readily retrievable. Requires memory search or reminding.
Learning	Learning not required. Interpretation substitutes for learning. How easy it is to interpret information in the world depends upon how well it exploits natural mappings and constraints.	Requires learning, which can be considerable. Learning is made easier if there is meaning of structure to the material (or if there is a good mental model).
Efficiency of use	Tends to be slowed up by the need to find and interpret the external information.	Can be very efficient.
Ease of use at first encounter	High.	Low.
Aesthetics	Can be unaesthetic and inelegant, especially if there is a need to maintain a lot of information. This can lead to clutter. In the end, aesthetic appeal depends upon the skill of the designer.	Nothing need be visible, which gives more freedom to the designer, which in turn can lead to better aesthetics.

off—gaining the advantages of knowledge in the world means losing the advantages of knowledge in the head (figure 3.6).

Knowledge in the world acts as its own reminder. It can help us recover structures that we otherwise would forget. Knowledge in the head is efficient: no search and interpretation of the environment is required. In order to use knowledge in the head we have to get it there, which might require considerable amounts of learning. Knowledge in the world is easier to learn, but often more difficult to use. And it relies heavily upon the continued physical presence of the information; change the environment and the information is changed. Performance relies upon the physical presence of the task environment.

Reminders provide a good example of the relative tradeoffs between the roles of internal versus external knowledge. Knowledge in the world is accessible. It is self-reminding. It is always there, waiting to be seen, waiting to be used. That is why we structure our offices and our places of work so carefully. We put piles of papers where they can be seen, or if we like a clean desk, we put them in standardized locations and teach ourselves (knowledge in the head) to look in these standard places routinely. We use clocks and calendars and notes. Knowledge in the mind is ephemeral: here now, gone later. We can't count on something being present in mind at any particular time, unless it is triggered by some external event or unless we deliberately keep it in mind through constant repetition (which then prevents us from having other conscious thoughts). Out of sight, out of mind.[17]

CHAPTER FOUR

KNOWING WHAT
TO DO

"Q. I read a news item about a new videotape-only player and rejoiced when the writer took a healthy swipe at the incomprehensible instructions that accompany VCRs. I can't even set the time of day on mine!

"There are many consumers out here like me—thwarted by an unfathomable machine and baffled by senseless instructions.

"Is there anyone, anywhere who will translate OR give a short course in VCR at play school level?"[1]

Video cassette recorders—VCRs—can be frightening to people who are unfamiliar with them. Indeed, the number of options, buttons, controls, displays, and possible courses of action is formidable. But at least when we have trouble operating a VCR we have something to blame: the machine's bewildering appearance and the lack of clues to suggest what can be done and how to do it. Even more frustrating, however, is that we often have trouble working devices that we expect to be simple.

The difficulty of dealing with novel situations is directly related to the number of possibilities. The user looks at the situation and tries to discover which parts can be operated and what operations can be done.

Problems occur whenever there is more than one possibility. If there is only one part that can be operated and only one possible action to do, there will be no difficulty. Of course, if the designer has been too clever, hiding all the visible clues, the user may believe there are no alternatives and not even know how to begin.

When we encounter a novel object, how can we tell what to do with it? Either we have dealt with something similar in the past and transfer old knowledge to the new object, or we obtain instruction. In these cases, the information we need is in the head. Another approach is to use information in the world, particularly if the design of the new object has presented us with information that can be interpreted.

How can design signal the appropriate actions? To answer the question we build upon the principles discussed in chapter 3. One important set of signals comes through the natural constraints of objects, physical constraints that limit what can be done. Another set of signals comes from the affordances of objects, which convey messages about their possible uses, actions, and functions. A flat plate affords pushing, an empty container affords filling, and so on. Affordances can signal how an object can be moved, what it will support, and whether anything will fit into its crevices, over it, or under it. Where do we grab it, which parts move, and which parts are fixed? Affordances suggest the range of possibilities, constraints limit the number of alternatives. The thoughtful use of affordances and constraints together in design lets a user determine readily the proper course of action, even in a novel situation.

A Classification
of Everyday Constraints

To understand the operation of constraints better, I did some simple experiments. I asked people to put things together from the parts given them; they had never seen the finished structure, and they were not even told what they should be constructing.[2] Let me illustrate with one of the examples: building a motorcycle from a Lego set (a children's construction toy).

The Lego motorcycle (figure 4.1) is a simple toy constructed of thirteen parts, some rather specialized. Of the thirteen parts, only two are alike—rectangles with the word *police* on them. One other piece is a blank rectangle of the same size. Three other pieces match in size and shape but are different colors. So there are two sets of three pieces in

4.1 Lego Motorcycle. The toy is shown assembled and in pieces. The thirteen parts are so cleverly constructed that even an adult can put them together. The design exploits constraints to specify just which pieces fit where. Physical constraints limit alternative placements. Semantic and cultural constraints provide the necessary clues for further decisions. For example, semantic constraints stop the user from putting the head backward on the body and cultural constraints dictate the placement of the three lights (the small rectangles, which are red, blue, and yellow).

which any of the three pieces are interchangeable, except for the semantic or cultural interpretation of the resulting construction. It turns out that the appropriate role for every single piece of the motorcycle is unambiguously determined by a set of physical, semantic, and cultural constraints. This means that people could construct the motorcycle without any instructions or assistance, although they had never seen it assembled. In this case, construction is entirely natural, if the builder knows about motorcycles and about the cultural assumptions that serve to constrain the placement of parts.

Affordances of the pieces were important in determining just how they fit together. The cylinders and holes characteristic of Lego suggested the major construction rule. The sizes and shapes of the parts suggested their operation. Physical constraints limited what parts would fit together. Other types of constraints also operated; all in all there were four different classes of constraints—physical, semantic, cultural, and logical. These classes are apparently universal, appearing in a wide variety of situations, and sufficient.

PHYSICAL CONSTRAINTS

Physical limitations constrain possible operations. Thus, a large peg cannot fit into a small hole. The motorcycle windshield would fit in only one place, with only one orientation. The value of physical constraints is that they rely upon properties of the physical world for their operation; no special training is necessary. With the proper use of physical constraints there should be only a limited number of possible actions—or, at least, desired actions can be made obvious, usually by being especially salient.

Physical constraints are made more effective and useful if they are easy to see and interpret, for then the set of actions is restricted before anything has been done. Otherwise, the physical constraint prevents the wrong action from succeeding only after it has been tried. The Lego windshield was sometimes tried in the wrong orientation first; the design could have made the correct position more visible. The everyday door key can be inserted into a vertical slot only if the key is held vertically. But this still leaves two possible orientations. A well-designed key will either work in both orientations or provide a clear physical signal for the correct one. Good automobile door keys are made so that orientation doesn't matter. A poorly designed car key can be yet another of those minor frustrations of everyday life—not so minor, perhaps, when you're standing outside the car in a storm with both arms full of packages.

SEMANTIC CONSTRAINTS

Semantic constraints rely upon the meaning of the situation to control the set of possible actions. In the case of the motorcycle, there is only one meaningful location for the rider, who must sit facing forward. The purpose of the windshield is to protect the rider's face, so it must be in front of the rider. Semantic constraints rely upon our knowledge of the situation and of the world. Such knowledge can be a powerful and important clue.

CULTURAL CONSTRAINTS

Some constraints rely upon accepted cultural conventions, even if they do not affect the physical or semantic operation of the device. One cultural convention is that signs are meant to be read; for the motorcycle, the pieces with the word *police* on them have to be placed right side up. Cultural constraints determine the locations of the three lights, which are otherwise physically interchangeable. Red is the culturally defined standard for a stop light, which is placed in the rear. White or yellow (in Europe) is the standard color for headlights, which go in front. And a police vehicle often has a blue flashing light on top.

Each culture has a set of allowable actions for social situations. Thus, we know how to behave in a restaurant, even one we have never been to before. This is how we manage to cope when our host leaves us alone in that strange room, at that strange party, with those strange people. And this is why we sometimes feel frustrated, so incapable of action, when we are confronted with a restaurant or group of people from an unfamiliar culture, where our normally accepted behavior is clearly inappropriate and frowned upon. Cultural issues are at the root of of many of the problems we have with new machines: there are as yet no accepted conventions or customs for dealing with them.

Those of us who study these things believe that guidelines for cultural behavior are represented in the mind by means of schemas, knowledge structures that contain the general rules and information necessary for interpreting situations and for guiding behavior. In some stereotypical situations (for example, in a restaurant), the schemas may be very specialized. Cognitive scientists Roger Schank and Bob Abelson have proposed that in these cases we follow "scripts" that can guide the sequence of behavior. The sociologist Ervin Goffman calls the social constraints on acceptable behavior frames, and he shows how they govern behavior even when a person is in a novel situation or novel culture. Danger awaits those who deliberately violate the frames for a culture.[3]

Next time you are in an elevator, stand facing the rear. Look at the strangers in the elevator and smile. Or scowl. Or say hello. Or say, "Are you feeling well? You don't look well." Walk up to random passersby and give them some money. Say something like, "You make me feel good, so here is some money." In a bus or streetcar, give your seat to the next athletic-looking teenager you see. The act is especially effective if you are elderly, or pregnant, or disabled.

LOGICAL CONSTRAINTS

In the case of the motorcycle, logic dictated that all the pieces should be used, with no gaps in the final product. The three lights of the Lego motorcycle presented a special problem for many people. They could use the cultural constraint to figure out that the red was the stop light and should go in the rear, that the yellow was the headlight and should go in the front, but what about the blue? Many people had no cultural or semantic information that would help them place the blue light. For them, logic provided the answer: only one piece left, only one possible place to go. The blue light was logically constrained.

Natural mappings work by providing logical constraints. There are no physical or cultural principles here; rather there is a logical relationship between the spatial or functional layout of components and the things that they affect or are affected by. If two switches control two lights, the left switch should work the left light, the right switch the right light. If the lights are mounted one way and the switches another, the natural mapping is destroyed. If two indicators reflect the state of two different parts of a system, the location and operation of the indicators should have a natural relationship to the spatial or functional layout of the system. Alas, natural mappings are not often exploited.

The characteristics of affordances and constraints can be applied to the design of everyday objects, much simplifying our encounters with them. Doors and switches present interesting examples, for poor design causes unnecessary problems for their users. Yet the common problems have simple solutions, which properly exploit affordances and natural constraints.

THE PROBLEM WITH DOORS

In chapter 1 we encountered the sad story of my friend who was trapped between sets of glass doors at a post office, trapped because there were no clues to the doors' operation. When we approach a door, we have to find both the side that opens and the part to be manipulated; in other words, we need to figure out what to do and where to do it. We expect to find some visible signal for the correct operation: a plate, an extension, a hollow, an indentation—something that allows the hand to touch, grasp, turn, or fit into. This tells us where to act. The next step is to figure out how: we must determine what operations are permitted, in part using the affordances, in part guided by constraints.

Doors come in amazing variety. Some open only if a button is pushed, and some don't appear to open at all, having neither buttons, nor hardware, nor any other sign of their operation. The door might be operated with a foot pedal. Or maybe it is voice operated, and we must speak the magic phrase. *("Open Simsim!")* In addition, some doors have signs on them: pull, push, slide, lift, ring bell, insert card, type password, smile, rotate, bow, dance, or, perhaps, just ask. Somehow, when a device as simple as a door has to come with an instruction manual— even a one-word manual—then it is a failure, poorly designed.

Appearances deceive. I have seen people trip and fall when they attempted to push open a door that worked automatically, the door opening inward just as they attempted to push against it. On most subway trains, the doors open automatically at each station. Not so in Paris. I watched someone on the Paris Métro try to get off the train and fail. When the train came to his station, he got up and stood patiently in front of the door, waiting for it to open. It never opened. The train simply started up again and went on to the next station. In the Métro, you have to open the doors yourself by pushing a button, or depressing a lever, or sliding them (depending upon which kind of car you happen to be on).

Consider the hardware for an unlocked door. It need not have any moving parts: it can be a fixed knob, plate, handle, or groove. Not only will the proper hardware operate the door smoothly, but it will also indicate just how the door is to be operated: it will exhibit the proper affordances. Suppose the door opens by being pushed. The easiest way to indicate this is to have a plate at the spot where the pushing should be done. A plate, if large enough for the hand, clearly and unambiguously marks the proper action. Moreover, the plate constrains the possible actions: there is little else that one can do with a plate except push. Unfortunately, even this simple clue is misused. Doors that should be pulled or slid sometimes have plates (figure 4.2). Doors that should be pushed sometimes have both plates and knobs or a handle and no plate.

The violation of the simple use of constraints on doors can have serious implications. Look at the door in figure 4.3 *A*: this fire exit door has a push bar, a good example of an unambiguous signal to push, and a good design (required by law in the United States) because it forces proper behavior when panicked people press against a door as they attempt to flee a fire. But look again. On which side should you push? There is no way of knowing. Add some paint to the part that is to be pushed, or fasten a plate over it (figure 4.3 *B*): these provide strong cultural signals to guide the action properly. Push bars offer strong physical constraints, simplifying the task of knowing what to do. The use of cultural constraints simplifies the task of figuring out where to do it.

Some hardware cries out to be pulled. Although anything that can be pulled can also be pushed, the proper design will use cultural constraints so that the signal to pull will dominate. But even this can be messed up. I have seen doors with a mixture of signals, one implying push, the other pull. I have watched people passing through the door of figure 4.3 (*A*). And they had trouble, even people who worked in the building and who therefore used the door several times every day.

Sliding doors seem to present special difficulties. In fact, there are several good ways to signal the operation of a sliding door unambiguously. For example, a vertical slit in the door can be used in only one

4.2 The Design of Doors. The doors at the left show two excellent examples of design: different handles, side by side on the same automobile, each neatly signaling its proper operation. The vertical placement of the lever on the handle to the left causes the hand to be held in a vertical plane, signifying a slide. The horizontal placement of the lever on the door handle to the right, coupled with the overhang and indentation that neatly afford entrance by the hand, signifies a pull. Two different types of doors, adjacent to one another, and yet there is no confusion between them.

The handle depicted at the left shows inappropriate signals. This form of handle clearly marks grasp, twist, or pull—except that this particular door slides: a classic case of inappropriate design.

At left and below are photographs of hardware for doors that open by being pulled. The large plates at the left are a signal to push, but in fact the door is supposed to be pulled: no wonder the door needs the signs. The simple U-shaped brackets below is a much better design, but they are ambiguous enough that a sign still seems to be needed. Contrast with the two handles at the top, neither of which needs a sign yet is always operated properly. If a door handle needs a sign, then its design is probably faulty.

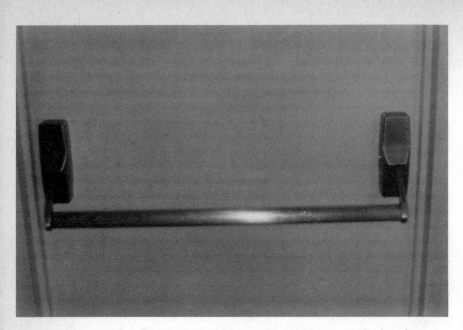

4.3 Doors in Two Commercial Buildings. Pushing the bar opens the door, but on which side do you push? Bar *A* (above) hides the signal, making it impossible to know on which side to push. A frustrating door. Bar *B* (below) has a flat plate mounted on the side that is to be pushed; this is a naturally interpreted signal. A nice design, no frustration for the user.

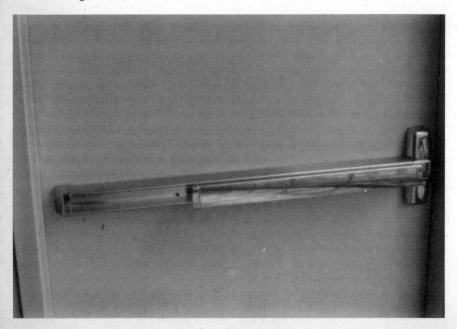

way: the fingers are inserted and the door slid. The location of the slit specifies not only where to exert the force but also in which direction. The critical signal is any depression in the door large enough for the fingers to fit into, but without an overhang. Similarly, any projection will also work, as long as it neither has an overhang nor is appropriate for being grasped with the hand. On a properly designed door, the fingers can exert pressure along the sides of the depression or projection—needed for sliding—but they can't pull or twist. I have seen elegant sliding doors, aesthetically pleasing, yet with clear signals to the user—in a conference room in Italy, on a door on a Métro train in Paris, on some Scandinavian furniture. Yet more often, it seems, sliding doors are built with the wrong signals, with clumsy hardware in positions that jam the fingers. Sliding doors somehow challenge the designer to get them wrong.

Some doors have appropriate hardware, well placed. The outside door handles of most modern automobiles are excellent examples of design. The handles are often recessed receptacles that simultaneously indicate the place and mode of action: the receptacle cannot be used except by inserting the fingers and pulling. Horizontal slits guide the hand into a pulling position; vertical slits signal a sliding motion. Strangely enough, the inside door handles for automobiles tell a different story. Here, the designer has faced a different kind of problem, and the appropriate solution has not yet been found. As a result, although the outside door handles of cars are often excellent, the inside ones are often difficult to find, hard to figure out how to operate, and difficult to use.

Unfortunately, the worst door hardware is found where we spend most of our time: at home and in the office. In many cases, the choice of hardware appears haphazard, used for convenience (or profitability). Architects and interior designers seem to prefer designs that are visually elegant and win prizes. This often means that a door and its hardware are designed to merge with the interior: the door may barely be visible, the hardware merges with door, and the operation is completely obscure. From my experience, the worst offenders are cabinet doors. It is sometimes not even possible to determine where the doors are, let alone whether and from where they are slid, lifted, pushed, or pulled. The focus on aesthetics may blind the designer (and the purchaser) to the lack of usability.

A particularly frustrating design is that of the door that opens outward by being pushed inward. The push releases the catch and ener-

gizes a spring, so that when the hand is taken away the door springs open. It's a very clever design, but most puzzling to the first-time user. A plate would be the appropriate signal, but designers sometimes do not wish to mar the smooth surface of the door. I have such a latch in the glass door of the cabinet in which I store phonograph records. You can see through the door, and it is obvious that there is no room for the door to open inward; to push on the door seems contradictory. New and infrequent users of this door usually reject pushing and open it instead by pulling, which often requires them to use fingernails, knife blades, or more ingenious methods to pry it open.

THE PROBLEM WITH SWITCHES

At any lecture I give, my first demonstration needs no preparation. I can count on the light switches of the room or auditorium to be unmanageable. "Lights please," someone will say. Then fumble, fumble, fumble. Who knows where the switches are and which lights they control? The lights seem to work smoothly only when a technician is hired to sit in a control room somewhere, turning them on and off.

The switch problems in an auditorium are annoying, but similar problems in airplanes and nuclear power plants are dangerous. The controls all look the same. How do the operators avoid the occasional mistake, confusion, or accidental bumping against the wrong control? Or misaim? They don't. Fortunately, airplanes and power plants are pretty robust. A few errors every hour are not important—usually.

One type of popular small airplane has identical-looking switches for flaps and landing gear right next to one another. You might be surprised to learn how many pilots, while on the ground, have decided to raise the flaps and instead raised the wheels. This very expensive error happened frequently enough that the National Transportation Safety Board wrote a report about it. The analysts politely pointed out that the proper design principles to avoid these errors have been known for thirty years. Why were those design errors still being made?

Basic switches and controls should be relatively simple to design well. But there are two fundamental difficulties. The first is the grouping problem, how to determine which switch goes with which function.

The second is the mapping problem. For example, when there are many lights and an array of switches, how can you determine which switch controls which light?

The switch problem becomes serious only where there are many of them. It isn't a problem in situations with one switch, and it is only a minor problem where there are two switches. But the difficulties mount rapidly with more than two switches at the same location. Multiple switches are more likely to occur in offices, auditoriums, and industrial locations than in homes (figure 4.4).

WHICH SWITCH CONTROLS WHICH FUNCTION?

Switches for unrelated functions are often placed together, usually with no distinguishing marks to help the user know which switch controls which function. Designers love rows of identical-looking switches. The switches look good, are easy to mount, are inexpensive to build, and please the aesthetic sensibilities of the viewer. But they

4.4 Typical Audio Mixing Control. This picture was taken in an auditorium in England. Fortunately, errors on panels like these are seldom serious, often not even noted.

4.5 A Clock Radio, "Human Engineered" to Simplify Operation. Note the row of identical-looking switches. (Copyright Tandy Corporation. Used with permission.)

make it easy to err. With identical switches all in a row, it is difficult to distinguish the switch for the coffee maker from the switch to the central power for the computer. Or the set-the-time switch from the turn-off-the-radio switch (figure 4.5). Or the landing gear switch from the flap control switch.

Consider my car radio: twenty-five controls, many apparently arbitrary. All tiny (so that they will fit the limited space available). Imagine trying to use the radio while driving at high speed, at night. Or in winter when wearing gloves, so that the attempt to push one button succeeds in pushing two, or the attempt to turn the loudness control also adjusts the tone control. You should be able to use things in the dark. A car radio should be usable with a minimum of visual cues. But the radio designers probably designed it in the laboratory, with little or no thought about the car, or the driver. For all I know the design won a prize for its visual aesthetics.

It should go without saying that controls that cause trouble should not be located where they can be operated by accident, especially in the dark, or when the person is trying to use the device without looking. It should go without saying, but in fact, it is necessary to say it.

There is a simple, well-known solution to the grouping problem: set the switches for one set of functions apart from the switches that control other functions. Another solution is to use different types of switches. The solutions can be combined. To solve the problem with the airplane flap and landing gear switches, separate the switches and don't line them up in a row. Also use shape coding: a tire-shaped switch can control the landing gear, and the flap switch can be a long, thin rectangle—the shape of a flap. Putting controls in different locations makes it less likely that a misaimed hand will throw the wrong switch. And using shape coding means that a potential error may be caught and that the correct switch can be found by feel alone (figure 4.6). That's how to solve this first problem, now let us turn to the other one.

HOW ARE THE SWITCHES ARRANGED?

With the lights in a room, you know that all the switches control lights. But which switch controls which light? Room lights are usually organized in a two-dimensional structure and they are usually horizontal (that is, they are on the ceiling or, if they are lamps, they are placed along the floor or on tables). But switches are usually arranged in a one-dimensional row mounted on the wall, a vertical surface. How can a one-dimensional row of switches map onto a two-dimensional array of lights? And with the switches being mounted on the wall and the

4.6 Make the Controls Look and Feel Different. The control-room operators in a nuclear power plant tried to overcome the problem of similar-looking knobs by placing beer-keg handles over them. This is good design, even if after the fact; the operators should be rewarded. (From Seminara, Gonzales, & Parsons, 1977. Photograph courtesy of Joseph L. Seminara.)

lights being on the ceiling, you have to do a mental rotation of the switches to get them to conform to the lights. The mapping problem is unsolvable with the current structure of switches.

Electricians usually try to lay out the switches in the same order as the lights they control, but the mismatch in the spatial arrangement of the lights and the switches makes it difficult, if not impossible, to produce a full natural mapping. Electricians have to use standard components, and the designers and manufacturers of those standard components worried only about fitting the proper number of switches into them safely. Nobody thought about how the lights were to be arranged or how the switches ought to be laid out.

My house was designed by two brash young architects, award winning, who, among other things, liked neat rows of light switches. We got a horizontal row of four identical switches in the front hall, a vertical column of six identical switches in the living room. "You will get used to it," the architects assured us when we complained. We never did. Finally we had to change the switches, making each one different. Even so we made lots of mistakes.

In my psychology laboratory, the lights and their switches were located in many different places, yet most people wanted to control the lights upon entering the area. The area is large, with three major hallways and approximately fifteen rooms. Moreover, this floor of the building has no windows, so it is dark unless the lights are turned on.

If light switches are placed on the wall, there is no way they can exactly correspond in position to the placement of the lights. Why place the switches flat against the wall? Why not redo things? Why not place the switches horizontally, in exact analogy to the things being controlled, with a two-dimensional layout so that the switches can be placed on a floorplan of the building in exact correspondence to the areas that they control? Match the layout of the lights with the layout of the switches: the principle of natural mapping. In my laboratory, as in my home, the solution was to construct a simple switchplate that mirrored the physical arrangement of the area, with small light switches placed in relevant locations.[4] Figure 4.7 shows the situation at my home, and figure 4.8 shows what we did at the laboratory.

How well do the new switch arrangements work? Quite well, I am happy to report. One laboratory user sent me the following note:

4.7 The vertical array of six switches at the right is what our architects provided to control the lights in our odd-shaped living room. We could never remember which switch did what.

The photograph below shows our solution: switches arranged to match the room layout. (One more switch, for a projection screen, will be mounted on the vertical plate just above the light switches. The switch panel was constructed for the author by David Wargo.)

4.8 The original layout of switches in my laboratory had the light switches scattered. We put all the switches in one convenient location, arranged on a floor plan of the laboratory. (The switch panel was constructed by David Wargo.)

"You know, I actually kind of like those new switches now—they seem easy to use, and it's nice to have all the switches in one location when you first walk in. You can just sort of swipe at them on your way past and light up the area you want—very quick. So while I was worried they wouldn't be advantageous for the experienced user, I was wrong."

Can the new switches be used everywhere? Probably not. But there is no reason they couldn't be widely adopted. There are a series of technical problems still to be addressed: builders and electricians need standardized components. How about making up standard light switch boxes, made to be mounted *on* the wall (instead of *in* the wall as they are today), where the switches are mounted on the top of the box, on the horizontal surface. And on the top, make up a matrix of supports so that there can be free, relatively unrestricted placement of the switches in whatever pattern best suits the room. Use smaller switches if necessary. Maybe get rid of those standardized light plates. The matrix design would require drilling holes differently for each room, but if the switches were designed to fit into standard sized circular or rectangular holes, the holes could be drilled or punched quite easily.

My suggestion requires that the switch box stick out from the wall, whereas today's boxes are mounted so that the switches are flush with the wall. Some might consider my solution ugly. Well, then, indent the boxes, placing them *in* the wall. After all, if there is room inside the wall for the existing switch boxes, there is also room for an indented horizontal surface. Or mount the switches on a little pedestal, or on a ledge.

Visibility and Feedback

So far we have concentrated upon constraints and mappings. But for knowing what to do there are other relevant principles, too, especially visibility and feedback:

1. *Visibility.* Make relevant parts visible.
2. *Feedback.* Give each action an immediate and obvious effect.

When we use a novel object, a number of questions guide our actions:

· Which parts move; which are fixed?

· Where should the object be grasped? What part is to be manipulated? What is to be held? Where is the hand to be inserted? If it is speech sensitive, where does one talk?

· What kind of movement is possible: pushing, pulling, turning, rotating, touching, stroking?

· What are the relevant physical characteristics of the movements? With how great a force must the object be manipulated? How far can it be expected to move? How can success be gauged?

· What parts of the object are supporting surfaces? How much size and weight will the object support?

The same kinds of questions arise whether we are trying to decide what to do or attempting to evaluate the results of an action. In examining the object, we have to decide which parts signify the state of the object and which are solely decorative, or nonfunctional, or part of the background or supports. What things change? What has changed over the previous state? Where should we be watching or listening to detect any changes? The important things to watch should be visible and clearly marked; the results of any action should be immediately apparent.

MAKING VISIBLE THE INVISIBLE

The principle of visibility is violated over and over again in everyday things. In numerous designs crucial parts are carefully hidden away. Handles on cabinets distract from some design aesthetics, and so they are deliberately made invisible or left out. The cracks that signify the existence of a door can also distract from the pure lines of the design, so these significant cues are also minimized or eliminated. The result can be a smooth expanse of gleaming material, with no sign of doors or drawers, let alone of how those doors and drawers might be operated. Electric switches are often hidden: many electric typewriters have the on/off switch hidden underneath; many computers and computer terminals have the on/off switch in the rear, difficult to find and awkward to use;[5] and the switches that control kitchen garbage disposal units are often hidden away, sometimes nearly impossible to find.

Many systems are vastly improved by the act of making visible what was invisible before. Consider the VCR.

"UMPTEEN-DAY-UMPTEEN-EVENT PROGRAMMING. *Because time-shifting is so popular, manufacturers and retailers play up a VCR's ability to record automatically. The typical VCR can record four events (video jargon for programs) over a 4-day span. . . .*

"*It's one thing to know that a VCR can record eight events in 14 days. It's quite another to make the machine behave. You have to go through a tedious series of steps to tell the VCR when to start recording, what channel to record, how long to run the tape, and so on.*

"*Some VCR's are much easier to program than others. . . . Best of all, we think, is a feature called on-screen programming. Commands that appear on the TV screen help you enter the time, date, and channel of the program you want to tape.*"[6]

As the quotation from *Consumer Reports* indicates, the act of setting up these units to do the recording is horribly complex and difficult. The same article later warns that if you are not careful in your selection, "you could wind up with a VCR that brings out fear and loathing whenever you try to change the channel resets or set it up to record a program when you are away." It does not take much examination to discover the reason for the difficulties: there is no visual feedback. As a result, users (1) have trouble remembering their place in the lengthy sequence of required steps; (2) have trouble remembering what next needs to be done; and (3) cannot easily check the information just entered to see if it is what was intended, and then cannot easily change it, if they decide it is wrong.

The gulfs both in execution (the first two problems) and in evaluation (the last problem) are significant for these VCRs. Both can be bridged by the use of a display. Displays often cost money and take up room, which is why designers hesitate to use them, but in the case of a VCR, a display device is usually already available: the TV set. And, indeed, those VCRs that can be programmed through the use of an on-screen TV display are much easier to use. Visibility makes all the difference.

NOTHING SUCCEEDS LIKE A GOOD DISPLAY

Over and over again we find unwarranted complexity that could be avoided were the device to contain a good display. With the modern telephone (see chapter 1), a display that could prompt the user through the series of steps required for programming would make the difference between a valuable, usable system and a next-to-useless one. So, too, with any device of complexity, whether it be the washing machine, microwave oven, or office copying machine. Nothing succeeds like visual feedback, which in turn requires a good visual display.

WHAT CAN BE DONE?

New technologies, especially the inexpensive microprocessors available today (the heart of the computer) make possible the incorporation of powerful and intelligent systems even in simple, everyday things, from toys to kitchen appliances to office machines. But new capabilities must be accompanied by appropriate displays, also now relatively inexpensive. I asked the students in one of my classes to generate some possibilities for adding visibility to everyday devices. Here are some of them:

· *Display the song titles for compact discs.* Why not take advantage of the storage capacity of an audio compact disc (CD) and have it display not only the number of the song or track (as it now does) but also the title? Each title could be accompanied by other information, such as performers, composer, or playing time. Thus, in programming the CD, you could select by name rather than by number, and you would always know what you were hearing.

· *Display the names of television programs.* If each television station would also broadcast its station identification and the title of the current program, the viewer who tuned in during the middle of a show could easily find out what it was. The information could be sent in computer-readable format during the retrace interval (the time that the beam is off the screen).

· *Print the cooking information for foods on the food package in computer-readable form.* This is a scheme for bypassing the need to make things visible. The cooking of frozen foods often requires several different cooking times, waiting times, and heat settings. The programming is complex. If the cooking information were on the package in machine-readable form, one could put the food in the microwave oven, pass a scanner over the printed information, and let the oven program itself.

USING SOUND FOR VISIBILITY

Sometimes things can't be made visible. Enter sound: sound can provide information available in no other way. Sound can tell us that things are working properly or that they need maintenance or repair. It can even save us from accidents. Consider the information provided by:

· The click when the bolt on a door slides home
· The "zzz" sound when a zipper works properly
· The "tinny" sound when a door doesn't shut right
· The roaring sound when a car muffler gets a hole
· The rattle when things aren't secured
· The whistle of a tea kettle when the water boils
· The click when the toast pops up
· The increase in pitch when a vacuum cleaner gets clogged
· The indescribable change in sound when a complex piece of machinery starts to have problems

Many devices do use sound, but only for signals. Simple sounds, such as buzzers, bells, or tones. Computers use bleeping, whining, and clicking sounds. This use of sound is valuable and serves an important function, but it is very limited in power; it is as if the use of visual cues were limited to different colored, flashing lights. We could use sound for much more communciation than we do.

These days computers produce several sounds, and keypads, microwave ovens, and telephones beep and burp. These are not naturalistic sounds; they do not convey hidden information. When used properly, a beep can assure you that you've pressed a button, but the sound is as annoying as informative. Sounds should be generated so as to give information about the source. They should convey something about the actions that are taking place, actions that matter to the user but that would otherwise not be visible. The buzzes, clicks, and hums that you hear while a telephone call is being completed are one good example: take out those noises and you are less certain that the connection is being made.

Bill Gaver, who has been studying use of sound in my laboratory, points out that real, natural sound is as essential as visual information because sound tells us about things we can't see, and it does so while our eyes are occupied elsewhere. Natural sounds reflect the complex interaction of natural objects: the way one part moves against another; the material of which the parts are made—hollow or solid, metal or wood, soft or hard, rough or smooth. Sounds are generated when materials interact, and the sound tells us whether they are hitting, sliding, breaking, tearing, crumbling, or bouncing. Moreover, sounds differ according to the characteristics of the objects, according to their size, solidity, mass, tension, and material. And they differ with how fast things are going and how far away from us they are.

If they are to be useful, sounds must be generated intelligently, with an understanding of the natural relationship between the sounds and the information to be conveyed. Sounds on artificial devices should be as useful as sounds in the real world. Gaver has proposed that sound could play an important role in computer-based applications. Here, rich, naturalistic sounds could serve as auditory icons, caricatures of naturally occurring sounds that could provide information about the concepts being represented not easily conveyed in other ways.[7]

You have to be very careful with sound, however. It easily becomes cute rather than useful. It can annoy and distract as easily as it can aid. One of the virtues of sounds is that they can be detected even when attention is applied elsewhere. But this virtue is also a deficit, for sounds are often intrusive. Sounds are difficult to keep private unless the intensity is low or earphones are used. This means both that neighbors may be annoyed and that others can monitor your activities. The use of sound to convey information is a powerful and important idea, but still in its infancy.

Just as the presence of sound can serve a useful role in providing feedback about events, the absence of sound can lead to the same kinds of difficulties we have already encountered from a lack of feedback. The absence of sound can mean an absence of information, and if feedback from an action is expected to come from sound, silence can lead to problems.

I once stayed in the guest apartment of a technological institute in the Netherlands. The building was newly completed, with many interesting architectural features. The architect had gone to great lengths to keep the noise level low; the ventilation system could not be heard. In similar fashion, the ventilation for the room came and went through invisible slots in the ceiling (so I am told; I never did find them).

All was fine until I took a shower. The bathroom seemed to have no ventilation at all, so everything became wet, then eventually cold and clammy. There was a switch in the bathroom that I thought might be the control for an exhaust fan. When I pushed the switch, a light on it came on and stayed on. Further pushing had no effect.

I noticed that whenever I returned to the apartment after an absence, the light would be off. So each time I entered the apartment, I went into the bathroom and pushed the button. By listening closely, I could hear a slight "thump" in the distance the first time the button was depressed. I decided it was some kind of signal. Perhaps it was a call button, summoning the maid, or the janitor, or maybe even the fire department (though no one showed up). I did also consider that it might control a ventilation system, but I could hear no flow of air. I examined the inside of the entire bathroom with care, trying to find an air inlet. I even got a chair and a flashlight and examined the ceiling. Nothing.

At the end of my stay, the person driving me to the airport, explained that the button controlled the exhaust fan. The fan was on as long as the light was on, and it turned off, automatically, in about five minutes. The architect was very good at disguising the ventilation system and at keeping the noise level down.

Here is a case where the architect was too successful: the feedback was clearly lacking. The light was not enough—in fact, it was quite misleading. Noise would have been welcome. It would have signaled that there really was ventilation.

CHAPTER FIVE

TO ERR IS HUMAN

"LONDON—An inexperienced computer-operator pressed the wrong key on a terminal in early December, causing chaos at the London Stock Exchange. The error at stockbrokers Greenwell Montagu led to systems staff working through the night in an attempt to cure the problem."[1]

People make errors routinely. Hardly a minute of a normal conversation can go by without a stumble, a repetition, a phrase stopped midway through to be discarded or redone. Human language provides special mechanisms that make corrections so automatic that the participants hardly take notice; indeed, they may be surprised when errors are pointed out. Artificial devices do not have the same tolerance. Push the wrong button, and chaos may result.

Errors come in several forms. Two fundamental categories are slips and mistakes. Slips result from automatic behavior, when subconscious actions that are intended to satisfy our goals get waylaid en route. Mistakes result from conscious deliberations. The same processes that make us creative and insightful by allowing us to see relationships between apparently unrelated things, that let us leap to correct conclusions on the basis of partial or even faulty evidence, also lead to error.

Our ability to generalize from small amounts of information helps tremendously in new situations; but sometimes we generalize too rapidly, classifying a new situation as similar to an old one when, in fact, there are significant discrepancies. False generalizations can be hard to discover, let alone eliminate.

The differences between slips and mistakes are readily apparent in the analysis of the seven stages of action. Form an appropriate goal but mess up in the performance, and you've made a slip. Slips are almost always small things: a misplaced action, the wrong thing moved, a desired action undone. Moreover, they are relatively easy to discover by simple observation and monitoring. Form the wrong goal, and you've made a mistake. Mistakes can be major events, and they are difficult or even impossible to detect—after all, the action performed is appropriate for the goal.

Slips

A colleague reported that he went to his car to drive to work. As he drove away, he realized that he had forgotten his briefcase, so he turned around and went back. He stopped the car, turned off the engine, and unbuckled his wristwatch. Yes, wristwatch, instead of his seatbelt.

Most everyday errors are slips. Intend to do one action, find yourself doing another. Have a person say something clearly and distinctly to you, but "hear" something quite different. The study of slips is the study of the psychology of everyday errors—what Freud called "the psychopathology of everyday life." Some slips may indeed have hidden, darker meanings, but most are accounted for by rather simple events in our mental mechanisms.[2]

Slips show up most frequently in skilled behavior. We don't make so many slips in things we are still learning. In part, slips result from a lack of attention. On the whole, people can consciously attend to only one primary thing at a time. But we often do many things at once. We walk while we talk; we drive cars while we talk, sing, listen to the radio, use a telephone, take notes, or read a map. We can do more than one thing at a time only if most of the actions are done automatically, subconsciously, with little or no need for conscious attention.

Doing several things at once is essential even in carrying out a single task. To play the piano, we must move the fingers properly over the keyboard while reading the music, manipulating the pedals, and listening to the resulting sounds. But to play the piano well, we should do these things automatically. Our conscious attention should be focused on the higher levels of the music, on style, and on phrasing. So it is with every skill. The low-level, physical movements should be controlled subconsciously.

TYPES OF SLIPS

Some slips result from the similarities of actions. Or an event in the world may automatically trigger an action. Sometimes our thoughts and actions may remind us of unintended actions, which we then perform. We can place slips into one of six categories: capture errors, description errors, data-driven errors, associative activation errors, loss-of-activation errors, and mode errors.

CAPTURE ERRORS

"I was using a copying machine, and I was counting the pages. I found myself counting '1, 2, 3, 4, 5, 6, 7, 8, 9, 10, Jack, Queen, King.' I have been playing cards recently."[3]

Consider the common slip called the capture error, in which a frequently done activity suddenly takes charge instead of (captures) the one intended.[4] You are playing a piece of music (without too much attention) and it is similar to another (which you know better); suddenly you are playing the more familiar piece. Or you go off to your bedroom to change your clothes for dinner and find yourself in bed. (This slip was first reported by William James in 1890.) Or you finish typing your thoughts on your word processor or text editing program, turn off the power, and go off to other things, neglecting to save any of your work. Or you get into your car on Sunday to go to the store and find yourself at the office.

The capture error appears whenever two different action sequences have their initial stages in common, with one sequence being unfamiliar and the other being well practiced. Seldom, if ever, does the unfamiliar sequence capture the familiar one.

DESCRIPTION ERRORS

A former student reported that one day he came home from jogging, took off his sweaty shirt, and rolled it up in a ball, intending to throw it in the laundry basket. Instead he threw it in the toilet. (It wasn't poor aim: the laundry basket and toilet were in different rooms.)

In the common slip known as the description error, the intended action has much in common with others that are possible. As a result, unless the action sequence is completely and precisely specified, the intended action might fit several possibilities. Suppose that my tired student in the example formed a mental description of his intended action something like "throw the shirt into the opening at the top of the container." This description would be perfectly unambiguous and sufficient were the laundry basket the only open container in sight; but when the open toilet was visible, its characteristics matched the description and triggered the inappropriate action. This is a description error because the internal description of the intention was not sufficiently precise. Description errors usually result in performing the correct action on the wrong object. Obviously, the more the wrong and right objects have in common, the more likely the errors are to occur. Description errors, like all slips, are more likely when we are distracted, bored, involved in other activities, under extra stress, or otherwise not inclined to pay full attention to the task at hand.

Description errors occur most frequently when the wrong and right objects are physically near each other. People have reported a number of description errors to me.

Two clerks in a department store were both on the telephone to verify credit cards while simultaneously dealing with a customer and filling out a credit card form. One sales clerk had passed in back of the other to reach the charge forms. When this clerk finished preparing the sales slip, she hung up the handset on the wrong telephone, thereby terminating the other clerk's call.

A person intended to put the lid on a sugar bowl, but instead put it on a coffee cup (with the same size opening).

I had a report of someone who planned to to pour orange juice into a glass but instead poured it into a coffee cup (adjacent to the glass).

Another person told me of intending to pour rice from a storage jar into a measuring cup, but instead pouring cooking oil into the measuring cup (both the oil and the rice were kept in glass containers on the counter).

Some things seem designed to cause slips. Long rows of identical switches are perfect setups for description errors. Intend to flip one switch, instead flip a similar-looking one. It happens in industrial plants, aircraft, homes, anywhere. When different actions have similar descriptions, there is a good chance of mishap, especially when the operator is experienced and well practiced and therefore not paying full attention, and if there are more important things to do.

DATA-DRIVEN ERRORS

"I was assigning a visitor a room to use. I decided to call the department secretary to tell her the room number. I used the telephone in the alcove outside the room, with the room number in sight. Instead of dialing the secretary's phone number—which I use frequently and know very well—I dialed the room number."

Much human behavior is automatic, for example, brushing away an insect. Automatic actions are data driven—triggered by the arrival of the sensory data. But sometimes data-driven activities can intrude into an ongoing action sequence, causing behavior that was not intended.

ASSOCIATIVE ACTIVATION ERRORS

"My office phone rang. I picked up the receiver and bellowed 'Come in' at it."[5]

If external data can sometimes trigger actions, so, too, can internal thoughts and associations. The ringing of the telephone and knocking on the door both signal the need to greet someone. Other errors occur from associations among thoughts and ideas. Associative activation errors are the slips studied by Freud; you think something that ought not to be said and then, to your embarrassment, you say it.

LOSS-OF-ACTIVATION ERRORS

"I have to go to the bedroom before I start working in the dining room. I start going there and realize as I am walking that I have no idea why I am going there. Knowing myself, I keep going, hoping that something in the bedroom will remind me. . . . I get there but still cannot recall what I wanted . . . so I go back to the dining room. There I realize that my glasses are dirty. With great relief I go back to the bedroom, get my handkerchief, and wipe my glasses clean."

One of the more common slips is simply forgetting to do something. More interesting is forgetting part of the act, remembering the rest, as in the story above where the goal was forgotten, but the rest of the action continued unimpaired. One of my informants walked all the way through the house to the kitchen and opened the refrigerator door; then he wondered why he was there. Lack-of-activation errors occur because the presumed mechanism—the "activation" of the goals—has decayed. The less technical but more common term would be "forgetting."

MODE ERRORS

"I had just completed a long run from my university to my home in what I was convinced would be record time. It was dark when I got home, so I could not read the time on my stopwatch. As I walked up and down the street in front of my home, cooling off, I got more and more anxious to see how fast I had run. I then remembered that my watch had a built-in light, operated by the upper right-hand button. Elated, I depressed the button to illuminate the reading, only to read a time of zero seconds. I had forgotten that in stopwatch mode, the same button [that in the normal, time-reading mode would have turned on a light] cleared the time and reset the stopwatch."

Mode errors occur when devices have different modes of operation, and the action appropriate for one mode has different meanings in other modes. Mode errors are inevitable any time equipment is designed to have more possible actions than it has controls or displays, so the controls must do double duty. Mode errors are especially likely where the equipment does not make the mode visible, so the user is expected to remember what mode has been established, sometimes for many hours.

Mode errors are common with digital watches and computer systems (especially text editors). Several accidents in commercial aviation can be attributed to mode errors, especially in the use of the automatic pilots (which have a large number of complex modes).

DETECTING SLIPS

Although slips are relatively easy to detect because there is a clear discrepancy between goal and result, detection can only take place if there is feedback. If the result of the action is not visible, how can a misaction be detected? Even when a mismatch is noted, the person may not believe that the error occurred. Some trail of the sequence of actions that was performed is valuable.

Even when an error has been detected, it may not be clear what the error was.

"Alice" was driving a van and noticed that the rearview mirror on the passenger side was not adjusted properly. Alice meant to say to the passenger on the right, "Please adjust the mirror," but instead said "Please adjust the window."

The passenger, "Sally," was confused and asked, "What should I do? What do you want?"

Alice repeated the request: "Adjust the window for me."

The situation continued through several frustrating cycles of conversation and attempts by the passenger to understand just what adjustments should be made to the window. The error-correction mechanism adopted by the driver was to repeat the erroneous sentence more and more loudly.

In this example, it was easy to detect that something was wrong but hard to discover what. Alice believed the problem was that she couldn't be understood or heard. She was monitoring the wrong part of the action sequence—she had a problem of level.

Actions can be specified at many different levels. Suppose I were driving my car to the bank. At any given moment, the action being performed could be described at many different levels:

· Driving to the bank
· Turning into the parking lot
· Making a right turn
· Rotating the steering wheel clockwise
· Moving my left hand upward and to the right and my right hand downward
· Increasing the tension on the sternocostal portion of the pectoralis major muscle

All these levels are active at the same time. The most global description (the one at the top of the list), is called the high-level specification. The more detailed descriptions, the ones at the bottom of the list, are called the low-level specifications. Any one of them might be in error.

It is often possible to detect that the result of an action is not as planned, but then not to know at which level of specification the error has taken place.

Problems of level commonly thwart the correction of error. My collection of slips includes several examples in which a person detects a problem but attempts to correct it at the wrong level.

One frequent example is the nonworking key, reported to me both for cars and homes. Someone goes to his or her car and the key won't work. The first response is to try again, perhaps holding the key more level or straight. Then the key is reversed, tried upside down. When that fails, the key is examined and perhaps another tried in its stead. Then the door is wiggled, shaken, hit. Finally, the person decides that the lock has broken, and walks around the car to try the other door, at which point it is suddenly clear that this is the wrong car.

In all the situations I have examined the error correction mechanism seems to start at the lowest possible level and slowly works its way higher. Whether this is universally true I do not know, but the hypothesis warrants further examination.

DESIGN LESSONS FROM THE STUDY OF SLIPS

Two different kinds of design lessons can be drawn, one for preventing slips before they occur and one for detecting and correcting them when they do occur. In general, the solutions follow directly from the preceding analyses. For example, mode errors are minimized by minimizing modes, or at least by making modes visible.

Cars provide a number of examples of how design relates to error. A variety of fluids are required in the engine compartment of an automobile: engine oil, transmission oil, brake fluid, windshield washer solution, radiator coolant, battery water. Putting the wrong fluid into a reservoir could lead to serious damage or even an accident. Automobile manufacturers try to minimize these errors (a combination of description and mode errors) by making the different compartments look different—using different shapes and different-size openings—and by adding color to the fluids so that they can be distinguished. Here design by and large prevents errors. But, unfortunately, designers seem to prefer to encourage them.

I was in a taxi in Austin, Texas, admiring the large number of new devices in front of the driver. No more simple radio. In its place was a computer display, so that messages from the dispatcher were now printed on the screen. The driver took great delight in demonstrating all the features to me. On the radio transmitter I saw four identical-looking buttons laid out in a row.

"Oh," I said, "you have four different radio channels."

"Nope," he replied, "three. The fourth button resets all the settings. Then it takes me thirty minutes to get everything all set up properly again."

"Hmm," I said, "I bet you hit that every now and then by accident."

"I certainly do," he replied (in his own unprintable words).

In computer systems, it is common to prevent errors by requiring confirmation before a command will be executed, especially when the action will destroy a file. But the request is ill timed; it comes just after the person has initiated the action and is still fully content with the choice. The standard interaction goes something like this:

USER: Remove file "My-most-important-work."

COMPUTER: Are you certain you wish to remove the file "My-most-important-work"?

USER: Yes.

COMPUTER: Are you certain?

USER: Yes, of course.

COMPUTER: The file "My-most-important-work" has been removed.

USER: Oops, damn.

The user has requested deletion of the wrong file but the computer's request for confirmation is unlikely to catch the error; the user is confirming the action, not the file name. Thus asking for confirmation cannot catch all slips. It would be more appropriate to eliminate irreversible actions: in this example, the request to remove a file would be handled by the computer's moving the file to some temporary holding place. Then the user would have time for reconsideration and recovery.

At a research laboratory I once directed, we discovered that people would frequently throw away their records and notes, only to discover the next day that they needed them again. We solved the problem by getting seven trash cans and labeling them with the days of the week.

Then the trash can labeled Wednesday would be used only on Wednesdays. At the end of the day it was safely stored away and not emptied until the next Tuesday, just before it was to be used again.

People discovered that they kept neater records and books because they no longer hesitated to throw away things that they thought would probably never be used again; they figured it was safe to throw something away, for they still had a week in which to change their minds.

But design is often a tradeoff. We had to make room for the six reserve wastebaskets, and we had a never-ending struggle with the janitorial staff, who kept trying to empty all of the wastebaskets every evening. The users of the computer center came to depend upon the "soft" nature of the wastebaskets and would discard things that they otherwise might have kept for a while longer. When there was an error—sometimes on the part of the janitorial staff, sometimes on our part in cycling the wastebaskets properly—then it was a calamity. When you build an error-tolerant mechanism, people come to rely upon it, so it had better be reliable.

**Mistakes as
Errors of Thought**

Mistakes result from the choice of inappropriate goals. A person makes a poor decision, misclassifies a situation, or fails to take all the relevant factors into account. Many mistakes arise from the vagaries of human thought, often because people tend to rely upon remembered experiences rather than on more systematic analysis. We make decisions based upon what is in our memory; memory is biased toward overgeneralization and overregularization of the commonplace and overemphasis on the discrepant.

SOME MODELS OF HUMAN THOUGHT

Psychologists have chronicled the failures of thought, the nonrationality of real behavior. Even simple tasks can sometimes throw otherwise clever people into disarray. Even though principles of rationality seem as often violated as followed, we still cling to the notion that human thought should be rational, logical, and orderly. Much of law is based upon the concept of rational thought and behavior. Much of economic theory is based upon the model of the rational human who attempts to optimize personal benefit, utility, or comfort. Many scientists who study artificial intelligence use the mathematics of formal logic—the predicate calculus—as their major tool to simulate thought.

But human thought—and its close relatives, problem solving and planning—seem more rooted in past experience than in logical deduction. Mental life is not neat and orderly. It does not proceed smoothly and gracefully in neat, logical form. Instead, it hops, skips, and jumps its way from idea to idea, tying together things that have no business being put together; forming new creative leaps, new insights and concepts. Human thought is not like logic; it is fundamentally different in kind and in spirit. The difference is neither worse nor better. But it is the difference that leads to creative discovery and to great robustness of behavior.

Thought and memory are closely related, for thought relies heavily upon the experiences of life. Indeed, much problem solving and decision making takes place through attempts to remember some previous experience that can serve as a guide for the present. There have been many theories of human memory. For example, every method of filing things has shown up somewhere along the line as a model for human memory. Do you file photographs neatly in a scrapbook? One theory of memory has postulated that our experiences are neatly encoded and organized, as if in a photo album. This theory is wrong. Human memory is most definitely not like a set of photographs or a tape recording. It mushes things together too much, confuses one event with another, combines different events, and leaves out parts of individual events.

Another theory is based on the filing cabinet model, wherein there are lots of cross references and pointers to other records. This theory has a good deal going for it, and it is probably a reasonable characterization of the most prominent approach today. Of course, it is not called a file cabinet theory. It goes by the names of "schema theory," "frame theory," or sometimes "semantic networks" and "propositional encoding." The individual file folders are defined in the formal structure of the schemas or frames, and the connections and associations among the individual records make the structure into a vast and complex network. The essence of the theory consists of three beliefs, all reasonable and supported by considerable evidence: (1) that there is logic and order to the individual structures (this is what the schema or frame is about); (2) that human memory is associative, with each schema pointing and referring to multiple others to which it is related or that help define the components (thus the term "network"); and (3) that much of our power for deductive thought comes from using the information in one schema to deduce the properties of another (thus the term "propositional encoding").[6] To illustrate the third concept: once I learn that all living animals breathe, I know that any live animal I will ever meet will breathe. I don't have to learn this separately for all animals. We call this the "default value." Unless told otherwise, anything I learn for a general concept applies to all of its instances by default. Default values do not have to apply to everything—I can learn exceptions, such as that all birds fly except for penguins and ostriches. But defaults hold true unless an exception shows otherwise. Deduction is a most useful and powerful property of human memory.

THE CONNECTIONIST APPROACH

We still are a long way from understanding human memory and cognition. Today, in the developing field of cognitive science, two different views are emerging. The traditional view considers thought to be rational, logical, and orderly; this approach uses mathematical logic as the scientific means to explain thought. Adherents of this approach have pioneered the development of schemas as the mechanism of human memory. A newer approach is rooted in the working of the brain itself. Those of us who follow this new approach call it "connectionism," but it also goes under the names of "neural nets," "neural models," and "parallel distributed processing." It is an attempt to model the way in which the brain itself is structured, with billions of brain cells connected into groups, many cells connected to tens of thousands of others, many all working at the same time. This approach follows the rules of thermodynamics more than it does the rules of logic. Connectionism is still tentative, still unproven. I believe that it has the potential to explain much of what puzzled us before, but part of the scientific community thinks that it is fundamentally flawed.[7]

The brain consists of billions of nerve cells—neurons—each connected to thousands of other cells. Each neuron sends simple signals to the neurons to which it is connected, each signal attempting to increase or decrease the activity of its recipient. The connectionist approach to the study of thought mimics these connections. Each connectionist unit is connected to many other units. The signals are either positive in value (called "activation" signals) or negative in value (called "inhibition"). Each unit adds up the total influence of the signals that it receives and then sends along its outward connections a signal whose value is a function of that sum. That's about all there is to it. The elements are all simple: the complexity and power come from the fact that there are a large number of interconnected units trying to influence the activities of the others. All this interconnection leads to massive interaction among the units, with the signals sometimes leading to fights and conflicts, sometimes to cooperation and stability. After a while, however, the system of interconnected units will eventually settle down to a stable state that represents a compromise among the opposing forces.

Thoughts are represented by stable patterns of activity. New thoughts are triggered whenever there is some change in the system, oftentimes because some new information arrives at the senses and changes the pattern of activation and inhibition. We can think of the interactions as the computational part of thought: when one set of units sends signals activating another, this can be interpreted as offering support for a cooperative interpretation of events; when one set of units sends signals suppressing another, it is because the two usually offer competing interpretations. The result of all this support and competition is a compromise: not the correct interpretation, simply one that is as consistent as possible with all possibilities under active consideration. This approach suggests that much of thought results from a kind of pattern matching system, one that forces its solutions to be analogous to past experiences, and one that does not necessarily follow the formal rules of logical inference.

The relaxation of interacting connectionist structures into patterns happens relatively quickly and automatically, below the surface of consciousness. We are conscious only of the end states, not of the means for getting there. As a result, in this view of the mind, our explanations of our own behavior are always suspect, for they amount to stories made up after the fact to explain the thoughts that we already have.

Much of our knowledge is hidden beneath the surface of our minds, inaccessible to conscious inspection. We discover our own knowledge primarily through our actions. We can also find out by testing ourselves, by trying to retrieve examples from memory—self-generated examples. Think of an example, then think of another example. Find a story that explains them. Then we believe that story and call it the reason or explanation for our behavior. The problem is that the story changes dramatically depending upon what examples we select. And the examples we select depend upon a large set of factors, some under our control, some not.

The connectionist approach to memory might also be called the "multiple-exposure" theory of memory.

Suppose, unbeknownst to you, your camera broke so that the film wouldn't wind. Every picture you took went right on top of all the others. If you had taken pictures of different scenes, you might still be able to make out the individual parts. But suppose you had taken a picture of a high-school graduating class, one person at a time. Each person took a turn sitting in the chair in front of the fixed camera; each smiled; each had a picture taken. Afterward, when you developed the film, you would find just one picture, a composite of all those faces. All the individual records would still be there, but on top of one another, difficult to separate out. You'd have the average high-school graduate.

Throw everything into memory on top of one another. That is a crude approximation of the connectionist approach to memory. Actually, things aren't thrown together until after a lot of processing has gone on. And memory isn't really like a multiple exposure. Still, this is not a bad characterization of the connectionist approach.

Consider what happens when two similar events are experienced: they merge together to form a kind of average, a "prototypical event." This prototype governs interpretations and actions related to any other event that seems similar. What happens when something really discrepant occurs? If it is quite different from the prototype, it still manages to maintain its identity when thrown into memory. It stands out by itself.

If there were a thousand similar events, we would tend to remember them as one composite prototype. If there were just one discrepant event, we would remember it, too, for by being discrepant it didn't get smudged up with the rest. But the resulting memory is almost as if there had been only two events: the common one and the discrepant one. The common one is a thousand times more likely, but not to the memory; in memory there are two things, and the discrepant event hardly seems less likely than the everyday one.

So it is with human memory. We mush together details of things that are similar, and give undue weight to the discrepant. We relish discrepant and unusual memories. We remember them, talk about them, and bias behavior toward them in wholly inappropriate ways.

What has this to do with everyday thought? A lot. Everyday thought seems to be based upon past experiences, upon our ability to retrieve an event from the past and use it to model the present. This event-based reasoning is powerful, yet fundamentally flawed. Because thought is based on what can be recalled, the rare event can predominate. Think about it. Think of your experiences with computers, or VCRs, or home appliances; what probably come to mind are the unusual experiences, things that are discrepant. It doesn't matter that you may have used the device a hundred times successfully—it is the one time you got embarrassed that will come to mind.[8]

The limitations of human thought processes have important implications for everyday activities, and in fact can be called in to distinguish everyday activities from others.

The Structure of Tasks

Everyday activities are conceptually simple. We should be able to do most things without having to think about what we're doing. The simplicity lies in the nature of the structure of the tasks.

WIDE AND DEEP STRUCTURES

Consider the game of chess, an activity that is neither everyday nor simple, at least, not for most of us. When it is my turn to play, I have a number of possible moves. For each of my moves, my opponent has a number of possible responses. And for each of my opponent's responses, I have a number of possible counterresponses. The sequences can be represented on a decision tree, a diagram that in this case takes the current board position as a starting point and shows each of my possible moves, each of the possible countermoves, each possible counter-counter move, each possible counter-counter-counter move, and so on, as deep as time and energy permit. The size of the tree for chess is immense, for the number of choices increases exponentially. Suppose that at each spot there are 8 possible moves. At that spot I must consider 8 initial moves for me, $8 \times 8 = 64$ replies of my opponent, $64 \times 8 = 512$ replies I can make, $512 \times 8 = 4,096$ possible replies by my opponent, and then $4,096 \times 8 = 32,768$ more possibili-

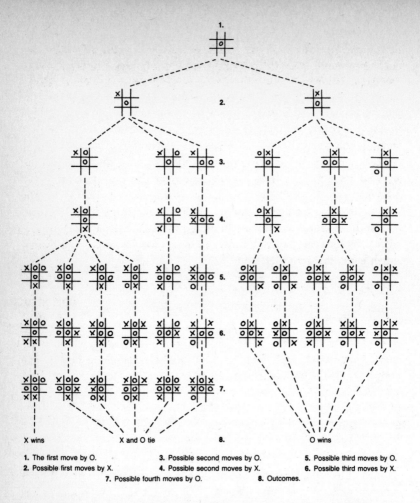

1. The first move by O.
2. Possible first moves by X.
3. Possible second moves by O.
4. Possible second moves by X.
5. Possible third moves by O.
6. Possible third moves by X.
7. Possible fourth moves by O.
8. Outcomes.

5.1 Wide and Deep Decision Tree. The game of tic-tac-toe (naughts and crosses). The tree starts at the top, with the initial state, then deepens as each successive layer considers all the alternative moves by each player. Although this diagram looks a bit complex, it is a pretty simple structure as these things go. First of all, this picture is much simplified. Only one possible first move by O is shown, and the symmetry of the board is used to reduce the number of alternatives being considered. (Only two first moves by X need be considered: the eight possibilities are really equivalent to the two shown because of the symmetry.) In the full game, there are nine possible first moves for O, eight possible replies by X, seven second moves by O, and so on, up to the third move by O, which is the first possible time for the game to be won; there are 15,120 possible sequences up to that point. Even this simple game leads to such a wide and deep decision tree that it is not possible to work out all the possibilities in the head. Expert players take advantage of simple strategies and memorized move sequences. (From *Human Information Processing*, Second Edition, by Peter H. Lindsay and Donald A. Norman, copyright © 1977 by Harcourt Brace Jovanovich, Inc. Reprinted by permission of the publisher.)

ties for me. As you can see, the decision tree gets large rapidly: looking ahead five moves means considering over 30,000 possibilities. The tree is characterized by a vast, spreading network of possibilities. There isn't space here for the decision tree for chess. But even a simple game like tic-tac-toe (or naughts and crosses) has a similar structure, shown in figure 5.1.

That decision tree for chess is even wider and deeper—wide in the sense that at each point in the tree there are many alternatives, so that the tree spreads out over a considerable area; deep in the sense that most branches of the tree go on for a considerable distance.

Everyday activities don't require the kind of complex analyses required for something like chess. In most everyday activities, we need only examine the alternatives and act. Everyday structures are either shallow or narrow.[9]

SHALLOW STRUCTURES

The menu of an ice cream store provides a good example of a shallow structure (figure 5.2). There are many alternative actions, but each is simple; there are few decisions to make after the single top-level choice. The major problem is to decide which action to do. Difficulties arise from competing alternatives, not from any prolonged search, problem solving, or trial and error. In shallow structures, there's no problem of planning or depth of analysis.

NARROW STRUCTURES

A cookbook recipe is a good example of a narrow structure (figure 5.3). A narrow structure arises when there are only a small number of alternatives, perhaps one or two. If each possibility leads to only one or two further choices, then the resulting tree structure can be said to be narrow and deep.

Just as the ice cream store menu is an example of a shallow structure, the multicourse, fixed menu meal can serve as an example of a deep structure. Although there may be many courses, for each course the diner is either automatically served the relevant dish or offered the choice of one or two dishes. The only action required is to accept one or to refuse: no deep thought is required.

5.2 Wide and Shallow Decision Tree. A lot of alternatives, but after the first decision, few or no further decisions. In this menu from an ice cream parlor, there are many choices, but once the flavor has been chosen, the remaining decisions are simple—what kind of cone, how many scoops, and what kind of topping. (Photograph by the author of a sign at a Baskin-Robbins store.)

Another example is the sequence of steps required to start a car. You must go to the car, select the proper key, insert it in the door lock, turn the key, open the door, remove the key, get into the car, close the door, put on the seatbelt, insert the proper key into the ignition, make sure

jnd Cabrillo Sea Bass

Saute onion and garlic.
Heat 2 bottles of beer to boiling.
Place sea bass in pan.
Pour beer over fish.
Add onion, garlic, and mushrooms.
Add 4 whole garlic cloves, unpeeled.
Add cilantro.
Poach for 10 minutes (approx.)
Remove fish from pan.
Reduce stock over high heat.
Put brown rice on serving plate.
Place fish over rice.
Cover fish with stock and
  *jnd*Jalepeño sauce.

jnd Jalepeño Sauce

Chop 1 large onion.
Peel and chop 6 tomatillos.
Slice 2 Jalapeño chiles lengthwise.
Peel and quarter 2 tomatoes.
Place onion, tomatillos, chile, and
  tomatoes in sauce pan.
Cover with 1 cup red wine.
Simmer for 15 minutes to 2 hours (the
  longer the milder).
Add cilantro.
Serve.

5.3 Deep and Narrow Decision Tree. Few decisions need be made at any level, but to complete the task, many steps (levels) must be followed. This decision structure is characteristic of any task that has a large number of steps, each of which is relatively straightforward. An example is the steps required to follow a recipe, such as my favorite fish recipe.

the car is not in gear, start the engine, and so on. This is a deep structure, but it is narrow. There is a long series of steps, but at each point, there are few, if any, alternatives to consider. Any task that involves a sequence of activities where the action to be done at any point is determined by its place in the sequence is an example of a narrow structure.

The modern superhighway offers the driver a series of exits. The driver either starts on the road with a predetermined exit in mind or else must decide at each exit whether to stay on the road or not. In fact, road designers attempt to linearize and simplify the decision-making tasks of the driver: the relevant information is fed slowly and sequentially to the driver to minimize the mental workload and the need for overlapping processing.

Freeway design is by now a science, with a well-defined set of procedures and with societies, books, and journals devoted to it. Different countries of the world have reached different solutions to the problem of guiding the driver.

A rather complete analysis was done in Britain for the design of the M series motorways. Each motorway exit has a carefully programmed sequence of six signs. The first precedes the exit by one mile and is intended to serve an alerting function, as well as to present route number information. The second precedes the exit by a half mile and gives the major towns reached by the exit (but no route number information). The third precedes the exit by a quarter mile and adds the "forward destination" (where you eventually get to if you don't exit). The fourth sign is at the exit and provides major route numbers and a few town names. The fifth sign is on the motorway beyond the exit; it is intended to play a "confirmatory" role: it displays the forward destinations and their distances. The sixth sign is on the exit ramp, in colors the reverse of all the preceding signs; it shows all the local destinations, usually on a map of the roundabout (traffic circle) found at most exits. [10]

THE NATURE OF EVERYDAY TASKS

Most tasks of daily life are routine, requiring little thought or planning—things like bathing and dressing, brushing teeth, eating at the table, getting to work, meeting with friends, going to the theater. These are the daily activities that occupy most of our time, and there are many of them. Yet each, by itself, is relatively simple: either shallow or narrow.

What are *not* everyday activities? Those with wide and deep structures, the ones that require considerable conscious planning and thought, deliberate trial and error: trying first this approach, then that—backtracking. Unusual tasks include writing a long document or letter, making a major or complex purchase, computing income tax, planning a special meal, arranging a vacation trip. And don't forget intellectual games: bridge, chess, poker, crossword puzzles, and so on.

The tasks most frequently studied by psychologists are *not* everyday tasks. They are things like chess or algebraic puzzles, which require much thought and effort; but indeed, these pursuits have just the sort of wide and deep structures that do not characterize everyday activities.

In general, we find wide and deep structures in games and leisure activities, where the structure is devised so as to occupy the mind or to make the task deliberately (and artificially) difficult. After all, what challenge would there be if games such as chess or bridge were conceptually simple? How would interest in a mystery novel—or any novel for that matter—be sustained if the plot were straightforward and the answers readily deducible? Recreational activities *should* be wide and deep, for we do them when we have the time and wish to expend the effort. In the everyday world, we want to get on with the important things of life, not spend our time in deep thought attempting to open a can of food or dial a telephone number.

Everyday activities must usually be done relatively quickly, often simultaneously with other activities. Neither time nor mental resources may be available. As a result, everyday activities structure themselves so as to minimize conscious mental activity, which means they must minimize planning (and especially any planning with extensive looking ahead and backing up) and mental computation. These characteristics restrict everyday tasks to those that are shallow (having no need for extensive looking ahead and backing up) and those that are narrow (having few choices at any point, and therefore requiring little planning). If the structure is shallow, width is not important. If the structure is narrow, depth is not important. In either case, the mental effort required for doing the task is minimized.

Conscious and Subconscious Behavior

Much human behavior is done subconsciously, without conscious awareness and not available to inspection. The exact relationship between conscious and subconscious thought is still under great debate. The resulting scientific puzzles are complex and not easily solved.

Subconscious thought matches patterns. It operates, I believe, by finding the best possible match of one's past experience to the current one. It proceeds rapidly and automatically, without effort. Subconscious processing is one of our strengths. It is good at detecting general trends, at recognizing the relationship between what we now experience and what has happened in the past. And it is good at generalizing, at making predictions about the general trend based on few examples. But subconscious thought can find matches that are inappropriate, or wrong, and it may not distinguish the common from the rare. Subconscious thought is biased toward regularity and structure, and it is limited in formal power. It may not be capable of symbolic manipulation, of careful reasoning through a sequence of steps.

Conscious thought is quite different. It is slow and labored. Here is where we slowly ponder decisions, think through alternatives, compare different choices. Conscious thought ponders first this approach, then that—comparing, rationalizing, finding explanations. Formal logic, mathematics, decision theory: these are the tools of conscious thought. Both conscious and subconscious modes of thought are powerful and essential aspects of human life. Both can provide insightful leaps and creative moments. And both are subject to errors, misconceptions, and failures.

Conscious thought tends to be slow and serial. Conscious processing seems to involve short-term memory and is thereby limited in the amount that can be readily available. Try consciously to solve the children's game called tic-tac-toe or naughts and crosses and you will discover that you can't, not if you try to explore all the alternatives. How can I claim that a trivial children's game cannot be done in the head? Because you don't really play by thinking it through; you play by memorizing the patterns, by transforming the game into something simpler. Try playing the following game:

Start with the nine numbers 1, 2, 3, 4, 5, 6, 7, 8, and 9. You and your opponent alternate turns, each time taking a number. Each number can be taken only once, so if your opponent has selected a number, you cannot also take it. The first person to have any three numbers that total 15 wins the game.

This is a difficult game. You will find it is very hard to play without writing it down. But this game is identical to tic-tac-toe. Why should it be hard if tic-tac-toe is easy?

To see the relationship between the game of 15 and tic-tac-toe, simply arrange the nine digits into the following pattern:

8 1 6

3 5 7

4 9 2

Now you can see the connection: any three numbers that solve the 15 problem also solve tic-tac-toe. And any tic-tac-toe solution is also a solution to 15. So why is one easy and the other hard? Because tic-tac-toe takes advantage of perceptual abilities, and because you simplify tic-tac-toe by changing it in several ways, by taking advantage of symmetries, and by memorizing ("learning") the basic opening moves and their appropriate responses. In the end, unless someone makes a slip, two players will always draw, neither one winning.

The transformations of tic-tac-toe have made a complex task into an everyday one. The everyday version doesn't require much mental effort, it does not require planning and thinking, and it is boring. Which is exactly what everyday tasks ought to be—boring, so that we can put our conscious attention on the important things of life, not the routine.

Conscious thought is severely limited by the small capacity of short-term memory. Five or six items is all that can be kept available at any one moment. But subconscious thought is one of the tools of the conscious mind, and the memory limitation can be overcome if only an appropriate organizational structure can be found. Take fifteen unrelated things and it is not possible to keep them in conscious memory at once. Organize them into a structure and it is easy, for only that one structure has to be kept in conscious memory. As a result of this power of organization to overcome the limits of working memory, explanation and understanding become essential components of conscious thought: with understanding and explanation, the number of things that can be kept consciously in mind expands enormously.

Now consider how mistakes might be made: by mismatch; by taking the current situation and falsely matching it with something in the past. Although we are really good at finding examples from the past to match the present, these examples are biased in one of two ways: toward the regularities of the past—the prototypical situation—or toward the unique, discrepant event. But suppose the current event is different from all that has been experienced before: it is neither common nor unique, it is simply rare. We won't deal well with it: we are apt to classify the rare with either the common or the unique, and either of these choices is wrong. The same powers that make us so good at dealing with the common and the unique lead to severe error with the rare.

EXPLAINING AWAY ERRORS

A reformed thief, telling of his success, put it this way: "I'm telling you . . . if I had a hundred dollars for every time I heard a dog owner tell their dog to 'shut up . . . go lie down,' while I was right outside their window, I'd be a millionaire."[11]

Mistakes, especially when they involve misinterpreting the situation, can take a very long time to be discovered. For one thing, the interpretation is quite reasonable at the time. This is a special problem in a novel situation. The situation may look very much like others we've been in; we tend to confuse the rare event with the frequent one.

How many times have you heard a strange noise while driving your car, only to dismiss it as not relevant, or unimportant? How many times does your dog bark in the night, causing you to get up and yell out, "Be quiet!" And what if the car turns out to be broken, and your mistake has increased the damage? Or there really is a burglar outside, but you've silenced the dog?

This problem is natural. There are lots of things we could pay attention to or worry about; most would be false alarms, irrelevant minor events. At the other extreme, we can ignore everything, rationally explain each apparent anomaly. Hear a noise that sounds like a pistol shot and explain it away: "Must be a car's exhaust backfiring." Hear someone yell out and think, Why can't my neighbors be quiet? Most of the time we are correct. But when we're not, our explanations seem stupid and hard to justify.

When there is a devastating accident, people's explaining away the signs of the impending disaster always seems implausible to others. Afterward, there is a tendency to read about what has taken place and to criticize: "How could those people be so stupid? Fire them. Pass a law against it. Redo the training." Look at the nuclear power accidents. Operators at Three Mile Island made numerous errors and misdiagnoses, but each one was logical and understandable at the time. The nuclear plant disaster at Chernobyl in the Soviet Union was triggered by a well-intentioned attempt to test the safety features of the plant. The actions seemed logical and sensible to the operators at the time, but now their judgments can be seen to have been erroneous.[12]

Explaining away errors is a common problem in commercial accidents. Most major accidents follow a series of breakdowns and errors, problem after problem, each making the next more likely. Seldom does a major accident occur without numerous failures: equipment malfunctions, unusual events, a series of apparently unrelated breakdowns and errors that culminate in major disaster; yet no single step has appeared to be serious. In many of these cases, the people involved noted the problem but explained it away, finding a logical explanation for the otherwise deviant observation.

The contrast in our understanding before and after an event can be dramatic. The psychologist Baruch Fischhoff has studied explanations given in hindsight, where events seem completely obvious and predictable after the fact but completely unpredictable beforehand.[13]

Fischhoff presented people with a number of situations and asked them to predict what would happen: they were correct only at the chance level. He then presented the same situation along with the actual outcome to another group of people, asking them to state how likely the outcome was: when the actual outcome was known, it appeared to be plausible and likely, whereas the others appeared unlikely. When the actual outcome was not known, the various alternatives had quite different plausibility. It is a lot easier to determine what is obvious after it has happened.

SOCIAL PRESSURE AND MISTAKES

A subtle issue that seems to figure in many accidents is social pressure. Although it may not at first seem to be relevant in design, it has strong influence on everyday behavior. In industrial settings social pressures can lead to misinterpretation, mistakes, and accidents. For understanding mistakes, social structure is every bit as essential as physical structure.

Look at airline accidents, not everyday activities for most of us, but subject to the same principles. In 1983, Korean Air flight 007 strayed over the Soviet Union and got shot down, probably because of an error in programming the flight path into the inertial navigation system (INS). Although each checkpoint was discrepant, apparently the deviations were easily explained away if the crew substituted for each point the checkpoint reading for the previous INS point. But there were significant social pressures operating as well.

The crew of flight 007 probably misprogrammed the INS, but the INS couldn't be reprogrammed in flight: if an error were detected the aircraft would have to go back to the original airport, land (jettisoning fuel to get to a safe landing weight), and then reset the INS and take off again—an expensive proposition. Three Korean Air flights had returned to their airport in the six months preceding the flight 007 incident, and the airline had told its pilots that the next pilot who returned would be punished. Was this a factor in the accident? It's hard to know, but the design of the INS sounds badly deficient. The social pressures on the crew not to find (or admit to) an error in the INS were clearly strong. But punishment for following a safety procedure is never wise. The proper approach would be to redesign either the INS's or the procedures for using them.[14]

The real culprit, almost always, is the design. Design that makes it easy to make wrong settings, or to misread an instrument, or to misclassify an event. Design of the social structure that makes false reporting of danger punishable. Turn a nuclear power plant off by mistake and you cost the company hundreds of thousands of dollars; you'll probably lose your job. Fail to turn it off when there is a real incident, and you might lose your life. If you refuse to fly a crowded airliner because the weather looks bad, the company loses lots of money and the passengers get very angry. Take off under those situations and most of the time it works out fine, which encourages risk taking. But every so often there is a disaster.

Tenerife, the Canary Islands, in 1977. A KLM Boeing 747 that was taking off crashed into a Pan American 747 that was taxiing on the runway, killing 583 people. The KLM plane should not have tried to take off then, but the weather was starting to get bad, and the crew had already been delayed for too long (even being on the Canary Islands was a diversion from the scheduled flight—they had to land there because bad weather had prevented them from landing at their scheduled destination); they had not received clearance to take off. And the Pan American flight should not have been on the runway, but there was considerable misunderstanding between the pilots and the air traffic controllers. Furthermore, the fog was coming in so neither plane could see the other.

There were time pressures and economic pressures acting together. The Pan American pilots questioned their orders to taxi on the runway, but they continued anyway. The co-pilot of the KLM flight voiced minor objections to the pilot, suggesting that they were not yet cleared for takeoff. All in all, a tragedy occurred due to a complex mixture of social pressures and logical explaining away of discrepant observations.

The Air Florida flight from National Airport, Washington, D.C., crashed at takeoff into the 14th Street bridge over the Potomac River, killing seventy-eight people, including four who were on the bridge. The plane should not have taken off because there was ice on the wings, but it had already been delayed over an hour and a half; this and other factors "may have predisposed the crew to hurry." The accident occurred despite the first officer's (the co-pilot's) concern: "Although the first officer expressed concern that something 'was not right' to the captain four times during the takeoff, the captain took no action to reject the takeoff." Again we see social pressures coupled with time and economic forces. [15]

Error is often thought of as something to be avoided or something done by unskilled or unmotivated people. But everyone makes errors. Designers make the mistake of not taking error into account. Inadvertently, they can make it easy to err and difficult or impossible to discover error or to recover from it. Consider the London stock market story that opened this chapter. The system was poorly designed. It should not be possible for one person, with one simple error, to cause such widespread damage. Here is what designers should do:

1. Understand the causes of error and design to minimize those causes.

2. Make it possible to reverse actions—to "undo" them—or make it harder to do what cannot be reversed.

3. Make it easier to discover the errors that do occur, and make them easier to correct.

4. Change the attitude toward errors. Think of an object's user as attempting to do a task, getting there by imperfect approximations. Don't think of the user as making errors; think of the actions as approximations of what is desired.

When someone makes an error, there usually is good reason for it. If it was a mistake, the information available was probably incomplete or misleading. The decision was probably sensible at the time. If it was a slip, it was probably due to poor design or distraction. Errors are usually understandable and logical, once you think through their causes. Don't punish the person for making errors. Don't take offense. But most of all, don't ignore it. Try to design the system to allow for errors. Realize that normal behavior isn't always accurate. Design so that errors are easy to discover and corrections are possible.

HOW TO DEAL WITH ERROR—AND HOW NOT TO

Consider the error of locking your keys into your car. Some cars have made this error much less likely. You simply can't lock the doors (not easily, anyway) except by using the key. So you're pretty much forced to have the keys with you. I call this kind of design a *forcing function.* (More on this topic in the next section.)

In the United States, cars are required to be designed so that if the door is opened while the keys are in the ignition, a warning sound comes on. In theory, if you walk away from your car, leaving the keys in the ignition, the buzzer will call you back. Yet the signal must be ignored as often as it must be attended to. It must be ignored when you open the door of your car while the engine is running so you can hand someone something. On these occasions it is annoying; you know the door is open. And sometimes you want to or need to leave the keys in the car. There goes the buzzer—it can't distinguish deliberate actions from erroneous ones.

Warning signals are usually not the answer. Consider the control room of a nuclear power plant or the cockpit of a commercial aircraft. Thousands of instruments, each designed by someone who thought it was necessary to put in a warning signal for it. Many of the signals sound the same. Most can be ignored anyway because they tell the operator about something that is already known. And when a real emergency happens, all the warning signals seem to go on at once. Each competes with the others to be heard, preventing the person from concentrating upon the problem.[16]

Built-in warning features are bypassed for several reasons. One is that they can go off in error, disrupting perfectly sensible, proper behavior. Another is that they often conflict, and the resulting cacophony is distracting enough to hamper performance. Finally, they are often inconvenient. You can't sit in the car on a warm day, open the door to get some air, and listen to the radio. The key must be in the ignition to make the radio work, but then the door buzzes all the time. So we disconnect those warning signals, tape them over, silence the bell, unscrew the lightbulbs. Warnings and safety methods must be used with care and intelligence, taking into account the tradeoffs for the people who are affected.

FORCING FUNCTIONS

Forcing functions are a form of physical constraint: situations in which the actions are constrained so that failure at one stage prevents the next step from happening. Starting a car has a forcing function associated with it—you must put the ignition key into the ignition switch. Some

The Born Loser, May 11, 1986. Copyright © 1986 NEA Inc.

time ago, the button that activated the starter motor was separate from the ignition key, so that it was possible to attempt to start the car without the keys; the error was made frequently. In most modern automobiles, the starter switch is activated by turning the key—an effective forcing function that makes you use the key to do the operation.

There is no analogous forcing function for removing the key upon leaving the automobile. As we have already seen, those automobiles that have door locks that can be operated only by a key (from outside the vehicle) do introduce a forcing function: if you want to lock the door you can't leave the key in the car. If a forcing function is really desired, it is usually possible to find one, although at some cost for normal behavior. It is important to think through the implications of that cost—to decide whether people will deliberately disable the forcing function.

The history of seatbelts in autos provides a good example. Despite all the evidence that seatbelts are an effective means of saving lives, some people dislike them enough that they refuse to wear them, probably because the perceived risk is so much less than the actual, statistical risk. For a short period, the United States tried a forcing function on seatbelts: a special interlock was installed on each new car. If the driver's and passengers' belts were not fastened, the car would not start (and a buzzer would sound). This forcing function was so disliked that most drivers had their mechanics disconnect it. The law was quickly changed.

There seemed to be three problems. First, many people did not want to wear seatbelts, and they resented the mechanical forcing function. Second, the forcing function couldn't distinguish legitimate cases in which the seatbelt should not be buckled from illegitimate ones. Thus, if you wanted to carry a package in the passenger's seat, the weight-sensing element in the seat registered a person, so the car wouldn't start unless the passenger seat's buckle was fastened. Third, the mechanisms were not reliable, so they often failed—buzzing, stopping the engine, and being an overall nuisance. Those people who couldn't figure out how to disconnect the forcing function simply buckled the belts permanently, fastening the buckle when the seat was unoccupied and stuffing it under the seat. So if a passenger really wanted to use the belt, it couldn't be done. Moral: it isn't easy to force unwanted behavior upon people. And if you are going to use a forcing function, make sure it works right, is reliable, and distinguishes legitimate violations from illegitimate ones.

Forcing functions are the extreme case of strong constraints that make it easy to discover erroneous behavior. Not every situation allows such strong constraints to operate, but the general principle can be extended to a wide variety of situations. In the field of safety engineering, forcing functions show up under other names, in particular as specialized methods for the prevention of accidents. Three such methods are *interlocks, lockins,* and *lockouts.*

An *interlock* forces operations to take place in proper sequence (figure 5.4). Microwave ovens and television sets use interlocks as forcing functions to prevent people from opening the door of the oven or taking off the back of the television set without first turning off the electric power: the interlock disconnects the power the instant the door is opened or the back removed. The pin on a fire extinguisher or hand grenade and the safety on a rifle are other examples of interlocks; these forcing functions prevent the accidental use of the devices.

A *lockin* keeps an operation active, preventing someone from prematurely stopping it. The sad stories of those who turn off word processors without first saving their work could be avoided with the use of a lockin. Suppose the on-off switch were a "soft" switch, not really disconnecting the power, but sending a signal to the program to quit, checking that all files had been saved, and then, after all the appropriate housekeeping operations had been completed, turning off the power. (Of course, a normal power switch should also exist as an override for special situations or for when a software problem causes the soft switch to fail.)

A *lockout* device is one that prevents someone from entering a place that is dangerous, or prevents an event from occurring. A good example of a lockout occurs in stairways of public buildings, at least in the United States (figure 5.5). In cases of fire, people have a tendency to flee in panic, down the stairs, down, down, down, past the ground floor and into the basement, where they are trapped. The solution (required by the fire laws) is not to allow simple passage from the ground floor to the basement.

In the building in which I work, at the ground floor the stairs seem to end, leading directly to the building's exit door. To go down further requires finding a different door, opening it, and proceeding down the

5.4 Use of an Interlock. The Nissan Stanza van was constructed with the access door for its fuel tank right in the path of the sliding passenger door (above). It could be dangerous for the door to be opened while someone was fueling the car. To overcome the problem, Nissan added a forcing function, a bar that prevented the sliding door from opening whenever the fuel tank was being filled. The bar is constructed in the form of an interlock: the cap to the fuel tank cannot be removed unless the bar is moved to its safety position (below). Furthermore, the fuel door cannot be shut again unless the bar is returned to its normal position. Finally, warning signals were added, so that if someone attempts to open the door during fueling, a buzzer sounds. All in all, a lot of effort was put into these forcing functions—which were needed only because of an unfortunate placement of the fuel tank access in the first place.

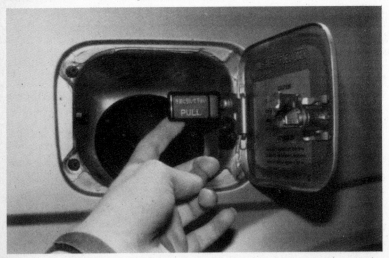

5.5 Lockout. A form of forcing function that prevents people from going down the stairs, past the ground floor, and into the basement. Although in normal times this is a nuisance, in times of fire, when people flee down the stairs in panic, the forcing function can save lives by preventing a mad dash into the basement. The bar encourages people to stop at the ground floor and leave the building.

stairs. This safety feature is usually a nuisance: we have never had a fire, yet I frequently must go from a higher floor into the basement. It's a minor nuisance, however, and it is worth the cost if it can save lives when there is a fire.

Forcing functions almost always are a nuisance in normal usage. The clever designer has to minimize the nuisance value while retaining the safety, forcing-function mechanism, to guard against the occasional tragedy.

There are other useful devices that make use of a forcing function. In some public restrooms there's a package shelf inconveniently placed on the wall just behind the cubicle door, held in a vertical position by a spring. You lower the shelf to the horizontal position, and the weight of a package keeps it there. Why not supply a permanent shelf, always horizontal, placed so that it wouldn't interfere with the opening of the door? There is room. A little thought reveals the answer: the shelf's position is a forcing function. When the shelf is lowered, it blocks the door. So to get out of the cubicle, you have to remove whatever is on the shelf and raise it out of the way. And that forces you to remember your packages. Clever design.

It is common to forget items. Examples spring readily to mind:

· Making copies of a document, but leaving the original inside the machine and walking off with only the copy.

· Using a bank or credit card to withdraw money from an automatic teller machine, then walking off without the card. This was a frequent enough error that many machines now have a forcing function: you must remove the card before the money will be delivered. Of course, you then can walk off without your money, but this is less likely than forgetting the card because money is the goal of using the machine. The possibility exists so the forcing function isn't perfect.

· Leaving a child behind at a rest stop during a car trip. I also heard about a new mother who left her infant in the dressing room of a department store.

· Losing a pen because it was taken out to write a note or a check in some public location, then put down for a moment while doing some other task—such as giving the check to the salesperson. The pen is forgotten in the activities of putting away the checkbook, picking up the goods, talking to the salesperson or friends, and so on. Or the reverse: borrowing a pen, using it, and then putting it away in pocket or purse, even though it is someone else's; this slip is an example of a capture error.

Forcing functions don't always show up where they should. Sometimes their absence causes all sorts of unnecessary confusion. Read the caution statement from the game instructions shown in figure 5.6.

All those exclamation marks! And the caution is repeated throughout the instruction manual. It won't do any good. The Nintendo Entertainment System is meant to be used by children. The instruction manual probably won't be around. Even if it is, a group of active children, anxious to try a different game, won't bother with it. I watched my own child follow the instruction faithfully for several days, then fail when asked to stop playing and come to dinner. I forgot on the few attempts I made to master the game. The only possible virtue of the warning is to protect the manufacturer: when the children repeatedly burn out the electronic circuits, the company can disclaim liability, asserting that the children violated the instructions.

4. OPERATING YOUR NES

●TO START PLAY

1. Turn your television on to Channel 3.

   Note: If Channel 3 is broadcasting in your area and interfering with the game, set the switch on the back of the Control Deck to Channel 4.

2. If your TV has an automatic fine tuning control (AFC), turn it off. (Use the manual fine tune dial to adjust the picture after inserting the game pak as described below.)
   Note: If you have a color TV that turns black and white when the AFC is turned off, leave the AFC on.

3. Make sure that the power switch on the Control Deck is off.

   CAUTION !! ALWAYS MAKE SURE THAT THE POWER SWITCH ON THE CONTROL DECK IS OFF BEFORE INSERTING OR REMOVING A GAME PAK !!

4. Open the Chamber Lid on the Control Deck.   Insert a Game Pak into the Chamber (Label Facing up) and Push it all the way in.   Press Down on the Game Pak until it locks into place and close the Chamber Lid.

  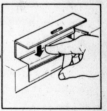

5.6   The Nintendo Children's Toy. This home video game set is intended for use by children. However, it has a complex safety instruction, one almost guaranteed to be ignored. To use the system, one inserts a "game pak" cartridge into the "chamber." The power switch should be off when inserting or removing the cartridge. In the absence of any forcing function, the instruction is almost universally disregarded (if anyone even knows about it). If order is important, there should be a forcing function. If order does not matter, the instruction should be dropped. (From the Nintendo instruction manual. Nintendo® and Nintendo Entertainment System® are trademarks of Nintendo of America Inc. © 1986 Nintendo.)

Proper design calls for a forcing function here. There are several viable schemes. The cover over the game pack compartment could control an interlock, so that it automatically turned off the power whenever it was opened. Or the power switch could move a lever blocking the top of the game pack compartment, so that the packs could not be removed or inserted unless the lever were out of the way, turning off the power. There are other possibilities. My point is, of course, that the design should have included one; without the forcing function, failure to heed the warning is almost guaranteed.

A Design Philosophy

There are lots of ways for a designer to deal with errors.[17] The critical thing, however, is to approach the topic with the proper philosophy. The designer shouldn't think of a simple dichotomy between errors and correct behavior; rather, the entire interaction should be treated as a cooperative endeavor between person and machine, one in which misconceptions can arise on either side. This philosophy is much easier to implement on something like a computer which has the ability to make decisions on its own than on things like doors and power plants, which do not have such intelligence. But the philosophy of user-centered system design still holds. Think of the user's point of view. Assume that every possible mishap will happen, so protect against it. Make actions reversible. Try to make them less costly. All the required principles have been thoroughly discussed in this book.

· Put the required knowledge in the world. Don't require all the knowledge to be in the head. Yet do allow for more efficient operation when the user has learned the operations, has gotten the knowledge in the head.

· Use the power of natural and artificial constraints: physical, logical, semantic, and cultural. Use forcing functions and natural mappings.

· Narrow the gulfs of execution and evaluation. Make things visible, both for execution and evaluation. On the execution side, make the options readily available. On the evaluation side, make the results of each action apparent. Make it possible to determine the system state readily, easily, and accurately, and in a form consistent with the person's goals, intentions, and expectations.

CHAPTER SIX

THE
DESIGN
CHALLENGE

They began work at once, and by the next September the first [typewriter] machine was finished, and letters were written with it. It worked successfully so far as to write rapidly and correctly, but trial and experience showed it to be far short of an acceptable, practicable writing machine. . . .

One device after another was conceived and developed till twenty-five or thirty experimental instruments were made, each succeeding one a little different from and a little better than the one preceding. They were put into the hands of stenographers, practical persons who were presumed to know better than anyone else what would be needed and satisfactory. Of these, James O. Clephane, of Washington, D.C., was one. He tried the instruments as no one else had tried them; he destroyed them, one after another, as fast as they could be made and sent him, till the patience of Mr. Sholes [the inventor] was exhausted. But Mr. Densmore insisted that this was the very salvation of the enterprise; that it showed the weak spots and defects, and that the machine must be made so that anybody could use it, or all efforts might as well be abandoned; that such a test was a blessing and not a misfortune, for which the enterprise should be thankful.[1]

Much good design evolves: the design is tested, problem areas are discovered and modified, and then it is continually retested and remodified until time, energy, and resources run out. This natural design process is characteristic of products built by craftspeople, especially folk objects. With handmade objects such as rugs, pottery, hand tools, or furniture, each new object can be modified slightly from the previous one, eliminating small problems, making small improvements, or testing new ideas. Over time, this process results in functional, aesthetically pleasing objects.

Improvements can take place through natural evolution as long as each previous design is studied and the craftsperson is willing to be flexible. The bad features have to be identified. The folk artists change the bad features and keep the good ones unchanged. If a change makes matters worse, well, it just gets changed again on the next go-around. Eventually the bad features get modified into good ones, while the good ones are kept. The technical term for this process is "hill-climbing," analogous to climbing a hill in the dark. Move your foot in one direction. If it is downhill, try another direction. If the direction is uphill, take one step. Keep doing this until you have reached a point where all steps would be downhill; then you are at the top of the hill—or at least at a local peak.[2]

FORCES THAT WORK AGAINST EVOLUTIONARY DESIGN

Natural design does not work in every situation: there must be enough time for the process to be carried out, and the item must be simple. Modern designers are subject to many forces that do not allow for the slow, careful crafting of an object over decades and generations. Most of today's items are too complex, with too many variables, for this slow sifting of improvements. But simple improvements ought to be possible. You would think that objects such as automobiles, appliances, or computers, which periodically come out in new models, could benefit from the experience of the previous model. Alas, the multiple forces of a competitive market seem not to allow this.

One negative force is the demands of time: new models are already into their design process before the old ones have even been released to customers. Moreover, mechanisms for collecting and feeding back the experiences of customers seldom exist. Another force is the pressure to be distinctive, to stand out, to make each design look different from what has gone before. It is the rare organization that is content to let a good product stand or to let natural evolution perfect it slowly. No, each year a "new, improved" model must come out, usually incorporating new features that do not use the old as a starting point. In far too many instances, the results spell disaster for the consumer.

There is yet another problem: the curse of individuality. Designers have to make an individual stamp, their mark, their signature. And if different companies manufacture the same type of item, each must do it differently to allow its product to be distinguished from others'. A mixed curse, individuality, for through the desire to be different come some of our best ideas and innovations. But in the world of sales, if a company were to make the perfect product, any other company would have to change it—which would make it worse—in order to promote its own innovation, to show that it was different. How can natural design work under these circumstances? It can't.

Consider the telephone. The early telephone evolved slowly, over several generations. It once was a most awkward device, with handset and microphone, one held with each hand. You had to turn a crank to generate a signal that would ring the bell at the other end of the line. Voice transmission was poor. Over the years improvements were slowly made in size and shape, reliability, and features that simplified its use. The instrument was heavy and robust: drop it on the floor, and not only did it still work but you seldom lost the telephone connection. The layout of the dial or the push buttons resulted from careful experimentation in the laboratory. The size and spacing of the keys were carefully selected to work for a wide variety of the population, including the very young and the very old. The sounds of the telephone were also carefully designed to produce feedback. Push a button and you heard a tone in the earphone. Speak into the microphone, and a carefully determined percentage of your own voice was fed back into the earphone, the better to help you regulate how loudly you were talking. The clicks, buzzes, and other noises you heard while a connection was being established provided useful indications of progress.

All these minor aspects of the telephone were arrived at slowly, over years of development protected by the monopoly status of most national telephone systems. In today's wildly competitive market, there is a fierce desire to bring out a product that appeals to a wide body of people and that is distinctive and different—the market demands speed and novelty. Many of the most useful refinements are being lost. Push buttons are apt to be arranged haphazardly, with the keys oversize or tiny. The sounds have been taken away. Many telephones don't even give feedback when the buttons are pushed. All the folklore of design has been lost with the brash new engineers who can't wait to add yet the latest electronic gimmickry to the telephone, whether needed or not.

One simple detail can make the point: the ridge of plastic next to the switch hook—the button under the receiver that, when depressed, hangs up the call. Ever knock the telephone off the table and onto the floor while you were talking? Wasn't it nice when you didn't get disconnected, frustrating when you did? The monopolistic Bell System designers explicitly recognized this problem and designed with it in mind. They made the telephone heavy and sturdy enough to withstand the fall. And they protected the critical button with a shield that prevents the switch hook from hitting the ground. Look carefully at

6.1 Design Subtleties. In the older Bell System instrument, the prongs that held the receiver also prevented the switch hook from being accidentally depressed. More recent telephones often lack such niceties.

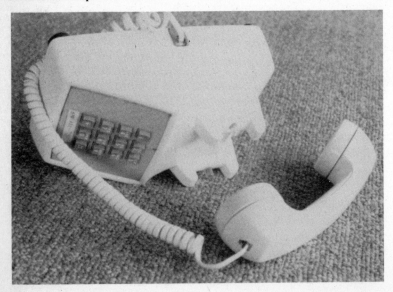

figure 6.1: see that on the one telephone the buttons cannot reach the ground and so are not depressed. A small feature, but an important one. Economic pressures have made the newer telephones lighter, less expensive, and less sturdy—throwaway phones, they are often called. And the protective shield? Often as not, there is none—in this case not because of cost, but because the new designers probably never thought of it, probably never realized its function. The result? This scenario, repeated in office over office.

Mark is sitting at his desk when the phone rings. "Hello," he answers. "Yeah, I can help you—let me get out the manual." He reaches, pulling the telephone with him. Bang! Crash! The phone falls on the floor, hanging itself up. "Damn," mutters Mark, "I don't even know who that was."

THE TYPEWRITER: A CASE HISTORY IN THE EVOLUTION OF DESIGN

"Among all the mechanical inventions for which the age is noted, none, perhaps, has more rapidly come into general use than the typewriter. . . . The time is coming when it will almost, or quite as much, supersede the steel pen as that has the good, gray goose quill."[3]

The history of the typewriter is the story of dedicated inventors in many countries, each striving to develop a machine for rapid writing. They tried many versions in their struggle to get the one that fit all the constraints—that worked, could be manufactured at reasonable cost, and could be used.

Consider the typewriter keyboard, with its arbitrary, diagonally sloping arrangement of keys and its even more arbitrary arrangement of letters on the keys. The current standard keyboard was designed by Charles Latham Sholes in the 1870s. The design is called the "qwerty" keyboard (because in the American version the top row of letters begins with "qwerty"), or sometimes the Sholes keyboard. The Sholes typewriter was not the first, but it was the most successful of the early versions; it eventually became the Remington typewriter, the model upon which most manual typewriters were constructed. Why such a weird keyboard?

The design of the keyboard has a long and peculiar history. Early typewriters experimented with a wide variety of layouts, using three basic themes. One was circular, with the letters laid out alphabetically; the operator would find the proper spot and depress a lever, lift a rod, or do whatever other mechanical operation the device required. Another popular layout was like the piano keyboard, with the letters laid out in a long row; some of the early keyboards, including an early version by Sholes, even had black and white keys. Both the circular layout and the piano keyboard proved awkward. In the end, a third arrangement was adopted by all: a rectangular arrangement of keys, still in alphabetical order. The levers manipulated by the keys were large and ungainly, and the size, spacing, and arrangement of the keys were dictated by these mechanical considerations, not by the characteristics of the human hand.

Why did the alphabetical ordering change? To overcome a mechanical problem. When the typist went too quickly the typebars would collide, jamming the mechanism. The solution was to change the locations of the keys: letters such as *i* and *e* that were often typed in succession were placed on opposite sides of the machine so that their bars would not collide.[4] Other typewriting technologies did not follow the qwerty arrangement. Typesetting machines (such as the Linotype machine) use a completely different layout; the Linotype keyboard is called "shrdlu," after the pattern of keys it follows, and is modeled after the relative frequency of letters in English. This was how hand printers arranged the letters that they would remove from bins and insert manually into the printing forms. Ah, yes, the natural evolution of design.

Not all early keyboards had a backspace, and the "tabulation" key ("tab" on modern keyboards) was a revolutionary breakthrough. The first typewriters could print only upper case letters. The addition of lower case letters was, at first, accomplished by adding a new key for each lower case letter, so in effect there were two separate keyboards. Some early typewriters organized the keys for upper case differently than for lower case. Imagine how difficult it would be to learn that keyboard! It took years to develop the shift key so that both upper and lower case letters could share the same key. This was a nontrivial invention, combining mechanical ingenuity with a dual-faced typebar.

In the end, the keyboard was designed through an evolutionary process, but the main driving forces were mechanical. Modern keyboards do not have the same problems; jamming isn't a possibility with electronic keyboards and computers. Even the style of typing has changed. In the early years, people kept their eyes on the keyboard and typed with one or two fingers of each hand. Then one courageous person, Frank McGurrin of Salt Lake City, memorized the key locations and learned to type with all his fingers, without looking at the keyboard. His skills were not recognized at first; it took a national contest held in Cincinnati, Ohio, in 1877 to prove that this method was indeed superior.[5] In the end, the qwerty keyboard was adopted throughout the world with but minor variations. We are committed to it, even though it was designed to satisfy constraints that no longer apply, was based on a style of typing no longer used, and is difficult to learn.

Tinkering with keyboard design is a popular pastime (figure 6.2). Some schemes keep the existing mechanical layout of the keys, but arrange the assignments of letters more efficiently. Others improve the physical layout as well, arranging the keys to accommodate the mirror-image symmetry of the hands and the varied spacing and agility of the fingers. Still others reduce the number of keys dramatically by having patterns of keys—chords—represent the letters, permitting one-handed or faster two-handed typing. But none of these innovations takes hold because the qwerty keyboard, while deficient, is good enough. Although its antijamming arrangement no longer has mechanical justification, it does put many common letter pairs on opposing hands; one hand can be getting ready to type its letter while the other is finishing, so typing is speeded up.

What about alphabetical keyboards (figure 6.3)? Wouldn't they at least these be easier to learn? Nope.[6] Because the letters have to be laid out in rows, just knowing the alphabet isn't enough. You also have to know where the rows break. Even if you could learn that, it would still be easier to scan the keyboard than to compute where a key might be. Then you are better off if common letters are located where you are apt to find them by scanning—a property that the qwerty keyboard provides. If you don't know any keyboard, there is little difference in typing speed among a qwerty keyboard, an alphabetic keyboard, and even a random arrangement of keys. If you know even a little of the qwerty, that is enough to make it better than the others. And for expert typists, the alphabetical arrangements are always *slower* than qwerty.

There is a better way—the Dvorak keyboard—painstakingly developed by (and named after) one of the founders of industrial engineering. It is easier to learn and allows for about 10 percent faster typing, but that is simply not enough of an improvement to merit a revolution

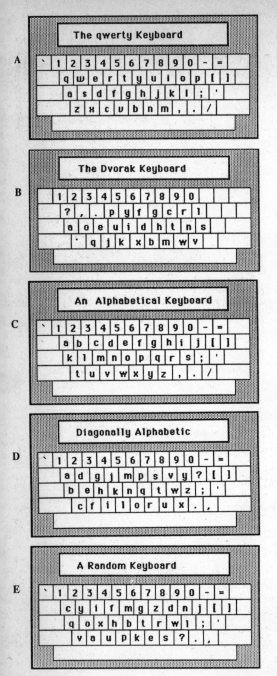

6.2 Typewriter Keyboards.

The standard American layout of keys —the Sholes or qwerty keyboard.

The American Simplified Keyboard (often called ASK), a simplified version of the original Dvorak keyboard; on the original, the numerals and punctuation keys are arranged differently.

Most alphabetically organized keyboards arrange the alphabet along horizontal rows, as shown (and in the keyboards of figure 6.3).

This alphabetical arrangement is superior, however: with its diagonal arrangement, letters increase systematically up the alphabet from left to right without major breaks.

The keyboard at left has randomly arranged letters.

Beginners succeed about the same on all these keyboards: alphabetical works barely better than random. For experts, ASK is best, followed by qwerty: alphabetical keyboards are quite inferior. Moral: Don't bother with alphabetical keyboards.

6.3 Products with Alphabetical Keyboards. Even though several experiments show that these are of no use to novices and detrimental to experts, every year designers plunge ahead and foist yet another alphabetical keyboard on us. Even if you manage to learn one, you will not have learned to use all the different ones.

in the keyboard. Millions of people would have to learn a new style of typing. Millions of typewriters would have to be changed. The severe constraints of existing practice prevent change, even where the change would be an improvement.[7]

Couldn't we at least do better with two hands at once? Yes, we could. Court stenographers can outtype anyone else. They use chord keyboards, typing syllables directly onto the page—syllables, not letters. Chord keyboards have very few keys—as few as five or six, but usually ten to fifteen. Many chord keyboards allow you to type single letters or whole words with one depression of the hand on several keys. If you use all ten fingers at the same time, then there are 1,023 possible combinations. That is enough for all the letters and numbers, lower case and upper case, plus a lot of words—if only you can learn the patterns. Chord keyboards have a horrible disadvantage: they are very hard to learn and very hard to retain; all the knowledge has to be in the head. Walk up to any regular keyboard and you can use it right away. Just search for the letter you want and push the key. With a chord keyboard, you have to press several keys simultaneously. There is no way to label the keys properly and no way to know what to do just by looking. Some chord keyboards are incredibly clever and remarkably easy to learn, considering. I tried to learn one of the easier ones. Thirty minutes' practice, and I knew the alphabet. But if I didn't use the keyboard for a week, I forgot the chords. The gain did not seem worth the effort. What about one-handed chord keyboards? Wouldn't it be worth a lot of time and effort to be able to type with one hand? Perhaps, if you are flying a jet aircraft with one hand and need to enter data into your computer with the other. But not for the rest of us.[8]

All this brings up an important lesson in design. Once a satisfactory product has been achieved, further change may be counterproductive, especially if the product is successful. You have to know when to stop.

You can observe the design iterations and experiments with the computer keyboard. The layout of the basic keyboard is now standardized through international agreement. But computer keyboards need extra keys, and these are not standardized. Some keyboards have an extra key between the shift key and the "z" key. The return key takes on different shapes and locations. The special keys of the computer keyboard—for example, control, escape, break, delete (not to be confused with backspace), and the "arrow" or cursor control keys—vary in location with the phases of the year, varying even among the products of a single manufacturer. Much confusion and strong emotions result.

Note, too, that the computer allows for flexible letter arrangements. It is a simple matter on some computers to switch the interpretation of the keys from qwerty to Dvorak: one command and the change is done. But unless the Dvorak fan also pries off and rearranges the keycaps, the Dvorak fan has to ignore the labels on the keys and rely on memory. Someday key labeling will be done by electronic displays on each key, so changing the labels will also become trivial. So computer technology may liberate users from forced standardization. Everyone could select the keyboard of personal choice.

Why Designers Go Astray

"[Frank Lloyd] Wright evidently wasn't very sympathetic about complaints. When Herbert F. Johnson, the late president of S. C. Johnson, Inc., in Racine, Wis., called Wright to say that his roof was leaking all over a dinner guest, the architect is said to have responded, 'Tell him to move his chair.' "[9]

If everyday design were ruled by aesthetics, life might be more pleasing to the eye but less comfortable; if ruled by usability, it might be more comfortable but uglier. If cost or ease of manufacture dominated, products might not be attractive, functional, or durable. Clearly, each consideration has its place. Trouble occurs when one dominates all the others.

Designers go astray for several reasons. First, the reward structure of the design community tends to put aesthetics first. Design collections feature prize-winning clocks that are unreadable, alarms that cannot easily be set, can openers that mystify. Second, designers are not typical users. They become so expert in using the object they have designed that they cannot believe that anyone else might have problems; only interaction and testing with actual users throughout the design process can forestall that. Third, designers must please their clients, and the clients may not be the users.

PUTTING AESTHETICS FIRST

"It probably won a prize" is a disparaging phrase in this book. Why? Because prizes tend to be given for some aspects of a design, to the neglect of all others—usually including usability. Consider the following example, in which a usable, livable design was penalized by the design profession. The assignment was to design the Seattle offices of the Federal Aviation Administration (FAA). The most noteworthy feature of the design process was that those who would work in the building had a major say in the planning. One of the members of the design team, Robert Sommer, describes the process as follows:

> "Architect Sam Sloan coordinated a project in which employees . . . were able to select their own office furniture and plan office layout. This represented a major departure from prevailing practices in the federal services where such matters were decided by those in authority. Since both the Seattle and Los Angeles branches of the FAA were scheduled to move into new buildings at about the same time, the client for the project, the General Services Administration, agreed with architect Sloan's proposal to involve employees in the design process in Seattle, while leaving the Los Angeles office as a control condition where traditional methods of space planning would be followed."[10]

So there really were two designs: one in Seattle, with heavy participation by the users, and one in Los Angeles, designed in the conventional manner by architects. Which design do the users prefer? Why the Seattle one, of course. Which one got the award? Why the Los Angeles one, of course. Here is Sommer's description of the outcome:

> "Several months following the move into the new buildings, surveys by the research team were made in Los Angeles and Seattle. The Seattle workers were more satisfied with their building and work areas than were the Los Angeles employees. . . . It is noteworthy that the Los Angeles building has been given repeated awards by the American Institute of Architects while the Seattle building received no recognition. One member of the AIA jury justified his denial of an award to the Seattle building on the basis of its 'residential quality' and 'lack of discipline and control of the interiors,' which was what the employees liked the most about it. This reflects the well-documented differences in preferences between architects and occupants. . . . The director of the Seattle office admitted that many visitors were surprised that this is a federal facility. Employees in both locations rated their satisfaction with their job performance before and after the move into the new building. There was no change in the Los Angeles office and a 7 percent improvement in rated job performance in the Seattle office."[11]

Aesthetics, not surprisingly, comes first at museums and design centers. I have spent much time in the science museum of my own city, San Diego, watching visitors try out the displays. The visitors try hard, and although they seem to enjoy themselves, it is quite clear that they usually miss the point of the display. The signs are highly decorative; but they are often poorly lit, difficult to read, and have lots of gushing language with little explanation. Certainly the visitors are not enlightened about science (which is supposed to be the point of the exhibit). Occasionally I help out when I see bewildered faces by explaining the scientific principles being demonstrated by the exhibit (after all, many of the exhibits in this sort of museum are really psychology demonstrations, many of which I explain in my own introductory classes). I am often rewarded with smiles and nods of understanding. I took one of my graduate classes there to observe and comment; we all agreed about the inadequacy of the signs, and, moreover, we had useful suggestions. We met with a museum official and tried to explain what was happening. He didn't understand. His problems were the cost and durability of the exhibits. "Are the visitors learning anything?" we asked. He still didn't understand. Attendance at the museum was high. It looked attractive. It had probably won a prize. Why were we wasting his time?

Many museums and design centers make prime examples of pretty displays and signs coupled with illegible and uninformative labels. Mostly, I suspect, it's because these buildings are judged as places of art, where the exhibits are meant to be admired, not to be learned from. I made several trips to the Design Centre in London to collect material for this book. I hoped it would have a good library and bookshop (it did) and good exhibits, demonstrating the proper principles for combining aesthetics, economics, usability, and manufacturability. I found the London Design Centre itself to be an exercise in poor design. Take the cafeteria: just about impossible to use. Behind the counter, the four workers continually get in each other's way. The layout of the back-counter facilities seems without structure or function. Food is carefully heated for the customer, but it gets cold by the time the customer gets through the line. The cafeteria has tiny round tables, which are also too high. There are elegant round stools to sit on. The set up is impossible to use if you are elderly or young or have your hands full of packages. Of course, the design may have been a deliberate attempt to discourage use of the cafeteria. Consider this scenario.

The cafeteria is well designed, with spacious tables and comfortable chairs. But it then becomes too popular, interfering with the true pur-

pose of the Design Centre, which is to encourage good design among British manufacturers. The popularity of the Centre and its cafeteria to tourists is unexpected. The Design Centre decides to discourage people from using the cafeteria. They take out the original tables and chairs and replace them with dysfunctional, uncomfortable ones, all in the name of good design—the goal in this case being to discourage people from using the cafeteria and lingering. Actually, restaurants often install uncomfortable chairs for just this reason. Fast-food places often have no chairs or tables. So my complaints provide evidence that the design criteria were met, that the design was successful. [12]

In London I visited the Boilerworks, a part of the Victoria and Albert Museum, to look at a special exhibit called "natural design." The exhibit itself was one of the best examples of unnatural design I have ever witnessed. Pretty, tasteful signs near each display. Dramatically striking layout of the objects. But you couldn't tell which sign went with which exhibit, or what the text meant. Alas, this seems typical of museums.

A major part of the design process ought to be the study of just how the objects being designed are to be used. In the case of the cafeteria at the London Design Centre, the designers should imagine a crowd of people in line, imagine where the line will start and end, and study what effect the line will have on the rest of the museum. Study the work patterns of the cafeteria employees: consider them responding to customer requests. Where will they have to move? What objects will they have to reach? If there are several employees, will they get in each other's way? And then consider the customers. Grandparents with heavy coats, umbrellas, packages, and perhaps three small children—how will they pay for their purchases? Is there a place for them to put down their packages so they can open their wallets or purses and get out their money? Can this be done in a way that minimizes the disruption for the next people in line and improves the speed and efficiency of the cashier? And finally, consider the customers at the tables. Struggling to get up on a high stool to eat off a tiny table. And don't just imagine: go out and look at the current design, or at other cafeterias. Interview potential customers, interview the cafeteria employees.

In the case of science museums, studies have to be made on people who are the same as the intended audience. The designers and employees already know too much: they can no longer put themselves into the role of the viewer.

Let me be positive for a change: there are science museums and exhibits that work well. The science museums in Boston and in Toronto, the Monterey Aquarium, the Exploratorium in San Francisco. There are probably many others that I do not know about. Consider the Exploratorium. It is dark and grungy on the outside, located in a remodeled, left-over building. Very little is devoted to sleekness or aesthetics. The emphasis is on using and understanding the exhibits. The staff is interested in explaining things.

It is possible to do things right. Just don't let the focus on cost, or durability, or aesthetics destroy the major point of the museum: to be used, to be understood. The problem of focus, I call this.

DESIGNERS ARE NOT TYPICAL USERS

Designers often think of themselves as typical users. After all, they are people too, and they are often users of their own designs. Why don't they notice, why don't they have the same problems as the rest of us? The designers I have spoken with are thoughtful, concerned people. They do want to do things properly. Why, then, are so many failing?

All of us develop an everyday psychology—professionals call it "folk psychology" or, sometimes, "naive psychology"—and it can be as erroneous and misleading as the naive physics that we examined in chapter 2. Worse, actually. As human beings, we have access to our conscious thoughts and beliefs but not to our subconscious ones. Conscious thoughts are often rationalizations of behavior, explanations after the fact. We tend to project our own rationalizations and beliefs onto the actions and beliefs of others. But the professional should be able to realize that human belief and behavior are complex and that the individual is in no position to discover all the relevant factors. There is no substitute for interaction with and study of actual users of a proposed design.

"Steve Wozniak, the whiz-kid co-founder of Apple Computer offered the first public glimpse of CORE, his latest brainchild. . . .

"CORE, which stands for controller of remote electronics, is a single device that allows consumers to fully operate their home equipment by remote control as long as the equipment is all in one room. . . .

"CORE comes with a 40-page user manual. But Wozniak says users of his gizmo . . . won't be daunted because, initially, most will be 'techies.' "[13]

There is a big difference between the expertise required to be a designer and that required to be a user. In their work, designers often become expert with the *device* they are designing. Users are often expert at the *task* they are trying to perform with the device.[14]

Steve Wozniak designs a device to help people like himself, people who complain that their house is cluttered with too many remote control devices for their electronic components. So he produces a single controller that replaces the many. But the task is complex, the instruction manual thick. Not a problem, we are told, the initial users will be "techies." Just like Wozniak, presumably. But how accurate is that characterization? Do we even know that the technically ambitious, the "techies," will really be able to understand and use the device? The only way to find out is to test the designs on users—people as similar to the eventual purchaser of the product as possible. Furthermore, the designer's interaction with potential users must take place from the very beginning of the design process, for it soon becomes too late to make fundamental changes.

Professional designers are usually aware of the pitfalls. But most design is not done by professional designers, it is done by engineers, programmers, and managers. One designer described the issues to me this way:

"People, generally engineers or managers, tend to feel that they are humans, therefore they can design something for other humans just as well as the trained interface expert. It's really interesting to watch engineers and computer scientists go about designing a product. They argue and argue about how to do things, generally with a sincere desire to do the right thing for the user. But when it comes to assessing the tradeoffs between the user interface and internal resources in a product, they almost always tend to simplify their own lives. They will have to do the work, they try to make the internal machine architecture as simple as possible. Internal design elegance sometimes maps to user interface elegance, but not always. Design teams really need vocal advocates for the people who will ultimately use the interface."[15]

Designers have become so proficient with the product that they can no longer perceive or understand the areas that are apt to cause difficulties. Even when designers become users, their deep understanding and close contact with the device they are designing means that they operate it almost entirely from knowledge in the head. The user, especially the first-time or infrequent user, must rely almost entirely on knowledge in the world. That is a big difference, fundamental to the design.

Innocence lost is not easily regained. The designer simply cannot predict the problems people will have, the misinterpretations that will arise, and the errors that will get made. And if the designer cannot anticipate errors, then the design cannot minimize their occurrence or their ramifications.

THE DESIGNER'S CLIENTS MAY NOT BE USERS

Designers must please their clients, who are often not the end users. Consider major household appliances such as stoves, refrigerators, dishwashers, and clothes washers and dryers; and faucets and thermostats for heating and air conditioning systems. They are often purchased by housing developers or landlords. In business, purchasing departments make decisions for large companies and owners or managers make decisions in small companies. In all these cases, the purchaser is probably interested primarily in price, perhaps in size or appearance, almost certainly not in usability. And once devices are purchased and installed, the purchaser has no further interest in them. The manufacturer is primarily concerned about these decision makers, its immediate customers, not the eventual users.

In some situations cost must be put first, especially in government or industry. In my university, copying machines are purchased by the Printing and Duplicating Center, then dispersed to the various departments. The copiers are purchased after a formal "request for proposals" has gone out to manufacturers and dealers of machines. The selection is almost always based solely on price, plus a consideration of the cost of maintenance. Usability? Not considered. The state of California requires by law that universities purchase things on a price basis; there are no legal requirements regarding understandability or usability of the product. That is one reason we get unusable copying machines and telephone systems. If users complained strongly enough, usability could become a requirement in the purchasing specifications, and that demand could trickle back to the designers. But without this feedback, designers must often design the cheapest possible products because those are what sell.

Designers face a tough task. They answer to their clients, and it may be hard to find out who the actual users are. Sometimes they are even prohibited from contacting the users for fear they will incidentally reveal company plans for new products or mislead users into believing that new products are about to be developed. The design process is a captive of corporate bureaucracy, with each stage in the process adding its own assessment and dictating the changes it believes essential for its concerns. The design is almost certainly altered as it leaves the designers and proceeds through manufacturing and marketing. All participants are well intentioned, and their particular concerns are legitimate. The factors should all be considered simultaneously, however, and not subject to the accidents of time sequence or the realities of corporate rank and clout. One designer wrote me this about his problems:

"Most designers live in a world where the gulf of evaluation is infinite. True, we often know the product too well to envision how people will use it, yet we are separated from the end users by multiple layers of corporate bureaucracy, marketing, customer services, etc. These people believe they know what customers want and feedback from the real world is limited by filters they impose. If you accept the problem definition (product requirements) from these outside sources without personal investigation you will design an inferior product regardless of your best intentions. If this initial hurdle is overcome you are only halfway home. The best design ideas are often ruined by the development-manufacturing process that takes place when they leave the design studio. What this really points out is that the process by which we design is flawed, probably more so than our conception of how to create quality designs."[16]

The Complexity of the Design Process

"Design is the successive application of constraints until only a unique product is left."[17]

You might think that a water faucet would be pretty easy to design. After all, you merely want to start or stop the flow of water. But consider some of the problems. Suppose the faucets are for use in public places, where users may fail to turn them off. You can make a spring-operated faucet, which operates only as long as the handle is held. This automatically turns the faucet off; but it is difficult for users to hold the handle while wetting their hands. Ok, so you add a timer; then one push on the faucet handle yields five or ten seconds of water flow. But the extra complexity of the faucet design adds to the cost and lowers the reliability of the faucet. Furthermore, it is difficult to decide how long the water should stay on. Somehow it never seems like long enough for the user.

How about a foot-operated faucet, which overcomes the problems of springs and timers because the water stops as soon as the foot leaves the pedal (figure 6.4 A)? This solution requires slightly more elaborate plumbing, again raising the cost. It also makes the control invisible, violating a major design principle and making it difficult for a new user to find the control. How about a high-technology solution, with automatic sensors that turn on the water as soon as a hand is placed in the sink, turning it off as soon as it leaves (figure 6.4 B)? This solution has several problems. First, it is expensive. Second, it makes the controls invisible, causing difficulty for new users. And third, it is not easy to see how the user could control either the volume of water or the temperature. More on this faucet later.

Not all faucets are designed under the constraints of public faucets. At home, aesthetic considerations tend to dominate. Styles often reflect the social and economic class of the user. And different kinds of users have different requirements.

The same considerations hold true for most everyday things. The variety of possible solutions to the usual problems is enormous. The range of expression permitted the designer is vast. Moreover, the number of tiny details that must be accounted for is astounding. Pick up almost any manufactured item and examine its details with care. The little wiggly bends on a hairpin are essential in keeping it from slipping out of the hair: someone had to think of that, then design special equipment to create the bends. The felt-tip pen I am examining as I write has six different sizes on the pen body, two different sizes on the cap. The pen changes its taper at numerous spots, each change serving some function. Four different substances comprise the pen body (and I am not counting the ink, the container that holds the ink, or the felt

Press floor stud for water
Adjust knob for temperature

Not drinking water

6.4 Nonstandard Faucets. There are often good reasons for using nonstandard means for operating faucets, but the result is that the user is apt to need help to operate them. *A* (above) shows the faucet and operating instructions from the sink in a British train. *B* (right) shows an advertisement for an automatic faucet: simply put the hand under it and the water comes out at a preset temperature and rate of flow. Convenient, but only for those who know the secret.

Hygienic—Efficient—Electronic Wonder

CUE-TEL® AUTOMATIC FAUCETS

TWO FAUCETS IN ONE

Automatic or Manual Mode Temperature Controlled

Adapter approved
patent pending

New state of the art ELECTRONIC faucets. Automatically activates sensors when hand or object approaches faucet. Water stops automatically when hand is withdrawn.

- Saves money, water and energy
- Solid brass, heavily chromed
- Interchangeable parts—warranted
- Easy to install, enhance your decor

Available at selected dealers or write to

COLUMBIA ELECTRONIC RESEARCH CORP
50 Doughty Blvd. Lawrence. N.Y. 11559 • 516-239-0265

tip). The cap is made of two kinds of plastic and one kind of metal. The inside of the cap has a number of subtle indentations and internal structures that clearly match up with corresponding parts of the pen body, both to hold the cap on firmly and to prevent the felt tip from drying out. There are more parts and variables than I would ever have imagined.

The pen's designer must be aware of hundreds of requirements. Make the pen too thin, and it will not be strong enough to stand up to the hard use of schoolchildren. Make the middle section too thick, and it can neither be grasped properly by the fingers nor controlled with enough precision. Yet people with arthritic hands may need a thick body because they can't close their fingers entirely. Leave out the tiny hole near the tip, and pressure changes in the atmosphere will cause the ink to leak out. And what of those who use the pen as a measuring device or as a mechanical implement to pry, poke, stab, and twist? For example, the instructions for the clock in my automobile say to set it by depressing the recessed button with the tip of a ball-point pen. How could the pen designer have known about this? What obligation does the designer have to consider varied and obscure uses?

DESIGNING FOR SPECIAL PEOPLE

There is no such thing as the average person. This poses a particular problem for the designer, who usually must come up with a single design for everyone; the task is difficult when all sorts of people are expected to use the item. The designer can consult handbooks with tables that show average arm reach and seated height, how far the average person can stretch backward while seated, and how much room is needed for average hips, knees, and elbows. Physical anthropometry the field is called. With the data the designer can try to meet the size requirements for almost everyone, say for the 90th, 95th, or even the 99th percentile. Suppose you design a product for the 95th percentile, that is, for everyone except the 5 percent of people who are smaller or larger. You're leaving out a lot of people. If the United States has 250 million people, 5 percent is 12.5 million. Even if you design for the 99th percentile you'll leave out 1 percent of the population—2.5 million.

Consider typists. Typists need to have their hands comfortably poised above the keyboard. Because of the thickness of typewriters, typing tables are designed to be lower than work tables. Of course, what matters is not the table height or the keyboard thickness, but the distance from the normal position of the typist's hands to the keyboard, which is determined by several factors:

· How big the typist is: legs, chest, hands
· How high the table is
· How thick the keyboard is
· How high the chair is

What can the designer do? One solution is to make everything adjustable: chair height, height and angle of the typing table. In fact, good typing tables have several parts: a part for the keyboard, a part for the computer screen, a part that holds working papers. Let each part be separately adjustable in height and angle. Then everyone can be accommodated.

Some problems are not solved by adjustments. Left-handed people, for example, present special problems. Simple adjustments won't work, nor will averages: average a left-hander with a right-hander and what do you get? Here is where special products help—left-handed scissors and knives, left-handed rulers (figure 6.5). These special-purpose devices don't always work, of course, not when one device is to be used by many, or where the items are too large or expensive for each person to own or to carry around. In such cases the only solution is to make the device itself ambidextrous, even if that makes it a bit less efficient for each person.

Consider the special problems of the aged and infirm, the handicapped, the blind or near-blind, the deaf or hard of hearing, the very short or very tall, or the foreign. Wheelchairs, for example, cannot easily manipulate curbs, stairs, or narrow aisles. As we age, our physical agility decreases, our reaction time slows, our visual skills deteriorate,

6.5 Left-handed Ruler. Writing from left to right with the left hand means that you cover what you write, making rulers hard to use, smearing the ink. A left-handed pen is a pen with fast-drying ink. This ruler for left-handers has the numbers going from right to left. One solution to the problem of diversity among individuals is to produce specialized objects.

LEFT HAND WORLD
Pier 39, P-8B
San Francisco, California 94133
"Left Is Right" ®

and our ability to attend to several things at once or to switch rapidly among competing events decreases.

High-speed highways pose special problems for the aged. An automobile traveling at high speed on a crowded highway at dusk is already pushing the limit of the driver's capabilities. The elderly are pushed beyond their limit. The solution adopted by many elderly drivers is to travel very slowly, to adjust their speed to what their processing can handle comfortably. Unfortunately, the slow driver poses a hazard to other drivers: on high-speed highways, things are considerably safer if everyone travels at approximately the same speed. I see no simple solution to this problem. In many cities, especially in the United States, there is no easy way to get from one place to another except by private automobile. Yet the elderly can't be expected to stay home. The solution has got to be either increased public transportation, or supplied drivers, or perhaps special streets or highway lanes with slower speed limits. Automated cars, the dream of science fiction writers and city planners, may still one day come about; they would take care of this problem.

Those of you who are young, do not smirk. Our abilities begin to deteriorate relatively early, starting in our mid-twenties. By our mid-forties our eyes can no longer adjust sufficiently to focus over the entire range of distances, so most of us need reading glasses or bifocals. Bifocals make it harder to do fine work, harder to use computer terminals (whose screens seem to be designed for twenty-year-olds).

I type these words seated in front of my computer terminal, head tilted upward at an uncomfortable angle so that I can see the screen out of the bottom half of my eyeglasses. I can't figure out how to get comfortable. Lower the screen and it gets in the way of my typing. Use special "computer" glasses adjusted for screen size and distance, and I can't read all the notes and outlines scattered about me at various distances. Fortunately, I can change the size of the type that appears on the screen. I use a twelve-point font, one whose letters are comfortably large. Alas, this is a tradeoff, for the larger the letters on the screen, the less material can fit. Change to nine-point font and I can see 78 percent more material (33 percent more lines, each with 33 percent more words): a non-trivial difference when I'm trying to write long sections. But the letters are 33 percent smaller, making it harder both to read and to correct them. At least my computer allows flexibility in type size; most do not.

By the time we're sixty, enough stray material has scattered about in our eyes that visual contrast is diminished, enough to be one of the major reasons that airline pilots are forced to retire at this age. At the age of sixty a person is still in good mental and physical shape, and the accumulated wisdom of the years leads to superior performance in many tasks. But physical strength is lessened, the agility of the body decreased, and the speed of some operations lessened. In a world where the average age is increasing, sixty is still relatively young: most sixty-year-olds have another twenty years to live, many have forty. We need to design with these people in mind—think of it as designing with our future selves in mind.

There is no simple solution, no one size fits all. But designing for flexibility helps. Flexibility in the size of the images on computer screens, in the sizes, heights, and angles of tables and chairs. Flexibility on our highways, perhaps making sure there are alternative routes with different speed limits. Fixed solutions will invariably fail with some people; flexible solutions at least offer a chance for those with special needs.

SELECTIVE ATTENTION: THE PROBLEM OF FOCUS

The ability of conscious attention is limited: focus on one thing and you reduce your attention to others. Psychologists call the phenomenon "selective attention." Excessive focus leads to a kind of tunnel vision, where peripheral items are ignored.

I watched a consumer show on British television on toasters that caught fire when the bread was too dry. The consumer representatives pointed out that people often inserted their fingers, a fork, or a knife into the toaster to extract the toast. This was very dangerous (even more dangerous in Britain than in the United States because the voltage is 240 volts, not the 120 of the United States). Yet some toasters had exposed wires very close to the top, quite reachable by the finger or the metal utensil. The consumer representatives argued that manufacturers should not have placed the wires so close to the opening.

The manufacturers denied that their toasters were dangerous. "Why," they asked, "would someone stick their fingers or a knife into a toaster?" Certainly the instructions warned them not to. Certainly they must know it is dangerous. To the designer, such an action is so unthinkable that prevention did not enter into the design considerations.

Consider the matter from the user's point of view. The person sees a problem—stuck or burning toast—and focuses on the solution—to extract it. The danger does not come to mind. To my own surprise, I did the same thing the very next day. I inserted two crumpets into the toaster; a few minutes later, smoke was pouring out. Quick, I ran over to the toaster, popped up the crumpets as far as they would go, and then quickly (but carefully?) inserted a knife blade into the toaster, down the side, to lift them out. What was I doing?

Selective attention: attend to the immediate problem, forget the rest. Sure I was being careful, but that is probably what the people who electrocuted themselves also believed. It just didn't seem dangerous, that's all.

The same story is repeated over and over again. Underwater divers focus so much on struggling to the surface that they fail to release the lead weights (on a special easy-to-release belt) that are keeping them underwater. People who are fleeing a fire push hard against a door, harder and harder, failing to recognize that the door opens by pulling. Someone is trapped behind a door, pushing against the left side when it opens from the right. Motorcyclists have their helmets strapped to their bike, not their head. People don't use seatbelts, or they drive too fast, because it is inconvenient to do otherwise and because they don't see the danger.

When there is a problem, people are apt to focus on it to the exclusion of other factors. The designer must design for the problem case, making other factors more salient, or easier to get to, or perhaps less necessary. That's what the forcing functions of chapter 5 were all about. Make the power cutoff switch of the toaster a forcing function, so that a person can't stick something into the toaster without flipping a power cutoff switch (which should be easy to get to and use). Or change the design of the wiring and heating elements so that lethal elements cannot be reached from outside, no matter what flesh or metal gets put into the toaster.

A corollary principle is that designers must guard against the problems of focus in their own design. Did their attention to one set of variables cause them to neglect another? Did safety suffer for usability? Usability for aesthetics? Aesthetics for manufacturability?

The Faucet: A Case History of Design Difficulties

It may be hard to believe that an everyday water faucet could need an instruction manual. I saw one, this time at the meeting of the British Psychological Society in Sheffield, England. The participants stayed in dormitories. Upon checking into one of these, the Ranmoor House, a guest was given a pamphlet that gave useful information: where the churches were, the times of meals, the location of the post office, and how to work the taps (faucets). "The taps on the washhand basin are operated by pushing down gently."

When it was my turn to speak at the conference, I asked the audience about those taps. How many had trouble using it? Polite, restrained titterings from the audience. How many tried to turn the handle? A large show of hands. How many had to seek help? A few honest folks raised their hands. Afterward, one woman came up to me and said that she had given up and had to walk up and down the halls until she found someone who could explain the taps to her.

A simple sink, a simple-looking faucet. But it looks like it should be turned, not pushed (figure 6.6 A). If you want the faucet to be pushed, make it look like it should be pushed. It can be done: the airlines do it right (figure 6.6 B).

Pity the poor house porters, always getting calls for help about the faucets. So instructions were put in the orientation sheet. Who would ever think of having to read instructions before using a faucet? At least put them on the faucets, where they can't be missed. But when simple things need instructions, it is a certain sign of poor design.

Why are faucets so hard to get right? Let us take a closer look at the two major variables (they will give us quite enough to do). The person who uses the faucets cares about two things: the water temperature and volume. Two things to control. We should be able to do that with two controls, one for each. Except that water comes in two pipes, hot and cold, and so the two things that are easiest to control—volume of hot water and volume of cold water—are not the two things we want to have controlled. Hence the designer's dilemma.

There are three problems; two relate to the mapping of intentions to actions, and the third is the problem of evaluation:

6.6 Contrasting Designs for "Push" Faucets. The faucets A (above) in the Ranmoor dormitory at the University of Sheffield give little clue to their mode of operation. As a result, occupants must be supplied with the instruction sheet for "the taps". The faucets B (below) on the sink of a commercial airline are designed properly. Pushing is clearly indicated. No instruction manual is required.

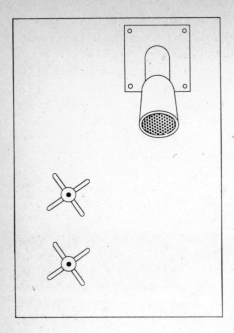

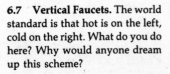

6.7 Vertical Faucets. The world standard is that hot is on the left, cold on the right. What do you do here? Why would anyone dream up this scheme?

· Which faucet controls the hot, which the cold?
· What do you do to the faucet to make it increase or decrease the water flow?
· How do you determine if the volume or temperature is correct?

The two mapping problems are solved through cultural conventions, or constraints. It is a worldwide convention that the left faucet should be hot, the right cold. It is also a universal convention that screw threads are made to tighten with clockwise turning, loosen with counterclockwise. You turn off a faucet by tightening a screw thread (tightening a washer against its seat), thereby shutting off the flow of water. So clockwise turning shuts off the water, counterclockwise turns it on.

Unfortunately, the constraints do not always hold. Most of the English people I asked were not aware that left/hot, right/cold was a convention; it is violated too often to be considered a convention in England. But the convention isn't universal in the United States. Look at the picture of a shower control from my own university (figure 6.7). Here we have vertical faucets. Vertical? If left is the standard for hot, how does that translate to vertical arrangements? Is hot the top or the bottom? Weird.

Sometimes a designer messes with the convention on purpose. The human body has a mirror-image symmetry, says this pseudopsychologist. So if the left hand moves clockwise, why, the right hand should move counterclockwise. Watch out, your plumber or architect may install a bathroom fixture where clockwise rotation turns the hot water off and the cold water on. Or is it the other way around? No matter, as you try to control the water temperature, soap running down over your eyes, groping to change the water control with one hand, soap or shampoo clutched in the other, you are guaranteed to get it wrong. The water is freezing, so you try to increase the amount of hot. You will probably turn on the shower, or the bath, or open the drain (or shut it), or turn off the hot water completely, or scald yourself.

Whoever invented that mirror-image nonsense should be forced to take a shower. Yes, there is some logic to it. To be a bit fair to the inventor of the scheme, it does work reasonably well as long as you always use the faucets by placing both hands on them at the same time, adjusting both controls simultaneously. It fails miserably, however, when one hand is used to alternate between the two controls. Then you cannot remember which direction does what.

What about the evaluation problem? Feedback in the use of most faucets is rapid and direct, so turning them the wrong way is easy to discover and correct—the evaluate-action cycle is easy to traverse. As a result, the discrepancy from normal rules is often not noticed. Unless you are in the shower and the feedback occurs when you scald yourself.

Older sinks have two separate spouts. Here evaluation is difficult. You can wave your hand rapidly back and forth between the spouts, hoping thereby to get a good mix of temperatures, or you can fill up the basin, adjusting the amount of hot and cold water so that the accumulating mixture reaches the desired temperature. Usually you settle for anything in the neighborhood. Each problem alone isn't a big deal. But the total sum of all the trivial mal-design unnecessarily adds to the trauma of everyday life.

Now consider the modern single-spout, single-control faucet. Technology to the rescue. Move the control one way, it adjusts temperature. Move it another, it adjusts volume. Hurrah! We control exactly the variables of interest, and the mixing spout solves the evaluation problem.

Yes, these new faucets are beautiful. Sleek, elegant, prize winning.

Unusable. They solved one set of problems only to create yet another. The mapping problems now predominate.

· Which control is associated with which action?
· What operations do you apply to the controls?

The problem is that it is very difficult to figure out which part of the sleek faucet is the control. And even if you figure that out, it is hard to figure out in which direction it moves. And once you figure that out, it is hard to figure out which direction controls which action. And when these fancy, multipurpose, sleek designs also control the basin plug and the diversion of water to shower or bath, disaster awaits.

There are two problems here. First, in the name of elegance, the moving parts sometimes meld invisibly into the faucet structure, making it nearly impossible even to find the controls, let alone figure out which way they move or what they control. Second, in the name of novelty, the new designs have forfeited the power of cultural constancy. Users don't want each new design to use a different method for controlling the water. Users need standardization. If all makers of faucets could agree on a standard set of motions to control amount and temperature (how about up and down to control amount—up meaning increase—and left and right to control temperature—left meaning hot?), then we could all learn the standards once, and forever afterward use the knowledge for every new faucet we encountered.

If you can't put the knowledge on the device, then develop a cultural constraint: standardize what has to be kept in the head.

There could be small variations in the standard. Suppose a designer wanted temperature to be controlled by a knob that turned rather than a lever that moved left and right. Fortunately, there is a natural mapping that relates turning to direction: a clockwise turning is the same as moving to the right—getting colder—and a counterclockwise turning is the same as moving to the left—hotter.

Technological development never ceases. There is yet another solution to the control problem, one that has a slight virtue over the others: it is cheaper. One control turns the water on or off and lets you adjust either temperature or volume, but not both (figure 6.8). All you have to do is to locate the control and operate it. Think of all the mental energy and confusion you have been saved. We finally have a control that is truly easy to use. Success.

6.8 Simpler Faucets. In *A* (above) the mapping problem is solved—the faucet is presumed to be easy to use. The problem is that you cannot control the amount of water. On top of that, once the knob has been turned 180°, it is no longer clear which way to turn it in order to make the water hotter or colder. Faucet *B* (below) couldn't be simpler. It certainly is easy to use. Of course, you can only turn it on; you get a fixed temperature and a fixed volume of water.

Wait, we really do want to control both amount and temperature independently. This solution gives us only one control. So we can adjust temperature, but we get out whatever amount of water the designer thought was good for us. Or we can adjust the amount while getting an arbitrary temperature. The story of progress.

Some variants on this faucet control only on or off: you have control over neither volume nor temperature. Sometimes there is no visible means to turn on the water. How does the novice user realize that one is supposed to wave the hands under the faucet? There is no sign of the required operation, no relevant information in the world.

Perhaps you have a big sign: "Do not adjust controls, simply place hand under spout." The sign ruins the elegance, doesn't it? Interesting choice—understandability or elegance. Of course, if such faucets became common, then people would know how to use them and the signs could come down. Someday.

Two Deadly Temptations for the Designer

Let's return to the designer's problems. I've mentioned the time and economic pressures on them. Now let me tell you of two deadly temptations that await the unwary, temptations that lead toward products that are overly complex, products that drive users to distraction—I call these creeping featurism and the worshipping of false images.

CREEPING FEATURISM

I recently attended a demonstration of a new word processing program, held in a large, crowded auditorium. A representative from the company sat in front of the computer, a video projector putting a large image of the computer screen onto the movie screen. The audience was skeptical: they were experts and knew the limitations of such programs. The demonstrator was smooth and convincing, composing an outline, expanding it into text, indenting the paragraphs, numbering them, changing their styles, flipping into a drawing program, drawing a figure, inserting the drawing into the text with the text flowing neatly around the drawing. "You want two columns?" asked the demonstra-

tor. "Here it is. Three columns? Four? Just name it." The screen flowed: three columns of text neatly lined up, illustrations just where they ought to be, page headers, footers, paragraph numbers, boldface italics. Large type, small type, footnotes neatly displayed at the end of columns. You could even highlight just the things that had been changed in the last revision. You could leave notes for yourself or a co-author, notes that would appear on the screen but need not be printed in the final text.

The audience applauded. They called out for their favorite features. Usually the demonstrator would say, "Yes, I am glad you asked, here it is," and whiz, bang, wave of hands, click of keys, swish of the mouse, and the screen would display the latest called-for feature. Sometimes the demonstrator would say, "Not yet, it will be in the second release—in a few months."

Creeping featurism is the tendency to add to the number of features that a device can do, often extending the number beyond all reason. There is no way that a program can remain usable and understandable by the time it has all of those special-purpose features. The word processor I use on my home computer comes with a 340-page reference manual, plus a 150-page introductory manual intended for first-time users (who probably can't understand the reference manual until they have first read the learning manual). EMACS, the text editor I use on my university computer, comes with a 250-page manual, which would be longer if you weren't assumed to be expert at many things.

How can users cope? How can users protect themselves from themselves? After all, as the story of the demonstration illustrates, it is the users who request the features; the designers are simply obliging them. But each new set of features adds immeasurably to the size and complexity of the system. More and more things have to be made invisible, in violation of all the principles of design. No constraints, no affordances; invisible, arbitrary mappings. And all because the users have demanded features.

Creeping featurism is a disease, fatal if not treated promptly. There are some cures, but, as usual, the best approach is to practice preventive medicine. The problem is that the disease comes so naturally, so innocently. Analyze a task, and you see how it can be made easier. Why, adding features seems so virtuous, following the very preachings of this book, simply trying to make life easier for everyone. But with extra features comes extra complexity. Each new feature adds yet another control, or display, or button, or instruction. Complexity probably increases as the square of the features: double the number of features, quadruple the complexity. Provide ten times as many features, multiply the complexity by one hundred.

There are two paths to treating featurism. One is avoidance, or at the least, great restraint. Yes, allow features that seem absolutely necessary, but steel yourself to the rigors of doing without the rest. Once a device has multiple functions, there is no way to avoid having multiple controls and operations, multiple pages of instructions, multiple difficulties and confusions.

The second path is organization. Organize, modularize, use the strategy of divide and conquer. Suppose we take each set of features and hide them away in separate locations, perhaps with dividing barriers between sets. The technical word is *modularization.* Create separate functional modules, each with a limited set of controls, each specialized for some different aspect of the task. The virtue is that each separate module has limited properties, limited features. Yet the sum total of features in the device is unchanged. The proper division of a complex set of controls into modules allows you to conquer complexity (as can be seen in figure 6.9).

THE WORSHIPPING
OF FALSE IMAGES

The designer—and user—may further be tempted to worship complexity. Some of my students did a study of office copying machines. They discovered that the most expensive, most feature-laden machines were best sellers among law firms. Did the firms need the extra features of the machines? No. It turns out that they liked to put them in the front offices where clients were waiting—impressive machines, with flashing lights and pretty displays. The firm gained an aura of being modern and up to date, capable of dealing with the rigors of modern high technology. The fact that the machines were too complex to be mastered by most of the people in the firms was irrelevant: the copiers did not even have to be used—appearance alone did the job. Ah, yes, the worshipping of false images, in this case, by the customers.

A colleague told me of her difficulties with her home audio/television set. It was comprised of separate components, each alone not too complex. But the combination was so overwhelming that she could not

6.9 Overcoming Complexity through Organization. The remote control device *A* (above) for the Bang & Olufsen audio set (there are no controls on the set itself) serves numerous features and options. The controls are made simple through several principles. First, the buttons are grouped into logical, functional modules. Second, the display on the remote gives good feedback about the operation. Third, infrequently used controls are hidden beneath a panel *B* (below), which reduces the visual complexity in normal use but is available when needed.

use it. Her solution was to work through each of the operations she wished to perform and write explicit instructions for herself (figure 6.10). And even with these instructions, operation was not easy. Here the culprit clearly is the interactions among components. Imagine having to write several pages of instructions in order to use your own audio set!

In the case of the overly complex audio/television set, the components were from different manufacturers. Nonetheless, they were intended to be purchased and used individually. I have seen equal complexity in components from a single manufacturer. Some salespeople try to create the impression that this is how it has to be, that anyone with any technical competence can manage to work the devices. No,

6.10 A Personal Instruction Manual. My colleague had to write out three pages of instructions to help herself set up any desired configuration of her audio/video components. Too many interacting parts, too much complexity.

that attitude won't work. The equipment is simply too complex, the interaction between components too overwhelming. There was nothing particularly elaborate about my colleague's equipment. This person was reasonably sophisticated in technical things—she has a Ph.D. in computer science—but was baffled by an everyday audio set.

One of the problems with audio/video equipment is that even if each component has been designed with care, the interaction between components causes problems. The tuner, cassette deck, television, VCR, CD player, and so on, all seem to be designed in relative isolation. Put them all together and there is chaos: an amazing proliferation of controls, lights, meters, and interconnections that can defeat even the most talented.

In this case, the false image is appearance of technical sophistication. This is the sin responsible for the extra complexity of many of our devices, from telephones and televisions to dishwashers and washing machines, from automobile dashboards to audiovisual sets. There is no remedy except through education. You might argue that this is a victimless sin, hurting only those who practice it, but this is not true. Manufacturers and designers produce products for what they perceive as their market demands; therefore, if enough people sin in this way—and the evidence is that they do—then all the rest of us must pay for the pleasures of a few. We pay in fancy, colorful-looking equipment that is nearly impossible to use.

The Foibles of Computer Systems

Now turn to the computer, an area where all the major difficulties of design can be found in profusion. In this realm the user is seldom considered. There is nothing particularly special about the computer; it is a machine, a human artifact, just like the other sorts of things we have looked at, and it poses few problems that we haven't encountered already. But designers of computer systems seem particularly oblivious to the needs of users, particularly susceptible to all the pitfalls of design. The professional design community is seldom called in to help with computer products. Instead, design is left in the hands of engineers and programmers, people who usually have no experience, and no expertise in designing for people.

The abstract nature of the computer poses a particular challenge for the designer. The computer works electronically, invisibly, with no sign of the actions it is performing. And it is instructed through an abstract language, one that specifies the internal flow of control and movement of information, but one that is not particularly suited for the needs of the user. Specialized programmers work in these languages to instruct the system to perform its operations. The task is complex, and programmers must have a variety of skills and talents. The design of a program requires a combination of expertise, including technical skills, knowledge of the task, and knowledge of the needs and abilities of the users.

Programmers should not be responsible for the computer's interaction with the user; that is not their expertise, nor should it be. Many existing programs for user applications are too abstract, requiring actions that make sense for the demands of the computer and to the computer professional but that are not cohesive, sensible, necessary, or understandable to the everyday user. To make the system easier to use and to understand requires a large amount of extra work. I sympathize with the problems of the programmer, but I cannot excuse the general lack of concern for the users.

HOW TO DO THINGS WRONG

Ever sit down to a typical computer? If so, you have encountered "the tyranny of the blank screen." The person sits in front of the computer screen, ready to begin. Begin what? How? The screen is either completely blank or contains noninformative symbols or words that give no hint of what is expected. There is a typewriterlike keyboard, but there is no reason to suppose that one key is preferable to any other. Anyway, isn't it true that one wrong keystroke can blow up the machine? Or destroy valuable data? Or accidentally get connected to some top-secret data bank and then be investigated by the Secret Service? Who knows what danger lurks in the keypress? It is almost as frightening as being taken to a party filled with strange people, being led to the center of the room and let go. Your host disappears, saying: "Make yourself at home. I'm sure there are lots of people you can talk to." Not me. I retreat to the fringes and try to find something to read.

What is the problem? Nothing special, just more of everything. The special powers of the computer can amplify all the usual problems to new levels of difficulty. If you set out to make something difficult to use, you could probably do no better than to copy the designers of modern computer systems. Do you want to do things wrong? Here is what to do:

· Make things invisible. Widen the Gulf of Execution: give no hints to the operations expected. Establish a Gulf of Evaluation: give no feedback, no visible results of the actions just taken. Exploit the tyranny of the blank screen.

· Be arbitrary. Computers make this easy. Use nonobvious command names or actions. Use arbitrary mappings between the intended action and what must actually be done.

· Be inconsistent: change the rules. Let something be done one way in one mode and another way in another mode. This is especially effective where it is necessary to go back and forth between the two modes.

· Make operations unintelligible. Use idiosyncratic language or abbreviations. Use uninformative error messages.

· Be impolite. Treat erroneous actions by the user as breaches of contract. Snarl. Insult. Mumble unintelligible verbiage.

· Make operations dangerous. Allow a single erroneous action to destroy invaluable work. Make it easy to do disastrous things. But put warnings in the manual; then, when people complain, you can ask, "But didn't you read the manual?"

This list is getting depressing, so let us turn to the good side. The computer has vast potential, more than enough to overcome all its problems. Because it has unlimited power, because it can accept almost any kind of control, and because it can create almost any kind of picture or sound, it has the potential to bridge the gulfs, to make life easier. If designed properly, systems can be tailored for (and by) each of us. But we must insist that the computer developers work for us—not for the technology, not for themselves. Programs and systems do exist that have shown us the potential; they take the user into account, and they make it easier for us to do our tasks—pleasurable, even. This is how it ought to be. Computers have the power not only to make everyday tasks easier, but to make them enjoyable as well.

IT'S NOT TOO LATE TO DO THINGS RIGHT

Computer technology is still young, still exploring its potential. The notion lingers that if you have not passed the secret rites of initiation into programming skills, you should not be allowed into the society of computer users. It is like the early days of the automobile: only the brave, the adventurous, and the mechanically sophisticated need apply.

Computer scientists have so far worked on developing powerful programming languages that make it possible to solve the technical problems of computation. Little effort has gone toward devising the languages of interaction. Every student programmer takes courses on the computational aspect of computers. But there are very few courses on the problems faced by the user; such courses are usually not required, and they are not easy to fit into the already crowded schedule of the fledgling computer scientist. As a result, most programmers fluently write computer programs that do wonderful things but that are unusable by the non-professional. Most programmers have never thought of the problems faced by the users. They are surprised to discover that their creations tyrannize the user. There is no longer any excuse for this. It is not that difficult to develop programs that make visible their actions, that allow the user to see what is going on, that make the set of possible actions visible, that display the current state of the system in a meaningful and clear way.[18]

Let me give some examples of excellent work, systems that do take into account the needs of the user. First, there is the spreadsheet, an accounting program that has changed the face of office bookkeeping. The first spreadsheet program, Visicalc, was so impressive that people bought computers just so they could use this one program. That is a strong argument for its usability. Spreadsheets have their problems; but on the whole, they allow people to work with numbers in a convenient way, with immediately visible results.

What did people like about the spreadsheet? The way it looked. You didn't seem to be using a computer—you were working on your problem. You organized the problem just the way you always would, except now it was easy to make changes, easy to see the results. Change one number and everything that depended on that number changed along with it, in just the proper way. What a painless way to do budget projections. All the benefits of the computer, without the technical impediments. In fact, the best computer programs are the ones in which the computer itself "disappears," in which you work directly on the problem without having to be aware of the computer.

Actually, Visicalc had numerous problems. The concept was brilliant, but the execution was flawed. I'm not complaining about the designers, for they were limited by the power of an earlier generation of personal computers. Today's personal computers are much more powerful, and the spreadsheet programs are much easier to use. But the program established the model: it felt as if you were working directly on the problem, not on a computer.

It is not easy to develop effective and usable computer systems. For one thing, it is expensive. Consider the principles described in this book: visibility, constraints, affordances, natural mappings, feedback. Applied to computer systems, these mean that, among other things, the computer must be capable of making things visible (or audible), which requires large and high quality visual displays, a variety of input devices, and plenty of computer memory. These require faster, more powerful computer circuits. And all this adds up to more expensive systems: more cost to manufacture, most cost to the consumer. It may not be immediately clear that the everyday users of computer systems are the ones who require the most powerful systems, with the most memory and the best displays. Professional programmers can get by with less, for they know how to deal with more complex interactions and less effective displays.

The first proper attempt to build an effective system was not a commercial success. This was the Xerox Star, a brainchild of the Xerox Corporation's Palo Alto Research Center. The developers recognized the importance of large, highly detailed display screens with plenty of graphics; they gave the machine the ability to have several different documents on the screen at the same time; and they introduced a pointing device—in this case, the "mouse"—for the user to specify a work area on the screen. The Xerox Star computer was a breakthrough in usable design.[19] But the system was too expensive and too slow. Users liked the power and the ease of operation, but they needed better performance. The benefits of easy to use commands were completely outweighed by the slow response speed. The display could not always keep up with typing, and requests for explanation (the "help" system) sometimes took so long that a user could go for a cup of coffee while waiting for an answer to even the simplest question. Xerox showed the way but suffered a common fate of pioneers: the spirit was willing but the implementation weak.

Fortunately for the consumer, the Apple Computer Company has followed through on Xerox's ideas, using the philosophy developed for the Xerox Star (and hiring away some of Xerox's people) to produce first the Apple Lisa (also too slow and expensive and a failure in the marketplace) and then the Macintosh, a success story.

The approach followed by Xerox has been well documented.[20] *The major goal was consistency of operations, to make things visible so that the available options could always be determined, and to test each idea with users at every step of the development process. These are all the important characteristics of good system design.*

Apple's Macintosh computer makes extensive use of visual displays. These eliminate the blank screen: the user can see what alternative actions are possible. The computer also makes the actions relatively easy to do, and it standardizes procedures so that methods learned for one program apply to most other programs. There is good feedback. Many actions are done by moving a mouse—a small, hand-held pointing device that causes a marker to move to the appropriate location on the screen. The mouse provides good mapping of action to result, and the use of menus—choices spelled out on the screen—makes the operations easy to perform. The Gulf of Execution and the Gulf of Evaluation are both securely bridged.

The Macintosh fails badly at many things, especially those for which it uses obscure combinations of keypresses to accomplish some task. Many of the problems arise from the use of the mouse. The mouse has one button, which simplifies its use but means that some actions must be specified by clicking the button several times or by simultaneously holding down various combinations of keys on the keyboard and clicking the mouse button. These actions violate the basic design philosophy. They are difficult to learn, difficult to remember, and difficult to do.

Ah, the buttons-on-the-mouse problem. How many buttons should the mouse have? Various models use one, two, or three, three being the most common number. Actually, some mice have more buttons; one design even has a chord keyboard on it. Fierce arguments rage over the correct number. The answer, of course, is that there is no correct answer. It is a tradeoff. Increase the number of buttons and you simplify some operations, but you also increase the complexity of the mapping problem. Even two buttons lead to an inconsistent mapping of functions to buttons. Reduce to one button and the mapping problem goes away, but so, too, does some of the functionality.

The Macintosh provides an example of what computer systems could be like. The design emphasizes visibility and feedback. Its "human interface guidelines" and its internal "toolbox" provide standards for the many programmers who design for it. It has emphasized consideration for the user. Yes, there are several serious drawbacks to the Macintosh: it is far from perfect. And it isn't unique. Still, for its relative success in making usability and understanding into primary design objectives, I'd give the Apple Macintosh a prize. If only I thought more of prizes.

COMPUTER AS CHAMELEON

The computer is unusual among machines in that its shape, form, and appearance are not fixed: they can be anything the designer wishes them to be. The computer can be like a chameleon, changing shape and outward appearance to match the situation. The operations of the computer can be soft, being done in appearance rather than substance. And the appearance can be reversed with a change of mind by the user. As users, we can create explorable systems that can be learned through experimentation, without fear of failure or damage. Furthermore, the computer can take on the appearance of the task; it can disappear behind a facade (its system image).

EXPLORABLE SYSTEMS: INVITING EXPERIMENTATION

One important method of making systems easier to learn and to use is to make them explorable, to encourage the user to experiment and learn the possibilities through active exploration. This is how many people learn about home appliances, or about a new stereo system, television set, or video game. Work the buttons while listening and looking to see what happens. The same can be true with computer systems. There are three requirements for a system to be explorable.

1. In each state of the system, the user must readily see and be able to do the allowable actions. The visibility acts as a suggestion, reminding the user of possibilities and inviting the exploration of new ideas and methods.

2. The effect of each action must be both visible and easy to interpret. This property allows users to learn the effects of each action, to

develop a good mental model of the system, and to learn the causal relationships between actions and outcomes. The system image plays a critical role in making such learning possible.

3. Actions should be without cost. When an action has an undesirable result, it must be readily reversible. This is especially important with computer systems. In the case of an irreversible action, the system should make clear what effect the contemplated action will have prior to its execution; there should be enough time to cancel the plan. Or the action should be difficult to do, nonexplorable. Most actions should be cost-free, explorable, discoverable.

TWO MODES OF COMPUTER USAGE

Compare two different ways of getting a task done. One way is to issue commands to someone else who does the actual work: call this "command mode" or "third-person" interaction. The other way is to do the operations yourself: call this "direct manipulation mode" or "first-person" interaction. The difference between these two is like the difference between being driven by a chauffeur and driving an automobile yourself. These two different modes exist with computers.[21]

Most computer systems offer command mode, third-person interactions. To use the computer, you type commands to it, using a special "command language" that you have to learn. Some computer systems offer direct manipulation, first-person interactions, good examples being the driving, flying, and sports games that are commonplace in arcades and on home machines. In these games, the feeling of direct control over the actions is an essential part of the task. This feeling of directness is also possible with everyday computer tasks, such as writing or bookkeeping. Spreadsheet programs and many text editors and word processing programs are good examples of direct manipulation systems used in business.

Both forms of interaction are needed. Third-person interaction is well suited for situations in which the job is laborious or repetitive, as well as those in which you can trust the system (or other person) to do the job for you properly. Sometimes it is nice to have a chauffeur. But if the job is critical, novel, or ill-specified, or if you do not yet know exactly what is to be done, then you need direct, first-person interaction. Now direct control is essential; an intermediary gets in the way.

But direct manipulation, first-person systems have their drawbacks. Although they are often easy to use, fun, and entertaining, it is often difficult to do a really good job with them. They require the user to do the task directly, and the user may not be very good at it. Colored pencils and musical instruments are good examples of direct manipulation systems. But I, for one, am not a good artist or musician. When I want good art or good music, I need professional assistance. So, too, with many direct manipulation computer systems. I find that I often need first-person systems for which there is a backup intermediary, ready to take over when asked, available for advice when needed.

When I use a direct manipulation system—whether for text editing, drawing pictures, or creating and playing games—I do think of myself not as using a computer but as doing the particular task. The computer is, in effect, invisible. The point cannot be overstressed: make the computer system invisible. This principle can be applied with any form of system interaction, direct or indirect.

THE INVISIBLE COMPUTER OF THE FUTURE

Consider what the computer of the future might look like. Suppose I told you it wouldn't even be visible, that you wouldn't even know you were using one? What do I mean? Well, this is already true: you use computers when you use many modern automobiles, microwave ovens, and games. Or CD players and calculators. You don't notice the computer because you think of yourself as doing the task, not as using the computer.[22]

In the same sense, you don't go to the kitchen to use an electric motor; you go to use the refrigerator, or the blender, or the dishwasher. The motors are part of the task, even in the case of the blender, mixer, or food processor, which are essentially pure motors and the specialized attachments they drive.

The computer of the future is perhaps best illustrated by my imaginary perfect calendar. Suppose I am home one evening, deciding whether to accept an invitation to attend a conference next May. I pick up my appointment calendar and turn to the appropriate page. I tentatively decide that I can attend and pencil in the topic. The calendar flashes at me and displays a note reminding me that the university will still be in session during that period and that the trip overlaps my wife's birthday. I decide that the conference is important, so I make a note to check whether I can get someone to take over my classes and to see whether I can leave the conference early for the birthday. I close the calendar and get back to other things. The next day, when I arrive at my office I find two notes on my message screen: one to find a substitute for my classes next May, the other to check with the conference organizers to see if I can leave early.

This imaginary calendar looks like a calendar. It's about the size of a standard pad of paper, it opens up to display dates. But it really is a computer, so it can do things that today's appointment calendar cannot. It can, for example, present its information in different formats: it can display the pages compressed so that a whole year fits on one page; it can expand the display so that I see a single day in thirty-minute intervals. Because I frequently use my calendar in conjunction with my travels, the calendar is also an address book, notepad, and expense account record. Most important, it can also connect itself to my other systems (via a wireless infrared or electromagnetic channel). Thus, whatever I enter into the calendar gets transmitted to my office and home systems so that they are always in synchrony. If I make an appointment or change someone's address or telephone number on one system, the others get told. When I finish a trip, the expense record can be transferred to the expense account form. The computer is invisible, hidden beneath the surface; only the task is visible. Although I may actually be using a computer, I feel as if I am using my appointment calendar.

CHAPTER SEVEN

USER-CENTERED DESIGN

OFF THE LEASH By W.B. Park

"Darn these hooves! I hit the wrong switch again! Who designs these instrument panels, raccoons?"

The point of POET is to advocate a user-centered design, a philosophy based on the needs and interests of the user, with an emphasis on making products usable and understandable. In this chapter I summarize the main principles, discuss some implications, and offer suggestions for the design of everyday things.

Design should:

· Make it easy to determine what actions are possible at any moment (make use of constraints).

· Make things visible, including the conceptual model of the system, the alternative actions, and the results of actions.

· Make it easy to evaluate the current state of the system.

· Follow natural mappings between intentions and the required actions; between actions and the resulting effect; and between the information that is visible and the interpretation of the system state.

In other words, make sure that (1) the user can figure out what to do, and (2) the user can tell what is going on.

Design should make use of the natural properties of people and of the world: it should exploit natural relationships and natural constraints. As much as possible, it should operate without instructions or labels. Any necessary instruction or training should be needed only once; with each explanation the person should be able to say, "Of course," or "Yes, I see." A simple explanation will suffice if there is reason to the design, if everything has its place and its function, and if the outcomes of actions are visible. If the explanation leads the person to think or say, "How am I going to remember that?" the design has failed.

Seven Principles for Transforming Difficult Tasks into Simple Ones

How does the designer go about the task? As I've argued in POET, the principles of design are straightforward.

1. Use both knowledge in the world and knowledge in the head.
2. Simplify the structure of tasks.
3. Make things visible: bridge the gulfs of Execution and Evaluation.
4. Get the mappings right.

5. Exploit the power of constraints, both natural and artificial.

6. Design for error.

7. When all else fails, standardize.

USE BOTH KNOWLEDGE
IN THE WORLD AND KNOWLEDGE IN THE HEAD

I have argued that people learn better and feel more comfortable when the knowledge required for a task is available externally—either explicit in the world or readily derived through constraints. But knowledge in the world is useful only if there is a natural, easily interpreted relationship between that knowledge and the information it is intended to convey about possible actions and outcomes.

Note, however, that when a user is able to internalize the required knowledge—that is, to get it into the head—performance can be faster and more efficient. Therefore, the design should not impede action, especially for those well-practiced, experienced users who have internalized the knowledge. It should be easy to go back and forth, to combine the knowledge in the head with that in the world. Let whichever is more readily available at the moment be used without interfering with the other, and allow for mutual support.

THREE CONCEPTUAL MODELS

The operation of any device—whether it be a can opener, a power generating plant, or a computer system—is learned more readily, and the problems are tracked down more accurately and easily, if the user has a good conceptual model. This requires that the principles of operation be observable, that all actions be consistent with the conceptual model, and that the visible parts of the device reflect the current state of the device in a way consistent with that model. The designer must develop a conceptual model that is appropriate for the user, that captures the important parts of the operation of the device, and that is understandable by the user.

Three different aspects of mental models must be distinguished: the *design model,* the *user's model,* and the *system image* (figure 7.1). The design model is the conceptualization that the designer has in mind. The user's model is what the user develops to explain the operation of the system. Ideally, the user's model and the design model are equivalent. How-

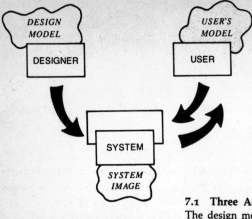

7.1 Three Aspects of Mental Models. The design model, the user's model, and the system image. (From Norman, 1986.)

ever, the user and designer communicate only through the system itself: its physical appearance, its operation, the way it responds, and the manuals and instructions that accompany it. Thus the *system image* is critical: the designer must ensure that everything about the product is consistent with and exemplifies the operation of the proper conceptual model.

All three aspects are important. The user's model is essential, of course, for that determines what is understood. In turn, it is up to the designer to start with a design model that is functional, learnable, and usable. The designer must ensure that the system reveals the appropriate system image. Only then can the user acquire the proper user's model and find support for the translation of intentions into actions and system state into interpretations. Remember, the user acquires all knowledge of the system from that system image.

THE ROLE OF MANUALS

The system image includes instruction manuals and documentation.

Manuals tend to be less helpful than they should be. They are often written hastily, after the product is designed, under severe time pressures and with insufficient resources, and by people who are overworked and underappreciated. In the best of worlds, the manuals would be written first, then the design would follow the manual. While the product was being designed, potential users could simultaneously test the manuals and mock-ups of the system, giving important design feedback about both.

Alas, even the best manuals cannot be counted on; many users do not read them. Obviously it is wrong to expect to operate complex devices without instruction of some sort, but the designers of complex devices have to deal with human nature as it is.

SIMPLIFY THE STRUCTURE OF TASKS

Tasks should be simple in structure, minimizing the amount of planning or problem solving they require. Unnecessarily complex tasks can be restructured, usually by using technological innovations.

Here is where the designer must pay attention to the psychology of the person, to the limits on how much a person can hold in memory at one time, to the limits on how many active thoughts can be pursued at once. These are the limitations of short-term and long-term memory and of attention. The limitations of short-term memory (STM) are such that a person should not be required to remember more than about five unrelated items at one time. If necessary, the system should provide technological assistance for any temporary memory requirements. The limitations of long-term memory (LTM) mean that information is better and more easily acquired if it makes sense, if it can be integrated into some conceptual framework. Moreover, retrieval from LTM is apt to be slow and to contain errors. Here is where information in the world is important, to remind us of what can be done and how to do it. Limitations on attention are also severe; the system should help by minimizing interruption, by providing aids to allow for recovery of the exact status of the operations that were interrupted.

A major role of new technology should be to make tasks simpler. A task can be restructured through technology, or technology might provide aids to reduce the mental load. Technological aids can show the alternative courses of action; help evaluate implications; and portray outcomes in a more complete, more easily interpretable manner. These aids can make the mappings more visible or, better, make the mappings more natural. Four major technological approaches can be followed:

· Keep the task much the same, but provide mental aids.
· Use technology to make visible what would otherwise be invisible, thus improving feedback and the ability to keep control.

- Automate, but keep the task much the same.
- Change the nature of the task.

Let us look separately at each of these possibilities.

KEEP THE TASK MUCH THE SAME, BUT PROVIDE MENTAL AIDS

Don't underestimate the power or importance of simple mental aids. Consider, for example, the value of simple, everyday notes to ourselves. Without them, we might fail. Or simple notepads for telephone numbers, names, addresses—for the facts that are essential to everyday functioning, but that we cannot trust our own memory structures to provide. Some mental aids are also technological advances; these include watches, timers, calculators, pocket dictating machines, computer notepads, and computer alarms. Some aids are still to come: the pocket computer with a powerful display, which will keep our notes, remind us of our appointments, and smooth our passage through the schedules and interactions of life.

USE TECHNOLOGY TO MAKE VISIBLE WHAT WOULD OTHERWISE BE INVISIBLE, THUS IMPROVING FEEDBACK AND THE ABILITY TO KEEP CONTROL

The instruments in the automobile or aircraft do not change the task, but they do make visible the state of the engine and the other parts of the vehicle, even though you cannot physically get access to them. Similarly, the microscope and telescope, television set, camera, microphone, and loudspeaker all provide ways of getting information about a remote object, making visible (or audible) what is happening, making possible tasks and pursuits that would otherwise not be possible. With modern computers and their powerful graphic displays, we now have the power to show what is really happening, to provide a good, complete image that matches the person's mental model of the task— thereby simplifying both understanding and performance. Today, computer graphics are used more for show than for legitimate purposes. Their powers are wasted. But there exists great potential to make visible what should be visible (and to keep hidden what is irrelevant).

These first two approaches to mental aids keep the main tasks unchanged. They act as reminders. They reduce memory load by provid-

ing external memory devices (providing knowledge in the world rather than requiring it to be in the head). They supplement our perceptual abilities. Sometimes they enhance human skills sufficiently so that a job that was not possible before, or was possible only for the most highly skilled performers, becomes available to many.

Don't these so-called advances also cause us to lose valuable mental skills? Each technological advance that provides a mental aid also brings along critics who decry the loss of the human skill that has been made less valuable. Fine, I say: if the skill is easily automated, it wasn't essential.

I prefer to remember things by writing them on a pad of paper rather than spending hours of study on the art of memory. I prefer using a pocket calculator to spending hours of pencil pushing and grinding, usually only to make an arithmetic mistake and not discover it until after the harm has been done. I prefer prerecorded music to no music, even if I risk becoming complacent about the power and beauty of the rare performance. And I prefer writing on a text editor or word processor so that I can concentrate on the ideas and the style, not on making marks on the paper. Then I can go back later and correct ideas, redo the grammar. And with the aid of my all-important spelling correction program, I can be confident of my presentation.

Do I fear that I will lose my ability to spell as a result of overreliance on this technological crutch? What ability? Actually, my spelling is improving through the use of this spelling corrector that continually points out my errors and suggests the correction, but won't make a change unless I approve. It is certainly a lot more patient than my teachers used to be. And it is always there when I need it, day or night. So I get continual feedback about my errors, plus useful advice. My typing does seem to be deteriorating because I can now type even more sloppily, confident that my mistakes will be detected and corrected.

In general, I welcome any technological advance that reduces my need for mental work but still gives me the control and enjoyment of the task. That way I can exert my mental efforts on the core of the task, the thing to be remembered, the purpose of the arithmetic or the music. I want to use my mental powers for the important things, not fritter them away on the mechanics.

AUTOMATE, BUT KEEP THE TASK MUCH THE SAME

There are dangers in simplification: unless we are careful, the automation can harm as well as help. Consider one impact of automation.

As before, the task will stay essentially the same, but parts of it will disappear. In some cases the change is confirmed as a universal blessing. I don't know of anyone who misses the automatic spark advance in automobiles or cranking the engine to get it started. Just a few people miss having manual control over the automobile choke. On the whole, this type of automation has resulted in useful advances, replacing tedious or unnecessary tasks and reducing what must be monitored. The automatic controls and instruments of ships and aircraft have been great improvements. Some automation is more problematic. Automatic shift on a car: Do we lose some control, or does it help lighten the mental burden of driving? After all, we drive to get to a destination, so the need to monitor engine speed and gearshift position would seem quite irrelevant. But some people take pleasure in performing the task itself; for them, part of driving is using the engine well, believing that they can operate more efficiently than can the automatic device.

What about the automatic pilot of an aircraft, or the automatic navigation systems that have eliminated the sextant and lengthy computations? Or what about frozen, precooked meals? Do the changes destroy the essence of the task? Here there's more debate. In the best of worlds we would be able to choose automation or full control.

CHANGE THE NATURE OF THE TASK

When a task seems inherently complex because of the manual skill required, certain technological aids can dramatically change which type of skill is required by restructuring the task. In general, technology can help transform deep, wide structures into narrower, shallower ones.

Tying a shoelace is one of the standard, everyday tasks that is actually quite difficult to learn. Adults may have forgotten how long it took them to learn (but they will be reminded if their fingers stiffen with injury, age, or disease). The introduction of new fastening materials—for example, Velcro hook-and-loop fasteners—has eliminated the need for a complex sequence of skilled motor actions by changing the task to one that is considerably simpler, one that requires less skill. The task has become possible for both young children and infirm adults. The example of shoelaces may seem trivial, but it isn't; like many everyday activities, it is difficult for a large segment of the population and its difficulties can be overcome through the restructuring provided by a simple technology.

The hook-and-loop fasteners provide another example of design tradeoffs (figure 7.2). Hook-and-loop fasteners dramatically simplify shoe fastening for the young and infirm. But they add to the problems of parents and teachers, for children delight in fastening and unfastening their shoes; so a fastener that is more difficult to work has certain virtues. And for sports for which precise support of the foot is required, the best solution still appears to be the shoelace, which can be adjusted so as to offer different tensions at different parts of the foot. The current generation of hook-and-loop fasteners does not have the flexibility of laces.

Digital watches represent another example of how a new technology can supplant an old one; it has delayed or eliminated the need for children to learn the mapping of the analog hands of the traditional clockface onto the hours, minutes, and seconds of the day. Digital timepieces are controversial: in changing the representation of time, the

7.2 Hook-and-Loop Fastener. With the use of hook-and-loop fasteners, the act of tying shoes is much simplified: a good example of the power of technology to change the nature of the task. But there is a cost. Children find the task so easy they gleefully untie their shoes. And these fasteners are not yet as flexible as shoelaces for the support needed for sports.

power of the analog form has been lost, and it has become more difficult to make quick judgments about time. The digital display makes it easier to determine the exact time, but harder to make estimates or to see approximately how much time has passed since an earlier reading. This might serve as a useful reminder that task simplification, by itself, is not necessarily a virtue.

I do not want to argue for digital timepieces, but let me remind you how difficult and arbitrary the analog timepiece really is. After all, it, too, was an arbitrary imposition of a notational scheme, imposed upon the world by the early technologists. Today, because we can no longer remember the origins, we think of the analog system as necessary, virtuous, and proper. It presents a horrid, classic example of the mapping problem. Yes, the notion that time should be represented by the distance a hand moves around a circle is a good one. The problem is that we use two or three different hands moving around the same circle, each one meaning something different and operating on a different scale. Which hand is which? (Do you remember how hard it is to teach a child the difference between the little hand and the big hand, and not to confuse the second hand—which is sometimes big, sometimes little—with the minute hand or the hour hand?)

Do I exaggerate? Read what Kevin Lynch says about this in his delightful book on city planning, What time is this place?

"Telling time is a simple technical problem, but unfortunately the clock is a rather obscure perceptual device. Its first widespread use in the thirteenth century was to ring the hours for clerical devotions. The clockface which translated time into spatial alteration, came later. That form was dictated by its works, not by any principle of perception. Two (sometimes three) superimposed cycles give duplicate readings, according to angular displacement around a finely marked rim. Neither minutes nor hours nor half days correspond to the natural cycles of our bodies or the sun. And so teaching a child to read a clock is not a childish undertaking. When asked why a clock had two hands, a four-year-old replied, 'God thought it would be a good idea.' "[1]

Aircraft designers started using meters that looked like clockfaces to represent altitude. As airplanes were able to fly higher and higher, the meters needed more hands. Guess what? Pilots made errors—serious errors. Multihanded analog altimeters have been largely abandoned in favor of digital ones because of the prevalence of reading errors. Even so, many contemporary altimeters maintain a mixed mode: information about rate and direction of altitude change is determined from a single analog hand, while precise judgments of height come from the digital display.

DON'T TAKE AWAY CONTROL

Automation has its virtues, but automation is dangerous when it takes too much control from the user. "Overautomation"—too great a degree of automation—has become a technical term in the study of automated aircraft and factories.[2] One problem is that overreliance on automated equipment can eliminate a person's ability to function without it, a prescription for disaster if, for example, one of the highly automated mechanisms of an aircraft suddenly fails. A second problem is that a system may not always do things exactly the way we would like, but we are forced to accept what happens because it is too difficult (or impossible) to change the operation. A third problem is that the person becomes a servant of the system, no longer able to control or influence what is happening. This is the essence of the assembly line: it depersonalizes the job, it takes away control, it provides, at best, a passive or third-person experience.

All tasks have several layers of control. The lowest level is the details of the operation, the nimble finger work of sewing or playing the piano, the nimble mental work of arithmetic. Higher levels of control affect the overall task, the direction in which the work is going. Here we determine, supervise, and control the overall structure and goals. Automation can work at any level. Sometimes we really want to maintain control at the lower level. For some of us, it is the nimble execution of the finger or mind that matters. Some of us want to play music with skill. Or we like the feel of tools against wood. Or we enjoy wielding a paintbrush. In cases like these, we would not want automation to interfere. At other times we want to concentrate on higher level things. Perhaps our goal is to listen to music, and we find the radio more effective for us than the piano; perhaps our artistic skill can't get us as far as can a computer program.

MAKE THINGS VISIBLE: BRIDGE
THE GULFS OF EXECUTION AND EVALUATION

This has been a focal theme of POET. Make things visible on the execution side of an action so that people know what is possible and how actions should be done; make things visible on the evaluation side so that people can tell the effects of their actions.

There is more. The system should provide actions that match intentions. It should provide indications of system state that are readily perceivable and interpretable and that match intentions and expectations. And, of course, the system state should be visible (or audible) and readily interpretable. Make the outcomes of an action obvious.

Sometimes the wrong things are visible. A friend of mine, a professor of computer science at my university, proudly showed me his new CD player and its associated remote control. Sleek, functional. The remote control unit had a little metal loop protruding from one end. When I asked what it was for, my friend told a story. When he first got the set, he assumed that the loop was an antenna for the remote unit, so he always aimed it at the CD player. It didn't seem to work well; he had to stand within a few feet of the CD while using the remote. He mumbled to himself that he had bought a poorly designed unit. Weeks later he discovered that the metal hook was just a hook for hanging up the device. He had been aiming the remote at his own body. When he turned the remote around, it worked from far across the room.

Here is a case of natural mappings that fails. The hook provided a natural mapping for function: it indicated which side of the remote control device should be pointed at the CD set. Unfortunately, it provided erroneous information. In making things visible, it is important to make the correct things visible. Otherwise people form explanations for the things they can see, explanations that are likely to be false. And then they find some reason for poor performance—in this example, that the remote was not very powerful. People are very good at forming explanations, at creating mental models. It is the designer's task to make sure that they form the correct interpretations, the correct mental models: the system image plays the key role.

Remote transmitter units that need to be pointed at a receiver should have some visible evidence of the transmitting mechanism. Modern units carefully hide any indication of the signaling method, violating the rules of visibility. My friend searched hard for some clue of the direction to point the device in, and he found one: the hook. And, no, the instruction manual did not say which end of the unit should be pointed at the CD player.

GET THE MAPPINGS RIGHT

Exploit natural mappings. Make sure that the user can determine the relationships:

· Between intentions and possible actions
· Between actions and their effects on the system
· Between actual system state and what is perceivable by sight, sound, or feel
· Between the perceived system state and the needs, intentions, and expectations of the user

Natural mappings are the basis of what has been called "response compatibility" within the fields of human factors and ergonomics. The major requirement of response compatibility is that the spatial relationship between the positioning of controls and the system or objects upon which they operate should be as direct as possible, with the controls either on the objects themselves or arranged to have an analogical relationship to them. In similar fashion, the movement of the controls should be similar or analogous to the expected operation of the system. Difficulties arise wherever the positioning and movements of the controls deviate from strict proximity, mimicry, or analogy to the things being controlled.

The same arguments apply to the relationship of system output to expectations. A critical part of an action is the evaluation of its effects. This requires timely feedback of the results. The feedback must provide information that matches the user's intentions and must be in a form that is easy to understand. Many systems omit the relevant visible outcomes of actions; even when information about the system state is provided, it may not be easy to interpret. The easiest way to make things understandable is to use graphics or pictures. Modern systems (especially computer systems) are quite capable of this, but the need seems not to have been recognized by designers.

EXPLOIT THE POWER OF CONSTRAINTS,
BOTH NATURAL AND ARTIFICIAL

Use constraints so that the user feels as if there is only one possible thing to do—the right thing, of course. In chapter 4 I used the example of the Lego toy motorcycle, which could be correctly put together by people who had never before seen it. Actually, the toy is not simple. It was carefully designed. It exploits a variety of constraints. It is a good example of the power of natural mappings and constraints, constraints that reduce the number of alternative actions at each step to at most a few.

DESIGN FOR ERROR

Assume that any error that can be made will be made. Plan for it. Think of each action by the user as an attempt to step in the right direction; an error is simply an action that is incompletely or improperly specified. Think of the action as part of a natural, constructive dialog between user and system. Try to support, not fight, the user's responses. Allow the user to recover from errors, to know what was done and what happened, and to reverse any unwanted outcome. Make it easy to reverse operations; make it hard to do irreversible actions. Design explorable systems. Exploit forcing functions.

WHEN ALL ELSE FAILS, STANDARDIZE

When something can't be designed without arbitrary mappings and difficulties, there is one last route: standardize. Standardize the actions, outcomes, layout, displays. Make related actions work in the same way. Standardize the system, the problem; create an international standard. The nice thing about standardization is that no matter how arbitrary the standardized mechanism, it has to be learned only once. People can learn it and use it effectively. This is true of typewriter keyboards, traffic signs and signals, units of measurement, and calendars. When followed consistently, standardization works well.

There are difficulties. It may be hard to obtain an agreement. And timing is crucial: it is important to standardize as soon as possible—to save everyone trouble—but late enough to take into account advanced technologies and procedures. The shortcomings of early standardization are often more than made up for by the increase in ease of use.[3]

Users have to be trained to the standards. The very conditions that require standardization require training, sometimes extensive training (that is OK: it takes months to learn the alphabet, or to type, or to drive

7.3 The Backward Clock.
(Drawing by Eileen Conway.)

a car). Remember, standardization is essential only when all the necessary information cannot be placed in the world or when natural mappings cannot be exploited. The role of training and practice is to make the mappings and required actions more available to the user, overcoming any shortcomings in the design, minimizing the need for planning and problem solving.

Take the everyday clock. It's standardized. Consider how much trouble you would have telling time with a backward clock, where the hands revolved counterclockwise. Such clocks do exist (figure 7.3). They make effective conversation pieces. Not so good for telling the time, though. Why not? There is nothing illogical about a clock that goes counterclockwise. It's just as logical as one that goes clockwise. The reason we dislike it is that we have standardized on a different scheme, on the very definition of the term "clockwise." Without such standardization, clock reading would be more difficult: you'd always have to figure out the mapping.

STANDARDIZATION AND TECHNOLOGY

If we examine the history of advances in all technological fields, we see that some improvements naturally come through technology, others come through standardization. The early history of the automobile is a good example. The first cars were very difficult to operate. They required strength and skill beyond the abilities of many. Some problems were solved through automation: the choke, the spark advance, and the starter engine.

Arbitrary aspects of cars and driving had to be standardized:

- Which side of the road people drove on
- Which side of the car the driver sat on
- Where the essential components were: steering wheel, brake, clutch pedal, and accelerator (in some early cars it was on a hand lever)

Standardization is simply another aspect of cultural constraints. With standardization, once you have learned to drive one car, you feel justifiably confident that you can drive any car, any place in the world.

Today's computers are still poorly designed, at least from the user's point of view. But one problem is simply that the technology is still very primitive—like the 1906 auto—and there is no standardization. Standardization is the solution of last resort, an admission that we cannot solve the problems in any other way. So we must at least all agree to a common solution. When we have standardization of our keyboard layouts, our input and output formats, our operating systems, our text editors and word processors, and the basic means of operating any program, then suddenly we will have a major breakthrough in usability.[4]

THE TIMING OF STANDARDIZATION

Standardize and you simplify lives: everyone learns the system only once. But don't standardize too soon; you may be locked into a primitive technology, or you may have introduced rules that turn out to be grossly inefficient, even error-inducing. Standardize too late and there may already be so many ways of doing the task that no international standard can be agreed on; if there is agreement on an old-fashioned technology, it may be too expensive to change. The metric system is a good example: it is a far simpler and more usable scheme for representing distance, weight, volume, and temperature than the older, British system (feet, pounds, seconds, degrees on the Fahrenheit scale). But industrial nations with a heavy commitment to the old measurement standards claim they cannot afford the massive costs and confusion of conversion. So we are stuck with two standards, at least for a few more decades.

Would you consider changing how we specify time? The current system is arbitrary. The day is divided into twenty-four rather arbitrary units—hours. But we tell time in units of twelve, not twenty-four, so there have to be two cycles of twelve hours each, plus the special convention of A.M. and P.M. so we know which cycle we are talking about. Then we divide each hour into sixty minutes and each minute into sixty seconds. What if we switched to metric divisions: seconds divided into tenths, milliseconds, and microseconds? We would have days, millidays, and microdays. There would have to be a new hour, minute, and second: call them the newhour, the newminute, and the newsecond. It would be easy: ten newhours to the day, one hundred newminutes to the newhour, one hundred newseconds to the newminute.

Each newhour would last exactly 2.4 times an old hour: 144 old minutes. So the old one-hour period of the schoolroom or television program would be replaced with a half-newhour period—only 20 percent longer than the old. Each newminute would be quite similar to the current minute: 0.7 of an old minute, to be exact (each newminute would be about 42 old seconds). And each newsecond would be slightly shorter than an old second. The differences in durations could be gotten used to; they aren't that large. And computations would be so much easier. I can hear the everyday conversations now:

"I'll meet you at noon—5 newhours. Don't be late, it's only a half hour from now, 50 newminutes, OK?"

"What time is it? 7.85—15 minutes to the evening news."

What do I think of it? I wouldn't go near it.

Deliberately Making Things Difficult

"How can good design (design that is usable and understandable) be balanced with the need for 'secrecy' or privacy, or protection? That is, some applications of design involve areas which are sensitive and necessitate strict control over who uses and understands them. Perhaps we don't want any user-in-the-street to understand enough of a system to compromise its security. Couldn't it be argued that some things shouldn't be designed well? Can't things be left cryptic, so that only those who have clearance, extended education, or whatever, can make use of the system? Sure, we have passwords, keys, and other types of

7.4   A School Door, Deliberately Made Difficult to Use. The school is for handicapped children; the school officials did not want children to be able to go in and out of the school without adult supervision. The principles of usability espoused in POET can be followed in reverse to make difficult those tasks that ought to be difficult.

security checks, but this can become wearisome for the privileged user. It appears that if good design is not ignored in some contexts, the purpose for the existence of the system will be nullified."[5]

Consider figure 7.4, a door on a school in Stapleford, England: the latches are up at the very top of the door, where they are both hard to find and hard to reach. This is *good* design, deliberately and carefully done. The door is to a school for handicapped children, and the school didn't want the children to be able to get out to the street without an adult. Violating the rules of ease of use is just what is needed.

Most things are intended to be easy to use, but aren't. But some things are deliberately difficult to use—and ought to be. The number of things that should be difficult to use is surprisingly large:

- Any door designed to keep people in or out.
- Security systems, designed so that only authorized people will be able to use them.
- Dangerous equipment, which should be restricted.
- Dangerous operations, such as life-threatening actions. These can be designed so that one person alone can't complete the action. I worked for a summer setting off dynamite underwater (to study underwater sound transmission); the circuits were set up to require two people to work them. Two buttons had to be depressed at the same time in order to set off the charge: one button outside, one inside the electronic recording trailer. Similar precautions are taken at military installations.
- Secret doors, cabinets, safes: you don't want the average person even to know that they are there, let alone to be able to work them. These may require two different keys or combinations, meant to be carried or known by two people.
- Cases deliberately intended to disrupt the normal routine action (in chapter 5 I call these forcing functions). Examples include the acknowledgment required before permanently deleting a file from a computer storage system, safeties on pistols and guns, pins in fire extinguishers.
- Controls deliberately made big and spread far apart so that children will have difficulty operating them.
- Cabinets and bottles of medications and dangerous substances deliberately made difficult to open to keep them secure from children.
- Games, a category in which designers deliberately flout the laws of understandability and usability. Games are meant to be difficult. And in some games, such as the adventure or Dungeons and Dragons games popular on home (and office) computers, the whole point of the game is to figure out what is to be done, and how.
- *Not* the door on a train (figure 7.5).

Many things need to be designed for a certain lack of understandability or usability. The rules of design are equally important to know here, however, for two reasons. First, even deliberately difficult designs shouldn't be entirely difficult. Usually there is one difficult part, designed to keep unauthorized people from using the device; the rest of it should follow the normal good principles of design. Second, even if your job is to make something difficult to do, you need to know how to go about doing it. In this case, the rules are useful, for they state in reverse just how to go about the task. You systematically violate the rules.

- Hide critical components: make things invisible.
- Use unnatural mappings for the execution side of the action cycle, so that the relationship of the controls to the things being controlled is inappropriate or haphazard.
- Make the actions physically difficult to do.
- Require precise timing and physical manipulation.
- Do not give any feedback.
- Use unnatural mappings for the evaluation side of the action cycle, so that system state is difficult to interpret.

Safety systems pose a special problem in design. Oftentimes the design feature added to ensure safety eliminates one danger only to create a secondary one. When workers dig a hole in a street, they must put up barriers to prevent people from walking into the hole. The barriers solve one problem, but they themselves pose another danger, often circumvented by adding signs and flashing lights to warn of the barriers. Emergency doors, lights, and alarms must often be accompanied by warning signs or barriers that control when and how they can be used.

Consider the school door of figure 7.4. Under normal use, this design adds to the safety of the children. But what if there was a fire? Even nonhandicapped adults might have trouble with the door as they rushed to get out. What about short or handicapped teachers—how could they open the door? The solution to one problem—unauthorized exit of schoolchildren—can easily create a major new problem in times of fire. How could this problem be solved? Probably with a push bar located within everyone's reach on the door, but connected to an alarm so that in normal circumstances it would not be used.

DESIGNING A DUNGEONS AND DRAGONS GAME

One of my students worked for a computer game company helping develop a new Dungeons and Dragons game. He and his fellow students used his experience to do a class project on the difficulty of

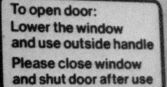

7.5 British Train Door, from the Inside. Clearly difficult to use, but why? I haven't the foggiest idea. To prevent accidental opening? To make it so that young children cannot open the door? None of the hypotheses I have tried stand up under close examination. I leave this to the reader.

games. In particular, they combined some research on what makes games interesting with the analysis of the seven stages of action (chapter 2) to determine what factors cause difficulties in dungeon games.[6] As you might imagine, making things difficult is a tricky business. If a game isn't difficult enough, experienced players lose interest. On the other hand, if it is too difficult, the initial enjoyment gives way to frustration. In fact, several psychological factors hang in a delicate balance: challenge, enjoyment, frustration, and curiosity. As the students reported, "Once the curiosity is lost and the frustration level becomes too high, it is hard to get a person's interest to return to the game." All this has to be considered, yet the game must maintain its appeal for players of many different levels, from first-time players to experienced players. One approach is to sprinkle the game with many different challenges of variable difficulty. Another is to have many little things continually happening, maintaining the curiosity motive.

The same rules that apply to make tasks understandable and usable also apply to make them more difficult and challenging; they can be applied perversely to show where the difficulty should be added. But difficulty and challenge should not be confused with frustration and error. The rules must be applied intelligently, for ease of use or difficulty of use.

EASY LOOKING IS NOT NECESSARILY EASY TO USE

Early in POET I examined the modern office telephone, simple looking but hard to use. I contrasted this with an automobile dashboard that has more than a hundred controls, complicated looking but easy to use. Apparent complexity and actual complexity are not at all the same.

Consider a surfboard, ice skates, parallel bars, or a bugle. All are simple looking. Yet years of study and practice are required to be good at using any of these objects.

The problem is that each of the apparently simple devices is capable of a wide repertoire of actions, but because there are few controls (and no moving parts), the rich complexity of action can be accomplished only through a rich complexity of execution by the user. Remember the office telephone system? When there are more actions than controls, each control must take part in a variety of different actions. If there are exactly the same number of controls as actions, then, in principle, the controls can be simple and the execution can be simple: find the correct control and activate it.

Actually, increasing the number of controls can both enhance and detract from ease of use. The more controls, the more complex things look and the more the user must learn about; it becomes harder to find the appropriate control at the appropriate time. On the other hand, as the number of controls increases up to the number of functions, there can be a better match between controls and functions, making things easier to use. So the number of controls and complexity of use is really a tradeoff between two opposing factors.

How many controls does a device need? The fewer the controls, the easier it looks to use and the easier it is to find the relevant controls. As the number of controls increases, specific controls can be tailored for specific functions. The device may look more and more complex, but it will be easier to use. We studied this relationship in our laboratory.[7] Complexity of appearance seems to be determined by the number of controls, whereas difficulty of use is jointly determined by the difficulty of finding the relevant controls (which increases with the number of controls) and difficulty of executing the functions (which may decrease with the number of controls).

We found that to make something easy to use, match the number of controls to the number of functions and organize the panels according to function. To make something look like it is easy, minimize the number of controls. How can these conflicting requirements be met simultaneously? Hide the controls not being used at the moment. By using a panel on which only the relevant controls are visible, you minimize the appearance of complexity. By having a separate control for each function, you minimize complexity of use. It is possible to eat your cake and have it, too.

Design and Society

Tools affect more than the ease with which we do things; they can dramatically affect our view of ourselves, society, and the world. It is hardly necessary to point out the dramatic changes in society that have resulted from the invention of today's everyday things: paper and pencil, the printed book, the typewriter, the automobile, the telephone, radio, and television. Even apparently simple innovations can bring about dramatic changes, most of which cannot be predicted. The telephone, for example, was widely misunderstood ("Why would we want one? Who would we want to talk to?"), as was the computer (fewer than ten were thought to be sufficient to satisfy all of America's computing needs).[8] Predictions of the future of the city were widely off the mark. And nuclear power was once thought destined to lead to atomic automobiles and airplanes. Some people expected private air transportation to become as widespread as the automobile—a helicopter in every garage.

HOW WRITING METHOD AFFECTS STYLE

The history of technology shows that we are not very good at prediction, but that does not diminish the need for sensitivity to possible changes. New concepts will transform society, for better or worse. Let us examine one simple situation: the effect of the gradual automation of the tools of writing on styles of writing.

FROM QUILL AND INK TO KEYBOARD AND MICROPHONE

In earlier times, when goose quill and ink were used on parchment, it was tedious and difficult to correct what had been written. Writers had to be careful. Sentences had to be thought through before being set to paper. One result was sentences that were long and embellished—the graceful rhetorical style we associate with our older literature. With the advent of easier to use writing tools, corrections became easier to make; so writing was done more rapidly, but also with less thought and care—more like everyday speech. Some critics decried the lack of literary niceties. Others argued that this was how people really communicated, and besides, it was easier to understand.

With changes in writing tools, the speed of writing increases. In handwriting, thought runs ahead, posing special demands on memory and encouraging slower, more thoughtful writing. With the typewriter keyboard, the skilled typist can almost keep up with thought. With the advent of dictation, the output and the thought seem reasonably well matched.

Even greater changes have come about with the popularity of dictation. Here the tool can have a dramatic effect, for there is no external record of what has been spoken; the author has to keep everything in memory. As a result, dictated letters often have a long, rambling style.

They are more colloquial and less structured—the former because they are based on speech, the latter because the writer can't easily keep track of what has been said. Style may change further when we get voice typewriters, where our spoken words will appear on the page as they are spoken. This will relieve the memory burden. The colloquial nature may remain and even be enhanced, but—because the printed record of the speech is immediately visible—perhaps the organization will improve.

The widespread availability of computer text editors has produced other changes in writing. On the one hand, it is satisfying to be able to type your thoughts without worrying about minor typographical errors or spelling. On the other hand, you may spend less time thinking and planning. Computer text editors affect structure through their limited real estate. With a paper manuscript, you can spread the pages upon the desk, couch, wall, or floor. Large sections of the text can be examined at one time, to be reorganized and structured. If you use only the computer, then the working area (or real estate) is limited to what shows on the screen. The conventional screens display about twenty-four lines of text. Even the largest screens now available can display no more than about two full printed pages of text. The result is that corrections tend to be made locally, on what is visible. Large-scale restructuring of the material is more difficult to do, and therefore seldom gets done. Sometimes the same text appears in different parts of the manuscript, without being discovered by the writer. (To the writer, everything seems familiar.)

OUTLINE PROCESSORS AND HYPERTEXT

The current fad in writing aids is the outline processor, a tool designed to encourage planning and reflection on the organization of material. The writer can compress the text into an outline or expand an outline to cover the entire manuscript. Moving a heading means moving an entire section. Outline processors attempt to overcome organizational problems by allowing collapsed views of the manuscript to be examined and manipulated. But the process seems to emphasize the organization that is visible in the outline or heading structure of the manuscript, thereby deemphasizing other aspects of the work. It is characteristic of thought processes that attention to one aspect comes at the cost of decreased attention to others. What a technology makes easy to do will get done; what it hides, or makes difficult, may very well not get done.

The next step in writing technology is already visible on the horizon: hypertext.[9] Here we have another set of possibilities, another set of difficulties, in this case for both writer and reader. Writers frequently complain that the material they are trying to explain is complex, multi-dimensional. The ideas are all interconnected, and there is no single sequence of words to convey them properly. Moreover, readers vary enormously in skill, interest, and prior knowledge. Some need expansion of the most elementary ideas, some want more technical details.[10] Some wish to focus on one set of topics, others find those uninteresting. How on earth can a single document satisfy them all, especially when that document must be in a linear sequence, words following words, chapters following chapters? It has always been considered part of the skill of a writer to be able to take otherwise chaotic material and order it appropriately for the reader. Hypertext relieves the author of this burden. In theory, it also frees the reader from the constraints of the linear order; the reader can pursue the material in whatever order seems most relevant or interesting.

Hypertext makes a virtue out of lack of organization, allowing ideas and thoughts to be juxtaposed at will. The writer throws out the ideas, attaching them to the page where they seem first relevant. The reader can take any path at all through the book. See an interesting word on the page, point at it, and the word expands into text. See a word you don't understand, and a touch gives the definition. Who could be against such a wonderful idea?

Imagine that this book was in hypertext. How would it work? Well, I've used several devices that relate to hypertext: one is the footnote,[11] another is parenthetical comments, and yet another is contrasting text. (I have tended not to use parenthetical asides in this book because I fear they distract, make the sentences longer, and add to the reader's memory burden, as this parenthetical statement demonstrates.)

Contrasting text, when used as a commentary, is a kind of hypertext. Here is a comment on the text itself, optional and not essential to a first reading. The typography gives signals to the reader.

Actual hypertext will be written and read using a computer, of course, so that this commentary wouldn't be visible unless it had been requested.

A footnote is essentially a signal that some comment is available to the reader. In hypertext, actual numbered footnotes will not be needed, but some sort of signal is still required. With hypertext, the signal that more information is available can be given through color, motion (such as flashing), or typeface. Touch the special word and the material appears; you don't need a number.

So, what do you think of hypertext? Imagine trying to write something using it. The extra freedom also poses extra requirements. If hypertext really becomes available, especially in the fancy versions now being talked about—where words, sounds, video, computer graphics, simulations, and more are all available at the touch of the screen—well, it is hard to imagine anyone capable of preparing the material. It will take teams of people. I predict that there will be much experimentation, and much failure, before the dimensions of this new technology are fully explored and understood.

One thing that does bother me, however, is the belief that hypertext will save the author from having to put material in linear order. Wrong. To think this is to allow for sloppiness in writing and presentation. It is hard work to organize material, but that effort on the part of the writer is essential for the ease of the reader. Take away the need for this discipline and I fear that you pass the burden on to the reader, who may not be able to cope, and may not care to try. The advent of hypertext is apt to make writing much more difficult, not easier. Good writing, that is.

THE HOME OF THE FUTURE: A PLACE OF COMFORT OR A NEW SOURCE OF FRUSTRATION

Even as this book is being completed, new sources of pleasure and frustration are entering our lives. Two developments are worthy of mention, both intended to serve the ever-promised "house of the future." One most wonderful development is the "smart house," the place where your every want is taken care of by intelligent, omniscient appliances. The other promised development is the house of knowledge: whole libraries available at our fingertips, the world's information resources available through our telephone/television set/home computer/rooftop satellite antenna. Both developments have great potential to transform lives in just the positive ways promised, but they are also apt to explode every fear and complexity discussed in this book into reality a thousand-times over.

Imagine all of our electric appliances connected together via an intelligent "information bus." This bus (the technical term for a set of wires that acts as communication channels among devices) allows home lamps, ovens, and dishwashers to talk to one another. The central home computer senses the car pulling into the driveway, so it signals the front door to unlock, the hall lights to go on, and the oven to start preparing the meal. By the time you arrive in the house, your television set has already turned on to your favorite news station, your favorite appetizer is available in the kitchen, and the cooking of the meal has begun. Some of these systems "speak" to you (with voice-synthesizers inside their computer brains), most have sensors that detect room temperature, the outside weather, and the presence of people. All assume a master controlling device through which the house occupants inform the system of their every want. Many allow for telephone control. Going to miss your favorite show on television? Call home and instruct your VCR to record it for you. Coming home an hour later than expected? Call your home oven and delay the starting time of the meal.

Can you imagine what it would take to control these devices? How would you tell your oven when to turn on? Would you do this through the buttons available at your friendly pay telephone? Or would you lug around a portable controlling unit? In either case, the complexity boggles the mind. Do the designers of these systems have some secret cure for the problems described throughout this book or have they perhaps already mastered the lessons within? Hardly. An article entitled "The 'smartest house' in America" in the technical magazine for design engineers, *Design News*, [12] shows the normal set of arbitrary control devices, overly complex panels, and conventional computer screens and keyboards. The modern cooktop (accompanied by the caption "for the ultimate chef") has two gas burners, four electric burners, and a barbecue grill controlled through a row of eight identical-looking, evenly spaced knobs.

It is easy to imagine positive uses for intelligent home appliances. The energy-saving virtues of a home that turns on the heat only for rooms that are occupied, or waters the yard only when the ground is dry and rain does not threaten, seem virtuous indeed. Not the most critical of the problems facing humankind, perhaps, but reassuring nonetheless. But it is difficult to see how the complex instructions required for such a system will be conveyed. I find it difficult to instruct my children how to do these tasks appropriately and I often fail at them myself. How will I manage the precise, clear instructions required for my intelligent dishwasher, especially through the very limited control mechanism I am sure to be provided with? I do not look forward to the day.

Now consider the information world of the future. The modern laser disk is capable of holding billions of characters of information.[13] This means that instead of purchasing individual books, we can now purchase whole libraries. One compact disk can hold hundreds of thousands (even millions) of printed pages of information. Whole encyclopaedias can be available at our fingertips, through our computer terminals and television screens. And when every home is connected to a central computer system through improved capacity telephone lines, or the cable television wire, or a rooftop antenna aimed at the neighborhood earth satellite, the information of the world is available to all.

There are two costs for these pleasures. One is economic: it may only cost a few dollars to manufacture a compact disk that contains the contents of one hundred books, but the cost to the consumer will be measured in the hundreds of dollars. After all, each book took an author several years of effort and a publishing house with editors and book designers another three to nine months. Connection to the world's libraries through the telephone, television, and satellite lines of the world cost money to the telephone, cable, and communication companies. These costs have to be recovered. Those of us who use the computer library search facilities available today know that it is most convenient to have them available but that each second of use is marked by the tension that the costs are piling up. Stop to reflect on something, and your bill increases astronomically. The true costs of these systems are high, and the user's continual thought that each use exacts a cost is not reassuring.

The second cost is the difficulty of finding anything in such large data bases. I can't always find my car keys or the book I was reading last night. When I read an interesting article and store it away in my files for some unknown but probable future use, I know at the time I stick it away that I may never be able to remember where I put it. If I already have these difficulties with my own limited possessions and books, imagine what it will be like when trying to find something in the libraries and data bases of the world, where the organization was done by someone else who had no idea of what my needs were. Chaos. Sheer chaos.

The society of the future: something to look forward to with pleasure, contemplation, and dread.

That design affects society is hardly news to designers. Many take the implications of their work seriously. But the conscious manipulation of society has severe drawbacks, not the least of which is the fact that not everyone agrees on the appropriate goals. Design, therefore, takes on political significance; indeed, design philosophies vary in important ways across political systems. In Western cultures, design has reflected the capitalistic importance of the marketplace, with an emphasis on exterior features deemed to be attractive to the purchaser. In the consumer economy taste is not the criterion in the marketing of expensive foods or drinks, usability is not the primary criterion in the marketing of home and office appliances. We are surrounded with objects of desire, not objects of use.[14]

Everyday tasks are not difficult because of their inherent complexity. They are difficult only because they require learning arbitrary relationships and arbitrary mappings, and because they sometimes require precision in their execution. The difficulties can be avoided through design that makes obvious what operations are necessary. Good design exploits constraints so that the user feels as if there is only one possible thing to do—the right thing, of course. The designer has to understand and exploit natural constraints of all kinds.

Errors are an unavoidable part of everyday life. Proper design can help decrease the incidence and severity of errors by eliminating the causes of some, minimizing the possibilities of others, and helping to make errors discoverable, once they have been made. Such design exploits the power of constraints and makes use of forcing functions and visible outcomes of actions. We do not have to experience confusion or suffer from undiscovered errors. Proper design can make a difference in our quality of life.

Now you are on your own. If you are a designer, help fight the battle for usability. If you are a user, then join your voice with those who cry for usable products. Write to manufacturers. Boycott unusable designs. Support good designs by purchasing them, even if it means going out of your way, even if it means spending a bit more. And voice your concerns to the stores that carry the products; manufacturers listen to their customers.

When you visit museums of science and technology, ask questions if you have trouble understanding. Provide feedback about the exhibits and whether they work well or poorly. Encourage museums to move toward better usability and understandability.

And enjoy yourself. Walk around the world examining the details of design. Take pride in the little things that help; think kindly of the person who so thoughtfully put them in. Realize that even details matter, that the designer may have had to fight to include something helpful. Give mental prizes to those who practice good design: send flowers. Jeer those who don't: send weeds.

NOTES

CHAPTER ONE: The Psychopathology of Everyday Things

1. Reprinted by permission of the *Wall Street Journal,* © Dow Jones & Co., Inc., 1986. All rights reserved.

2. W. H. Mayall (1979), *Principles in design,* 84.

3. The notion of affordance and the insights it provides originated with J. J. Gibson, a psychologist interested in how people see the world. I believe that affordances result from the mental interpretation of things, based on our past knowledge and experience applied to our perception of the things about us. My view is somewhat in conflict with the views of many Gibsonian psychologists, but this internal debate within modern psychology is of little relevance here. (See Gibson, 1977, 1979.)

4. D. Fisher & R. Bragonier, Jr. (1981), *What's what: A visual glossary of the physical world.* The list of the eleven parts of the sink came from this book. I thank James Grier Miller for telling me about the book and lending me his copy.

5. Biederman (1987) shows how he derives the number 30,000 on pages 127 and 128 of his paper, "Recognition-by-components: A theory of human image understanding," *Psychological Review, 94,* 115–147.

6. I thank Mike King for this example (and others).

7. More complex systems have already been successfully built. One example is the speech message system that recorded phone calls for later retrie-

val, built by IBM for the 1984 Olympics. Here was a rather complex telephone system, designed to record messages being sent to athletes by friends and colleagues from all over the world. The users spoke a variety of languages, and some were quite unfamiliar with the American telephone system and with high technology in general. But by careful application of psychological principles and continual testing with the user population during the design stage, the system was usable, understandable, and functional. Good design is possible to achieve, but it has to be one of the goals from the beginning. (See the description of the phone system by Gould, Boies, Levy, Richards, & Schoonard, 1987.)

CHAPTER TWO: The Psychology of Everyday Actions

1. Unfortunately, blaming the user is imbedded in the legal system. When major accidents occur, official courts of inquiry are set up to assess the blame. More and more often the blame is attributed to "human error." The person involved can be fined, punished, or fired. Maybe training procedures are revised. The law rests comfortably. But in my experience, human error usually is a result of poor design: it should be called system error. Humans err continually; it is an intrinsic part of our nature. System design should take this into account. Pinning the blame on the person may be a comfortable way to proceed, but why was the system ever designed so that a single act by a single person could cause calamity? An important book on this topic is Charles Perrow's *Normal accidents* (1984). I cover human error in detail in chapter 5.

2. This example is taken from White & Horwitz's (1987) technical report on "ThinkerTools," their system for teaching children physics, in part to overcome the beliefs in naive physics which are otherwise so strong.

3. The subject of naive views is treated at length in many reviews. The relationship between Aristotle's physics and modern naive physics is developed in McCloskey's (1983) *Scientific American* article, "Intuitive physics."

4. The valve theory of the thermostat is taken from Kempton (1986), a study published in the journal *Cognitive Science.*

5. Some thermostats are designed to anticipate the need to turn on or off. They avoid a common problem: the temperature in a cooling house continues to drop after the thermostat has turned on the furnace, and the temperature of a heating house continues to rise after the thermostat has turned off the furnace, due to the heat already in the system. The "intelligent" thermostat turns off or on a little before the desired temperature is reached.

6. National Transportation Safety Board (1984), *Aircraft accident report— Eastern Air Lines, Inc., Lockheed L-1011, N334EA, Miami International Airport, Miami, Florida, May 5, 1983.*

7. Surprisingly little is known about the nature of action sequences. The most relevant book to what I am describing is *Plans and the structure of behavior*, by Miller, Galanter, and Pribram (1960). The GOMS (Goals, Operators, Methods, and Selection) model of Card, Moran, and Newell (1983) is more recent and more relevant to applications. My work is described in more detail in Norman (1986). Sanders (1980) has reviewed a host of experimental studies that supports this breakdown of the sequence into seven stages. A fair amount of work on a theory of action is being done by social psychologists. On the whole, this is a rich, unexplored area, worthy of much study.

8. The story of these gulfs and the initial analyses came about from research performed with Ed Hutchins and Jim Hollan, then part of a joint research team between the Naval Personnel Research and Development Center and the University of California, San Diego. The work examined the development of computer systems that were easier to learn and easier to use and, in particular, of what has been called direct manipulation computer systems. I return to this in chapter 6. The initial work is described in the chapter "Direct manipulation interfaces" in the book *User centered system design* (Hutchins, Hollan, & Norman, 1986).

CHAPTER THREE: Knowledge in the Head and in the World

1. Many people are responsible for the development of these demonstrations. I do not know who first pointed out the problems with remembering the letter-number matchup on the telephone. Nickerson & Adams (1979) and Rubin & Kontis (1983) showed that people could neither recall nor recognize accurately the pictures and words on American coins. Jonathan Grudin did the demonstration of the typists' apparent lack of knowledge of the keyboard (unpublished study).

2. Thomas Malone, now at the MIT School of Business Administration, examined how people organize their work on their office desks. His studies of the importance of physical organization are often cited as justification for the frequent use of the desktop metaphor in some computer systems, especially the Xerox Star and the Apple Lisa and Macintosh (the Apple machines were derived from the Xerox Star; Malone was working for Xerox at the time he did his studies). See Malone's (1983) paper "How do people organize their desks: Implications for designing office automation systems."

3. I take this result from the work of Rubin & Kontis (1983), who attempted to determine the mental representation (the memory schema) that their students had for American coins.

4. Stanley Meisler, *Times* staff writer, in the *Los Angeles Times*, Dec. 31, 1986. Copyright 1986, *Los Angeles Times*. Reprinted by permission.

5. Confirmatory evidence comes from the fact that although long-term residents of Britain still complain that they confuse the one-pound coin with the five-pence coin, newcomers (and children) do not have the same confusion. This is because the long-term residents are working with their original set of descriptions, which did not easily accommodate the distinctions between these two coins. Newcomers, however, start off with no preconceptions and must form a set of descriptions to distinguish among all the coins; in this situation, the one-pound coin offers no particular problems. In the United States, the one-dollar coin never became popular and is no longer being made, so the equivalent observations cannot be made.

6. The suggestion that memory storage and retrieval is mediated through partial descriptions was put forth in a paper with Danny Bobrow (Norman & Bobrow, 1979). We argued that, in general, the required specificity of a description depends on the set of items among which a person is trying to distinguish. Memory retrieval can therefore involve a prolonged series of attempts when the initial retrieval description yields the wrong result, so that the person must keep trying to retrieve the desired item, each retrieval attempt coming closer to the answer and helping to make the description more precise.

7. D. C. Rubin & W. T. Wallace (1987), *Rhyme and reason: Integral properties of words* (Unpublished manuscript). Given just the cues for meaning (the first task), the people Rubin and Wallace tested could get the three target words used in these examples only 0 percent, 4 percent, and 0 percent of the time, respectively. Similarly, when the same target words were cued only by rhymes, they still did quite poorly, guessing the targets correctly only 0 percent, 0 percent, and 4 percent of the time, respectively. Thus, each cue alone offered little assistance. Combining the meaning cue with the rhyming cue led to perfect performance: the people got the target words 100 percent of the time.

8. A. B. Lord (1960), *The singer of tales* (Cambridge, MA: Harvard University Press), 27.

9. Lord (1960) points out that this length is excessive, probably produced only during the special circumstances in which Homer (or some other singer) dictated the story slowly and repetitively to the person who first wrote it down. Normally the length would be varied to accommodate the whims of the audience, and no normal audience could sit through 27,000 lines.

10. The quotation is from 'Ali Baba and the forty thieves, in *The Arabian nights: Tales of wonder and magnificence,* selected and edited by Padraic Colum, from the translation by Edward William Lane (New York: Macmillan, 1953). The names here are in an unfamiliar form. We are much more used to having the magic phrase be "Open Sesame," but according to Colum, "Simsim" is the authentic transliteration.

11. The quote comes from Winograd & Soloway's interesting study (1986), On forgetting the locations of things stored in special places, *Journal of Experimental Psychology: General, 115,* 366–372.

12. The description is taken from an earlier book, *Learning and memory* (Norman, 1982).

13. Landauer (1986) provides the most sophisticated attempt I have yet seen to estimate the amount of material people might know in his *Cognitive Science* article "How much do people remember? Some estimates of the quantity of learned information in long-term memory."

14. This story is taken from Hutchins, Hollan, & Norman (1986, p. 113), slightly reworded. I am of course indebted to our renamed colleague for allowing his thought processes to be aired in public.

15. Surprisingly little is known about the properties of mental models. There are two books with *Mental models* as their title, one the report of a conference, edited by Gentner and Stevens (1983), the other, by Johnson-Laird (1983), an examination of a particular form of mental model that might be used in problem solving and reasoning. The first is closer in spirit to the types being discussed here. The role mental models might play in the understanding of complex systems in general and computer systems in particular is discussed in our book on the design of computer systems (Norman & Draper, 1986). An excellent review is provided by Rouse and Morris (1986).

16. Readers conversant with information theory might consider how the various mappings reduce the information load on the user. The standard measure of information is the "bit," the amount of information required to distinguish between two items. With the completely arbitrary mapping of figure 3.3, each control could work any of four burners, so it takes 2 bits of information to specify which burner each control operates. If you wish to be able to look at any of the four controls and know immediately which burner it operates, 8 bits must be learned. Eight bits is a lot. (Technically, all four controls can be specified with a total of only 4.6 bits, but this makes use of the fact that once the first control is known [2 bits], the second one has to be selected from only three possibilities [1.5 bits], the third from the two remaining possibilities [1 bit], and then the last control becomes fully determined [0 bits]. This strategy requires less information to specify all four controls, but at the cost of more computation: you can't look directly at a control and know which burner it works—you have to figure it out.)

The partial mapping of arrangement figure 3.4 reduces the information load. Now, selection of each proper control is selection from two alternatives, or 1 bit. So a total of only 4 bits are required to let the person go to each control and know immediately which burner it operates. The full natural mappings of figure 3.5 have only one interpretation, so nothing has to be learned: 0 bits.

The change from an arbitrary mapping to a partial mapping to a full natural mapping reduces the number of alternatives from 24 to 4 to 1 and reduces the information theory content from 8 to 4 to 0 bits, respectively.

17. Despite the importance of reminding from both the practical and the theoretical point of view, little is known about it. Reminds, of course, occur in a number of different ways. One form of reminding occurs entirely internally, as when a thought or an experience "reminds" one of another thought or experience. As far as I know, only Roger Schank has written about it (in his book *Dynamic memory*, 1982). Another form of reminding comes from external cues: for example, as when seeing a clock reminds one of the time and of a task that needs to be done (or worse, that can no longer be done). Another form of reminding—the type I have been discussing—is deliberately invoked or set up, as when one tries to set up physical cues on one day of tasks that are to be done during another. We treat some of these issues in the chapters by Cypher and by Miyata and Norman in Norman & Draper (1986), *User centered system design*.

CHAPTER FOUR: Knowing What to Do

1. Letter to newspaper advice columnist Ellie Rucker, *Austin* [Texas] *American-Statesman*, Aug. 31, 1986. Reprinted by permission.

2. The results of my experiments are reminiscent of studies of chess masters who were allowed only ten seconds to examine a chess board with a configuration from the middle of a real game before being asked to reconstruct the board from memory. They did so very accurately. Novices reconstruct the board poorly. But show an illegal (or illogical) combination of those very same chess pieces to a master and a novice, and they perform about equally poorly. The expert has learned so much of the structure of the game that numerous natural and artificial constraints come into play, automatically ruling out all sorts of configurations and reducing what has to be remembered to a manageable amount. The novice does not have sufficient internal knowledge to make use of these constraints. Similarly, when faced with the illegal or illogical configuration, the expert's constraints and prior knowledge are no longer useful (see Chase & Simon, 1973).

3. See Schank & Abelson's (1977) *Scripts, plans, goals, and understanding* or Goffman's (1974) book *Frame analysis,* on social structures and conventions.

4. We had to overcome a number of technical problems to improve the mapping. The lights were already installed, and it was not possible to redo the wiring. We modified some light dimmers so that they could be used as controls for remotely located lights. The choice of electrical switches was also limited. Ideally, we would have made parts especially for our purpose. Still, the experiment has been remarkably successful. In this

work, I relied heavily on the electrical and mechanical ingenuity of Dave Wargo, who actually did the design, construction, and installation of the switches.

5. The reason for the awkward location of the switch is cost. One designer wrote me: "I fought the good battle to get the on/off switch to the front of the terminal. I lost the argument both times. The hardware engineers costed the front mounted switch at about $10 (about $30 to the consumer), plus the potential for the power to contaminate some nearby circuits." Those prices seem high to me, but this designer was speaking of professional equipment, where the terminal probably costs in the thousands of dollars. Here is the standard tradeoff of cost versus usability. What price are you willing to pay for usability? Does the cost really have to be that high? What if the switch had been designed to be on the front from the very beginning, as opposed to having to be moved after the rest of the layout had been completed?

6. Copyright 1987 by Consumers Union of United States, Inc., Mount Vernon, NY 10553. Excerpted by permission from *Consumer Reports,* Jan. 1987.

7. See Gaver (1986).

CHAPTER FIVE: To Err Is Human

1. *InfoWorld,* Dec. 22, 1986. Reprinted by permission.

2. See Sherry Turkle's (1984) analysis in her book *The second self.* The book is mostly about the impact of computers on people's lives, especially on the children who have grown up with daily, continual contact with machines—the "hackers" of the world. Turkle also presents an analysis of the changes that information-processing views of the human mind have made to our interpretation of Freud. All around, it is an intriguing and important book.

3. Unless otherwise noted, all the examples in this section were collected by me, primarily from the errors of myself, my research associates, my colleagues, and my students. Everyone diligently recorded their slips, with the requirement that only the ones that had been immediately recorded would be added to the collection. Many were first published in Norman (1980 and 1981).

4. The term "capture error" was invented by Jim Reason of Manchester, England (Reason, 1979). Reason has written widely on slips and other mishaps. I recommend as a good review of his work the book *Absent minded? The psychology of mental lapses and everyday errors* (Reason & Mycielska, 1982).

5. Reason (1979).

6. A simple introduction to schema theory can be found in my book *Learning and memory* (Norman, 1982).

7. The best source of information about the connectionist approach is the two-book series *Parallel Distributed Processing* (Rumelhart & McClelland, 1986; McClelland & Rumelhart, 1986).

8. An important set of studies has been performed by Danny Kahneman and Amos Tversky (Tversky & Kahneman, 1973). Kahneman and Miller's (1986) "Norm theory" applies a related set of ideas.

9. A standard objection to my claim that everyday tasks are conceptually simple—that they do not require extensive search and backtracking—is that perception and language are certainly everyday tasks, yet they violate these rules. I disagree.

Yes, perception and language are certainly everyday tasks. But I do not believe they violate my argument. I argue that the key to conceptual complexity is whether or not backtracking is required: Is there trial and error? Are multiple paths investigated? I want to argue that none of these are required for everyday tasks, including perception and language.

The study of perception is a difficult topic: we still do not know how it gets done. Clearly it involves a lot of computation. But I suspect that the computation is less complex than might be supposed. Perceptual systems are parallel structures, they use parallel algorithms. I believe they reach their solutions by pattern matching, by relaxation, by minimum energy constraints. With the proper hardware (the hardware of the brain), I believe these tasks are done without backtracking, without following false leads.

The rule I wish to invoke is that everyday language and perception are mostly conceptually simple. They are done without backtracking, without conscious involvement or even awareness. Both language and perception have situations that violate these assumptions, but they are relatively infrequent. When they occur, they require conscious involvement. And they provide patterns that are difficult to perceive or understand. In fact, a majority of these structures are created deliberately, as illusions, or puzzles, or brainteasers, or as the counterexamples and problems that linguists spend so many hours inventing and discussing.

10. There is a whole field devoted to the design and analysis of highway systems. These particular points are discussed in chapters by Alexander & Lunenfeld (1984) and by Kinner (1984).

My own experience is that while signs on the major national motorways may be well done, with considerable thought and planning, signs on the smaller roads are not. The signs on the local roads require more local knowledge, which visitors usually lack. In England, when I am offered a choice between Buxton and Whittlesford while I am trying to get to Oxford, what do I do? Or suppose I am home in San Diego trying to get to Mission Bay, when I am offered a choice between El Centro and Los Angeles, neither of which I wish to visit. When making long journeys on the secondary roads of England, I learned to go around each roundabout two or three times, each time eliminating a different exit until I finally could select what appeared to be the best. In this way I got lost only one in five times instead of every time. Fortunately, the good manners of British motorists made my circling possible, even safe. I have tried the same thing in the United States, but I was risking my life.

11. J. Maclean (1983), *Secrets of a superthief* (New York: Berkley Books), 108.

12. Although the nuclear power industry has done a good job of analyzing the situation, it has not been so responsive in actually changing anything, especially the design of the control rooms. It's almost impossible to redo an existing control room, a process that can cost millions of dollars and disrupt the plant for several years. We now know how to build much better control rooms, but there aren't any new plants being built in the United States. And, of course, management would have to take responsibility and recognize that human error results primarily from deficient design; I see few signs that this message is understood. The new control rooms of other countries' plants that I read about appear to have the same old misguided, inferior philosophy about how control rooms should be designed. The designs will definitely lead to error (which will be blamed on the operators, who will then be retrained and retrained, or, more likely, simply fired).

The aviation industry has been more responsive. But its costs are lower, and new cockpit designs and aircraft are continually being produced.

Other industries seem quite unaware of these problems, even though the documented accident and death rates to workers and innocent bystanders may be higher than for either nuclear power or commercial aviation. Human error, they call it, allowing them to fire the people involved and ignore the misdesign of the plant that led to the problem in the first place. The chemical, petroleum, and shipping industries seem particularly at fault, blaming training or operator incompetence when, in fact, the problems are inherent in the system. For an excellent analysis of these issues, read Charles Perrow's (1984) book, *Normal accidents.*

13. Fischhoff's (1975) study is called "Hindsight ≠ foresight: The effect of outcome knowledge on judgment under uncertainty." And while you are at it, see the very impressive book of readings entitled *Acceptable risk* (Fischhoff, Lichtenstein, Slovic, Derby, & Keeney, 1981).

14. The Korean Air flight 007 has been analyzed by Hersh (1986), who gives a plausible, detailed account of what might have gone wrong with the flight. Because the aircraft flight recorders were not recovered, we will never know with certainty what did happen. It appears that the actions on the Soviet side were probably equally confused, with pilots and the military under various social pressures to act. The information available about the Soviets' actions is insufficient to reach any reliable conclusions.

15. My source for information about the Tenerife crash is Roitsch, Babcock, & Edmunds (undated), the report issued by the American Airline

Pilots Association. It is perhaps not too surprising that it differs in interpretation from the Spanish government's report (Spanish Ministry of Transport and Communications, 1978), which in turn differs from the report by the Dutch Aircraft Accident Inquiry Board (1979). See also how Weiner treats the crash and its aftermath (Weiner, 1980; reprinted in Hurst & Hurst, 1982). (Weiner calls the episode the result of the *Realpolitik* of a system that "emphasizes airspace allocation and political compromise, rather than dealing directly with the variety of problems facing pilots and controllers.")

The information and quotations about the Air Florida crash are from the report of the National Transportation Safety Board (1982). An excellent review of the social pressures can be found in Weiner (1986) and in two books entitled *Pilot error* (Hurst, 1976; Hurst & Hurst, 1982). (The two books are quite different. The second is better than the first, in part because at the time the first book was written, not much scientific evidence was available.)

16. Warning signals can be designed properly. Roy Patterson at the Medical Research Council's Applied Psychology Unit in Cambridge, England, has devised a systematic set of procedures for conveying the meaning and importance of a problem with a carefully controlled sequence of sounds, where the frequency, intensity, and rate of presentation identifies the problem and indicates the seriousness. The scheme can be applied wherever a number of devices all require warning sounds, such as in aircraft cockpits or hospital operating rooms. It has been proposed as an international standard for warnings, and it is now working its way slowly through the societies and committees that must approve such things.

One problem has always been knowing how loud to make the signal. The common solution is to make it very loud. Patterson points out that the sound level that is required depends on what else is happening. When an airplane is taking off, loud warnings are needed. When it is in level, continuous flight, low levels will do. Patterson's system has a variable loudness: the warning sound starts off softly, then repeats with increasing sound intensity until the signal is acknowledged.

Modern technology makes it possible to have machines talk, either by storing a compressed waveform or by synthesizing a voice. This approach, like all approaches, has it strengths and weaknesses. It allows for precise information to be conveyed, especially when the person's visual attention is being directed elsewhere. But if several speech warnings operate at the same time, or if the environment is noisy, speech warnings cannot be understood. Or if conversations among the users or operators are necessary, speech warnings will interfere. Speech warning signals can be effective, but only if used intelligently.

17. I discuss the idea of designing for error in a paper in the *Communications of the ACM*, in which I analyze a number of the slips people make in using

computer systems and suggest system design principles that might minimize those errors (Norman, 1983). This philosophy also pervades the book that our research team put together: *User centered system design* (Norman & Draper, 1986). Here we discuss how to build systems for users. Two chapters are especially relevant to the discussions here: my "Cognitive engineering" and the one I wrote with Clayton Lewis, called "Designing for error."

CHAPTER SIX: The Design Challenge

1. Mares writes about the process used in the development of the first successful typewriter (1909, pp. 42–43). Mares said he was quoting "from an old catalog issued by the Remington Company, many years back."

2. There are very good descriptions of the hill-climbing process in Alexander's (1964) book *Notes on the synthesis of form* and Jones's book *Design methods;* also see Jones's (1984) *Essays in design.* Jones (1981) has a particularly good description of the evolution of the wheels of farm wagons: did you know they are "dished" or "cupped" outward, so that the rims bulge out more than the center? Did you know that the wagon will not function as well if the wheels are not cupped? This improvement resulted from a natural, hill-climbing design process.

All of Alexander's works describe this process of evolution, and his books on architectural design are influential. In addition to the one already mentioned, see *The timeless way of building* (Alexander, 1979) and *A pattern language: Towns, buildings, construction,* by Alexander, Ishikawa, and Silverstein (1977). I find the works fascinating to skim, frustrating to read, and difficult to put into practice, but his descriptions of the structure of homes and villages are very good.

While you're tracking down these classic books on design, by all means look at Simon's (1981) *The sciences of the artificial.*

3. *New York Daily Tribune* editorial from about 1890, quoted in G. C. Mares (1909), *The history of the typewriter, successor to the pen: An illustrated account of the origin, rise, and development of the writing machine* frontispiece.

4. The story makes sense, but the arrangement of the keys doesn't completely fit the story. Yes, *i* and *e* form a frequent pair and are far apart, but what about other frequent pairs, such as *e* and *r,* or *i, n, g?* And it seems suspicious that the letters of the word *typewriter* all appear on the top row; some other constraints seem to have been operating. Almost every country in the world uses a keyboard similar to qwerty. There are differences—the French, for example, replaced *q* and *w* with *a* and *z,* for "azerty"—but the changes are remarkably minor. Yet different languages have very different patterns of letter use, so an English-based keyboard would not be expected to work well for other languages.

5. The account of the "duel" is presented in Beeching's (1974) book, *Century of the typewriter* (pp. 40–41).

6. Fisher and I studied a variety of keyboard layouts. We thought that alphabetically organized keys would be superior for beginners. No, they weren't: we discovered that knowledge of the alphabet was not useful in finding the keys. Our studies of alphabetical and Dvorak keyboards were published in the journal *Human Factors* (Norman & Fisher, 1982).

7. Admirers of the Dvorak keyboard claim much more than a 10 percent improvement, as well as faster learning rates and less fatigue. But I will stick by my studies and my statements. If you want to read more, including a worthwhile treatment of the history of the typewriter, see the book *Cognitive aspects of skilled typewriting*, edited by Cooper (1983), which includes several chapters of research from my laboratory.

8. The Israeli psychologist Daniel Gopher has developed a clever single-hand chord keyboard for both the roman and Hebrew alphabets. He claims great success with the use of the Hebrew chord keyboard by pilots who have to enter data into their flight computer with one hand while flying the plane with the other (Gopher, Karis, & Koenig, 1985; Gopher & Raij, in press).

9. *Wall Street Journal*, Dec. 9, 1986. Reprinted by permission of the *Wall Street Journal*. © Dow Jones & Co., Inc., 1986. All rights reserved.

10. Sommer (1983), *Social design: Creating buildings with people in mind* (p. 126).

11. Sommer (1983, pp. 128–129).

12. "Wait a minute," you might say, "what has the design of the cafeteria got to do with the Design Centre? That isn't the purpose of the Centre. You are missing the whole point." I don't think so. The lack of concern for the user of the Centre reflects the attitude of the Centre as a whole. The exhibits are tasteful, pleasing to the eye. They emphasize artistic qualities and ease of manufacture. Those qualities are indeed important, but they aren't sufficient. The cafeteria was aesthetically pleasing but functionally inadequate. How many of the designs on display had the same characteristics? It isn't unreasonable to expect the Centre to show how design can be applied to all the relevant dimensions.

13. *Los Angeles Times*, June 1, 1987.

14. Most designers today work in teams. Nonetheless, the comments I make about "the designer" apply. In fact, the better the teamwork, the more apt members are to share common modes of thinking and common sets of approaches, and thereby to fall prey simultaneously to the same problems.

15. Mike King, a telephone company designer, commenting on an early draft of POET.

16. Dan Rosenberg, a design engineer, commenting on an early draft of POET.

17. Richard W. Pew, an authority on human factors and industrial design (personal communication, 1985).

18. There are some technical problems facing the programmer. It is up to each individual programmer to develop an appropriate system for representing the actions to be performed, to find out what is possible, and then to discover what has happened—to make judicious use of feedback, of intelligent interpretation. There should be a natural dialog, a comfortable interaction between computer and user in which both parties cooperate to reach the desired solution. All of this is too much of a burden to put upon the individual programmers. After all, the person skilled in a problem area or at programming is not likely also to be skilled in the psychology of human–computer interaction. The picture won't improve until there are better packages of tools for the user to make it easier to do things right. These packages are called "toolboxes," "workbenches," "rapid prototyping tools," and "user interface management systems," and they are now coming out.

Literature on how to do things right exists. A good starting point is Baecker & Buxton's (1987) *Readings in human-computer interaction;* Shneiderman's text, *Designing the user interface: Strategies for effective human-computer interaction* (1987); and my *User centered system design* (Norman & Draper, 1986). The book by Card, Moran, and Newell, *The psychology of human computer interaction* (1983) provides a beginning toward a set of computational design tools; it is also the most technical. For the most current work, see any of the proceedings of the annual conferences sponsored by the Association for Computing Machinery's subgroup, SIGCHI (Special Interest Group on Computer Human Interaction). Several international conference series meet at various locations in the United States and throughout Europe. Surely computer manufacturers can't be ignorant of all these activities.

19. Xerox did indeed make significant innovations in the usability of computer systems, but many of the basic ideas originated elsewhere. There is a long history of research on this topic. Light pens had been used as a pointing device for many years. Doug Engelbart invented the mouse in his project on augmented human reasoning at the Stanford Research Institute. It is not clear where the emphasis on graphics came from, but computer-aided design programs had already exploited the idea. Windows may have come from several sources, but Alan Kay, then at Xerox (now at Apple), commonly gets the credit.

20. Smith, Irby, Kimball, Verplank, & Harslem (1982), *Designing the star user interface.*

21. The understanding of these different modes of interaction has developed slowly: it still remains an active research topic. Ben Shneiderman (1974, 1983, 1987) invented the term direct manipulation and has done much to promote its use. The distinction between first-person and third-person interactions and the notion of direct engagement was developed by Brenda Laurel while she was working at Atari, at that time a major games

manufacturer. Computer games provide a modern form of dramatic experience. There are many varieties of games, from those that concentrate on emotions and motor skills to those that focus on the intellect. Most games, whether on the computer or not, present this feeling of direct engagement, of a first-person interaction with the environment. Similar feelings of being captured, of working directly at the task, are possible for other activities as well. See Laurel's (1986) chapter, "Interface as mimesis." Also see the chapter on direct manipulation interfaces by Hutchins, Hollan, and Norman (1986).

22. The ideas in this section were developed jointly with Jim Miller of the Microelectronics and Computer Technology Corporation (MCC), of Austin, Texas, the American research consortium for the development of future technologies for computers.

CHAPTER SEVEN: User-Centered Design

1. Lynch (1972), *What time is this place?* (pp. 66–67).

2. An excellent treatment of overautomation is Weiner and Curry's (1980) paper, "Flight-deck automation: Promises and problems."

3. I have enough friends on national and international standards committees for me to realize that the process of determining an internationally accepted standard is laborious. Even when all parties agree on the merits of standardization, the task of selecting standards becomes a lengthy and political issue. A small company or a single designer can standardize products without too much difficulty, but it is much more difficult for an industrial, national, or international body to agree to standards. There even exists a standardized procedure for establishing national and international standards. A set of national and international organizations works on standards; when a new standard is proposed, it must work its way up through the organizational hierarchy. Each step is complex, for if there are three ways of doing something, then there are sure to be strong proponents of each of the three ways, plus people who will argue that it is too early to standardize. Each proposal is debated at the meeting where it is presented, then taken back to the sponsoring organization—which is sometimes a company, sometimes a professional society—where objections and counterobjections are collected. Then the standards committee meets again to discuss the objections. And again and again and again. Any company that is already marketing a product that meets the proposed standard will have a huge economic advantage, and the debates are therefore often affected by the economics and politics of the issues as much as by real technological substance. The process is almost guaranteed to take five years, and quite often longer.

The resulting standard is usually a compromise among the various competing positions, oftentimes an inferior compromise. Sometimes the answer is to agree on several incompatible standards. Witness the existence of both metric and English units; of left-hand and right-hand drive automobiles; of three different kinds of color television, all incompatible. There are several international standards for the voltages and frequency of electricity and several different kinds of electrical plugs and sockets—which cannot be interchanged.

Actually, my description of how standards are achieved is more hope than reality. One of my colleagues, Jonathan Grudin, who has worked on national and international standards for the design of computer work stations, commented on my paragraphs this way:

> You said standards development "must work its way up through the organizational hierarchy" but in fact with the international standard increasingly the goal, it is a vastly more iterative procedure, at least in the ANSI-ISO arena [ANSI is American National Standards Institute: the standards are labeled things like ANSC X3V1, where the I for Institute is replaced with a C for Committee. ISO is International Standards Organization]. What happens is that someone draws up a proposal or parts of one, and it is quickly hashed up a bit at the national meeting then carried to the next international meeting. There it gets hashed up a lot more, often rewritten or extended, and brought back to all of the national meetings. They chew it over, and at the next international meeting it typically gets a real working over, this being the first input from various national working groups. Then it goes back to the national groups again, who really sink their teeth in it, the original sponsor moaning with pain at what they've done to its song, often. Then this process goes through many more iterations; in the case of a major standard, it could go through a dozen or more over several years.
>
> A compromise among existing approaches is generally not the *result* of the standards process, but an initial aim of the developers. Your tactful phrasing makes the process sound slightly more scientific and less political than it is, though I don't object to it. On the other hand, the standards developers are surely always utterly convinced that they are producing a compromise that is *superior,* not inferior, to any of the contributions to it, and they are well aware of the camel-is-a-horse-designed-by-committee problem. I have not studied enough cases to know that they are wrong. I would have guessed that they might often be right.

4. One reason the Apple Macintosh computer is such a usable machine is because Apple enforced a set of standard procedures for all the people who wrote programs for the Macintosh. The procedures governed the look and style of the interface, most especially the way that information could be

modified, the way the menus were used, the way information was displayed, the heavy use of the mouse, the ability to "undo" the just-previous action if the user wished to, and the format for working with text, working with windows, displaying choices, getting at files, and telling about errors. The result is that once the basic principles are learned, they carry over to most of the programs available for the system. Now if we could enlarge a similar spirit of standardization to the machines of all manufacturers, all over the world, we would have a major breakthrough in usability.

5. A computer mail question sent to me by a student, Dina Kurktchi. It is just the right question.

6. The company was FTL Games. The students were Dennis Walker, Rod Hartley, Steve Parker, and Joey Garon. An earlier study on games was performed by Tom Malone (1981), who examined how to develop educational programs that would be both interesting to students and of educational value.

7. These studies were carried out by Henry Strub at the University of California, San Diego.

8. P. Ceruzzi (1986), An unforeseen revolution: Computers and expectations, 1935–1985.

9. Hypertext can't be defined; it has to be experienced. I will attempt to convey what it would be like. This note is a kind of hypertext, for it is a commentary on the text itself. That is what the "hyper" of the name means: a higher-level text that comments on and expands the main text, allowing the reader freedom to explore or ignore the material as interests dictate.

Hypertext requires a computer with high-resolution display, good graphics, a pointing device, and a tremendous amount of memory. It is only today that technology is starting to make such systems affordable. At the time of this writing, only a few hypertext systems are available, but a lot have been talked about. In fact, as I travel from research laboratory to research laboratory across the country, everyone seems to be talking about doing a hypertext system. But there is a big difference between talking about doing something and actually doing it.

Hypertext was invented by Ted Nelson, although the basic idea can probably be traced to Vannevar Bush's prophetic *Atlantic Monthly* article "As we may think" (1945). Nelson's books are pretty good examples of how close one can come to hypertext without the use of a computer. The books are fun and insightful (see, for example, Nelson, 1981).

10. Some of you already know all about hypertext and wish I would get on with it; you might simply want to see whether I am for or against it. Others of you have never heard of the concept and need even more description than I am able to provide. How are we going to manage to satisfy all of you? Viva hypertext! (At this point I need a footnote to this

note, but that isn't allowed, my publisher tells me. So, into contrasting text.)

I am not going to tell you whether I am for or against it. Actually, that is because I am both. It is a really exciting concept. But I don't believe it can work for most material. For an encyclopaedia, yes; or a dictionary; or an instruction manual. But not for a text, or a novel. Imagine a mystery novel in hypertext. Hmm, it might be very interesting.

11. But what a pain these notes are. If positioned at the bottom of the page, they distract. If at the end of the text, as in this book, they are awkward to use. How much nicer if one could just touch the footnoted word and have it instantly expand into a note—on the side of the page, of course, where it wouldn't get in the way. Ah yes, hypertext.

12. D. Bulkeley (1987), The 'smartest house in America,' *Design News, 43,* 56–61.

13. The small compact disk now used for audio recordings is capable of holding $\frac{1}{2}$ gigabyte of information, where a gigabyte is the technical term for one billion characters (10^9). This number is sure to increase in the coming years, and larger size disks already hold considerably more information.

14. An excellent treatment of how design affects and is affected by society is given in Adrian Forty's *Objects of desire* (1986). The full assessment of the emptiness of the architectural revolution is provided most effectively by Tom Wolfe (1981), in his *From Bauhaus to our house,* and in a more scholarly way by Peter Blake (1977) in *Form follows fiasco: Why modern architecture hasn't worked.*

SUGGESTED
READINGS

Throughout the course of my research on design I have come across a number of relevant works. In this section I comment on the ones I have found most valuable, especially for those readers who wish to continue their investigations of the psychology of everyday things and the design process. I concentrate primarily on design, and especially on works that I feel did not receive sufficient acknowledgment within the chapters of POET. This list is not exhaustive but rather includes the books that I have found most helpful and that I recommend most strongly to others.

Everyday Things

Here are two fascinating books, which deal not with design but rather with the structures of everyday life—structures that, to a large extent, determine why things are designed. One book, Braudel's (1981) *The structures of everyday life,* talks about the development of civilization and capitalism in the fifteenth through eighteenth centuries and outlines the impact on ordinary people of rapid developments in agriculture, eating habits, clothing, housing, and fashion, as well as the general spread of technological developments in energy, metallurgy, and transport. (This is volume one of a three-volume series, *Civilization and capital-*

ism. Highly recommended as a masterful treatment, for those who are interested in such things.) The other book, Panati's (1987) *Extraordinary origins of everyday things,* discusses the origins of many of our popular objects, habits, and customs. Panati includes excellent sections of references and suggested readings. Braudel's book is a scholarly (but well written), systematic, cohesive treatment of the rise of modern civilization by a noted French historian. Panati's book is a popular treatment consisting of hundreds of unrelated, short essays, each treating a different topic, including the development of tableware, table manners, toilets, and everyday superstitions and customs.

Architectural Design

Architecture plays a major role in design, in part because its many schools provide a natural home for the study of design, in part because architects so deliberately use the construction of homes and buildings as design statements. The Bauhaus in Germany was probably the origin of the modern extremes, but the emphasis started long before then. The most engaging discussion of the excesses of modern architecture is that of Tom Wolfe (1981), *From Bauhaus to our house.* Blake's (1977) *Form follows fiasco: Why modern architecture hasn't worked,* is a bit more scholarly, but especially readable. There is, of course, a huge literature on architecture and it is not kind simply to cite two critiques. Nonetheless, that is what I shall do, especially as mine is not a book about architecture. The other architects whose work has influenced me are not builders; they are thinkers and designers, in particular, Alexander and his colleagues at the University of California, Berkeley (see Alexander, 1964, 1979; Alexander, Ishikawa, & Silverstein, 1977.)

Industrial Design

The classic books on industrial design are Dreyfuss's *Designing for people* (1951) and Loewy's *Never leave well enough alone* (1951), although I cannot state that they had much impact on me. Much more important books were Caplan (1982), *By design: Why there are no locks on the bathroom doors in Hotel Louis XIV and other object lessons;* Lynch (1960), *The image of the city;* and Lynch (1972), *What time is this place?*

Several good histories of design exist. I have found Forty's (1986) *Objects of desire: Design and society from Wedgewood to IBM* especially useful. Rybczynski's (1986) *Home: A short history of an idea* provides an excellent and engaging summary of the design of homes and furnishings. If you thought that comfort might be relevant to the design of furniture, you are naive; read Rybczynski's book and be informed. Comfort, like usability, won't be a design factor unless and until the purchasers demand it.

In the text I comment on the usefulness of Jones's several books on design philosophy and methods, especially the problem of going from original specification to realization (Jones, 1970, 1981, 1984).

Papanek has been a major critic of modern industrial design, especially scornful of the emphasis on frivolous excesses that make products expensive, ill-conceived, and ill-operating. His own designs emphasize low cost, durability, and ease of construction (especially for third-world economies), all useful and important attributes, but not necessarily relevant to the usability of the designs (see Papanek, 1971, and Papanek & Hennessey, 1977). Illich's cogent arguments for "convivial tools" help define the philosophy aimed for in POET (see his book *Tools for conviviality* [1973]).

A good way to find out what the design world cares about is to read the magazines of industrial design. In the United States, this is *ID,* a "magazine of International Design."* It's a fascinating magazine with clever innovative design. But I detect little interest in making designs usable, functional, or understandable. The professionals read *Innovation,* the journal of the Industrial Designers Society of America.

General Issues in Design

Petroski's (1985) *To engineer is human: The role of failure in successful design* provides an excellent analysis of the role of failures in the advancement of industrial and civil design, showing how, for example, each collapse of a bridge advances the design profession (but only if detailed study of the reasons for the collapse is made and the lessons propagated to the other designers); it's a truly excellent book. Perrow (1984) has written an extremely important book, *Normal accidents,* in which he looks at the structure of large systems (things such as oil drilling platforms, nuclear power plants, and ocean-going ships) and demonstrates that the combination of complexity and "tight-coupling" makes such systems highly susceptible to catastrophic failure. This book is essential

*Design Publications, Inc., 330 W. 42 St., New York, NY 10036.

reading for everyone involved in the design and operation of large-scale plants and systems.

It should come as no surprise to learn that I think that three excellent essays on the role model provided by architecture as well as the importance of social factors can be found in the chapters by Bannon, Brown, and Hooper in my *User centered system design*. An excellent treatment of the social aspects of design is provided by Sommer (1983) in his *Social design: Creating buildings with people in mind* (which I quote from extensively in chapter 6).

My work has been heavily influenced by Simon, especially by his ideas developed in *The sciences of the artificial* (1981), which, among other things, pointed out that much of the complexity of our behavior reflects the complexity of the world, not of our thought processes. In part I am complementing that argument, arguing that through design the world can be made simpler. A second, related idea was Simon's introduction of the concept of "satisficing," for which he argued that we do not necessarily examine all the alternatives available to us and choose the optimum, but rather we tend to minimize mental effort and take the first one that seems satisfactory.

Computers, of course, play an ever increasing role in modern design, both as tools for the design process and as the object of design. Smith, Irby, Kimball, Verplank, & Harslem (1982) present an excellent description of the design of a computer system (the Xerox Star) that heavily emphasized usability and understandability: this is recommended reading for people interested in computer systems. (The Star was not a commercial success, but later versions have been more successful; the design principles and philosophies were taken over by the Apple Computer Corporation and have accounted for the success of the Macintosh.) Ted Nelson (1981) presents an engaging description of the possible future of machines in his *Literary machines* (and other volumes). Illuminating discussions of the importance of the social context in which tools are used are provided in two new, important studies: Winograd and Flores (1986), *Understanding computers and cognition: A new foundation for design;* and Suchman's (1987) *Plans and situated actions: The problem of human-machine communication.*

REFERENCES

Alexander, C. (1964). *Notes on the synthesis of form.* Cambridge, MA: Harvard University Press.

Alexander, C. (1979). *The timeless way of building.* New York: Oxford University Press.

Alexander, C., Ishikawa, S., & Silverstein, M. (1977). *A pattern language: Towns, buildings, construction.* New York: Oxford University Press.

Alexander, G. J., & Lunenfeld, H. (1984). A users' guide to positive guidance in highway control. In R. Easterby & H. Zwaga (Eds.), *Information design: The design and evaluation of signs and printed material.* Chichester, England: Wiley.

Baeker, R., & Buxton, W. (1987). *Readings in human-computer interaction.* Los Altos, CA: Morgan Kaufmann.

Bannon, L. J. (1986). Issues in design. In D. A. Norman & S. W. Draper (Eds.), *User centered system design: New perspectives on human-computer interaction.* Hillsdale, NJ: Erlbaum Associates.

Beeching, W. A. (1974). *Century of the typewriter.* New York: St. Martin's Press.

Biederman, I. (1987). Recognition-by-components: A theory of human image understanding. *Psychological Review, 94,* 115–147.

Blake, P. (1977). *Form follows fiasco: Why modern architecture hasn't worked.* Boston: Little, Brown.

Braudel, F. (1981). *Civilization and capitalism: 15th–18th century: Vol. 1. The structures of everyday life.* London: William Collins Sons. New York: Harper & Row. Paperback edition, London: Fontana Paperbacks.

Brown, J. S. (1986). From cognitive to social ergonomics and beyond. In D. A. Norman & S. W. Draper (Eds.), *User centered system design: New perspectives on human-computer interaction.* Hillsdale, NJ: Erlbaum Associates.

Bulkeley, D. (1987, October 19). The 'smartest house in America.' *Design News,* pp. 56–61.

Bush, V. (1945, July). As we may think. *Atlantic Monthly,* pp. 101–108.

Caplan, R. (1982). *By design: Why there are no locks on the bathroom doors in Hotel Louis XIV and other object lessons.* New York: St. Martin's Press. Paperback edition, McGraw-Hill (1984).

Card, S., Moran, T., & Newell, A. (1983). *The Psychology of human-computer interaction.* Hillsdale, NJ: Erlbaum Associates.

Carelman, J. (1984). *Catalog d' Objets Introuvables.* Paris: André Balland. (First published in 1969.)

Ceruzzi, P. (1986.) An unforeseen revolution: Computers and expectations, 1935–1985. In J. P. Corn (Ed.), *Imagining tomorrow: History, technology, and the American future.* Cambridge, MA: MIT Press.

Chase, W., & Simon, H. A. (1973). Perception in chess. *Cognitive Psychology, 4,* 55–81.

Cooper, J. K. (Ed.). (1983). *Cognitive aspects of skilled typewriting.* New York: Springer-Verlag.

Cypher, A. (1986). The structure of users' activities. In D. A. Norman & S. W. Draper (Eds.), *User centered system design: New perspectives on human-computer interaction.* Hillsdale, NJ: Erlbaum Associates.

Dreyfuss, H. (1951). *Designing for people.* New York: Simon & Schuster.

Dutch Aircraft Accident Inquiry Board. (1979). *Verdict of aircraft accident inquiry board regarding the accident at Los Rodeos Airport, Tenerife (Spain).* The Hague.

Fischhoff, B. (1975). Hindsight ≠ foresight: The effect of outcome knowledge on judgment under uncertainty. *Journal of Experimental Psychology: Human Perception and Performance, 1,* 288–299.

Fischhoff, B., Lichtenstein, S., Slovic, P., Derby, S., & Keeney, R. (Eds.). (1981). *Acceptable risk.* New York: Cambridge University Press.

Fisher, D., & Bragonier, R., Jr. (1981). *What's what: A visual glossary of the physical world.* Maplewood, NJ: Hammond.

Forty, A. (1986). *Objects of desire: Design and society from Wedgewood to IBM.* New York: Pantheon Books.

Gaver, W. W. 1986. Auditory icons: Using sound in computer interfaces. *Human Computer Interaction, 2,* 167–177.

Gaver, W. W. (in press). Listening to computers. Paper presented at the ACM SIGCHI Workshop on Mixed Modes of Interaction, Dec. 15–17, 1986, Key West, Florida. To be published in a book of collected papers from that conference.

Gentner, D., & Stevens, A. (1983). *Mental models.* Hillsdale, NJ: Erlbaum Associates.

Gibson, J. J. (1977). The theory of affordances. In R. E. Shaw & J. Bransford (Eds.), *Perceiving, acting, and knowing.* Hillsdale, NJ: Erlbaum Associates.

Gibson, J. J. (1979). *The ecological approach to visual perception.* Boston: Houghton Mifflin.

Goffman, E. (1974). *Frame analysis.* New York: Harper & Row.

Gopher, D., Karis, D., & Koenig, W. (1985). The representation of movement schemas in long-term memory: Lessons from the acquisition of a transcription skill. *Acta Psychologica, 60,* 105–134.

Gopher, D., & Raij, D. (in press). Typing with a two hand chord keyboard: Will the QWERTY become obsolete? *IEEE Transactions on Systems, Man, and Cybernetics.*

Gould, J. D., Boies, S. J., Levy, S., Richards, J. T., & Schoonard, J. (1987). The 1984 Olympic message system: A test of behavioral principles of system design. *Communications of the ACM, 30,* 758–769.

Hersh, S. M. (1986). *The target is destroyed.* New York: Random House.

Hooper, K. (1986). Architectural design: An analogy. In D. A. Norman & S. W. Draper (Eds.), *User centered system design: New perspectives on human-computer interaction.* Hillsdale, NJ: Erlbaum Associates.

Hurst, R. (Ed.). (1976). *Pilot error: A professional study of contributory factors.* London: Granada.

Hurst, R., & Hurst, L. (Eds.). (1982). *Pilot error: The human factors.* London: Granada. (Also New York: Jason Aronson.)

Hutchins, E., Hollan, J. D., & Norman, D. A. (1986). Direct manipulation interfaces. In D. A. Norman & S. W. Draper (Eds.), *User centered system design: New perspectives on human-computer interaction.* Hillsdale, NJ: Erlbaum Associates.

Illich, I. (1973). *Tools for conviviality.* New York: Harper & Row.

Johnson-Laird, P. N. (1983). *Mental models.* Cambridge, MA: Harvard University Press. (Also Cambridge, England: Cambridge University Press.)

Jones, J. C. (1970). *Design methods: Seeds of human futures.* New York: Wiley.

Jones, J. C. (1981). *Design methods: Seeds of human futures* (1980 ed., with a review of new topics). New York: Wiley.

Jones, J. C. (1984). *Essays in design.* New York: Wiley.

Kahneman, D., & Miller, D. T. (1986). Norm theory: Comparing reality to its alternatives. *Psychological Review, 93,* 136–153.

Kempton, W. (1986). Two theories of home heat control. *Cognitive Science,* *10,* 75–90.

Kinner, J. (1984). The practical and graphic problem of road sign design. In R. Easterby & H. Zwaga (Eds.), *Information design: The design and evaluation of signs and printed material.* Chichester, England: Wiley.

Landauer, T. K. (1986). How much do people remember? Some estimates of the quantity of learned information in long-term memory. *Cognitive Science, 10,* 477–493.

Laurel, B. (1986). Interface as mimesis. In D. A. Norman & S. W. Draper (Eds.), *User centered system design: New perspectives on human-computer interaction.* Hillsdale, NJ: Erlbaum Associates.

Lewis, C., & Norman, D. A. (1986). Designing for error. In D. A. Norman & S. W. Draper (Eds.), *User centered system design: New perspectives on human-computer interaction.* Hillsdale, NJ: Erlbaum Associates.

Lindsay, P. H., & Norman, D. A. (1977). *Human information processing* (2nd ed.). New York: Academic Press. (Now San Diego: Harcourt Brace Jovanovich.)

Loewy, R. (1950). *Never leave well enough alone.* New York: Simon & Schuster.

Lord, A. B. (1960). *The singer of tales.* Cambridge, MA: Harvard University Press.

Lynch, K. (1960). *The image of the city.* Cambridge, MA: MIT Press.

Lynch, K. (1972). *What time is this place?* Cambridge, MA: MIT Press.

Malone, T. (1981). Toward a theory of intrinsically motivating instruction. *Cognitive Science, 4,* 333–369.

Malone, T. W. (1983). How do people organize their desks: Implications for designing office automation systems. *ACM Transactions on Office Automation Systems, 1,* 99–112.

Mares, G. C. (1909). *The history of the typewriter, successor to the pen: An illustrated account of the origin, rise, and development of the writing machine.* London: Guilbert Putnam. Reprinted by Post-era Books, Arcadia, CA, 1985.

Mayall, W. H. (1979). *Principles in design.* London: Design Council.

McClelland, J. L., Rumelhart, D. E., & the PDP Research Group. (1986). *Parallel distributed processing: Explorations in the microstructure of cognition. Vol. 2: Psychological and biological models.* Cambridge, MA: MIT Press.

McCloskey, M. (1983). Intuitive physics. *Scientific American, 248*(4), 122–130.

Miller, G. A., Galanter, E., & Pribram, K. (1960). *Plans and the structure of behavior.* New York: Holt, Rinehart & Winston.

Miyake, N. (1986). Constructive interaction. *Cognitive Science, 10,* 151–177.

Miyata, Y., & Norman, D. A. (1986). Psychological issues in support of multiple activities. In D. A. Norman & S. W. Draper (Eds.), *User centered system design: New perspectives on human-computer interaction.* Hillsdale, NJ: Erlbaum Associates.

National Transportation Safety Board. (1982). *Aircraft accident report: Air Florida, Inc., Boeing 737-222, N62AF collision with 14th Street bridge, near Washington National Airport, Washington, D.C., January 13, 1982.* (Report No. NTSB/AAR-82-8). Washington, D.C.: National Transportation Safety Board, Bureau of Accident Investigation.

National Transportation Safety Board. (1984). *Aircraft accident report: Eastern Air Lines, Inc., Lockheed L-1011, N334EA, Miami International Airport, Miami, Florida, May 5, 1983.* (Report No. NTSB/AAR-84-04.) Washington, D.C.: National Transportation Safety Board, Bureau of Accident Investigation.

Nelson, T. (1981). *Literary machines.* South Bend, IN: The Distributers (702 South Michigan St., South Bend, IN 46618, [219] 232–8500).

Nickerson, R. S., & Adams, M. J. (1979). Long-term memory for a common object. *Cognitive Psychology, 11,* 287–307.

Norman, D. A. (1980, April). Post-Freudian slips. *Psychology Today.*

Norman, D. A. (1981). Categorization of action slips. *Psychological Review, 88,* 1–15.

Norman, D. A. (1982). *Learning and memory.* San Francisco: W. H. Freeman.

Norman, D. A. (1983). Design rules based on analyses of human error. *Communications of the ACM, 4,* 254–258.

Norman, D. A. (1986). Cognitive engineering. In D. A. Norman & S. W. Draper (Eds.), *User centered system design: New perspectives on human-computer interaction.* Hillsdale, NJ: Erlbaum Associates.

Norman, D. A., & Bobrow, D. G. (1979). Descriptions: An intermediate stage in memory retrieval. *Cognitive Psychology, 11,* 107–123.

Norman, D. A., & Draper, S. W. (Eds.). (1986). *User centered system design: New perspectives on human-computer interaction.* Hillsdale, NJ: Erlbaum Associates.

Norman, D. A., & Fisher, D. (1982). Why alphabetic keyboards are not easy to use: Keyboard layout doesn't much matter. *Human Factors, 24,* 509–519.

Norman, D. A., & Lewis, C. (1986). Designing for error. In D. A. Norman & S. W. Draper (Eds.), *User centered system design: New perspectives on human-computer interaction.* Hillsdale, NJ: Erlbaum Associates.

Panati, C. (1987). *Extraordinary origins of everyday things.* New York: Harper & Row.

Papanek, V. (1971). *Design for the real world.* London: Thames & Hudson. (In 1985 there was a 2nd ed., "completely revised with 121 illustrations.")

Papanek, V., & Hennessey, J. (1977). *How things don't work.* New York: Pantheon Books.

Perrow, C. (1984). *Normal accidents.* New York: Basic Books.

Petroski, Henry. (1985). *To engineer is human: The role of failure in successful design.* New York: St. Martin's Press.

Reason, J. T. (1979). Actions not as planned. In G. Underwood & R. Stevens (Eds.), *Aspects of consciousness.* London: Academic Press.

Reason, J. T., & Mycieslka, K. (1982). *Absent minded? The psychology of mental lapses and everyday errors.* Englewood Cliffs, NJ: Prentice-Hall.

Roitsch, P. A., Babcock, G. L., & Edmunds W. W. (Undated). *Human factors report on the Tenerife accident.* Washington, D.C.: Air Line Pilots Association.

Rouse, W. B., & Morris, N. M. (1986). On looking into the black box: Prospects and limits in the search for mental models. *Psychological Bulletin, 100,* 349–363.

Rubin, D. C., & Kontis, T. C. (1983). A schema for common cents. *Memory and Cognition, 11,* 333–341.

Rubin, D. C., & Wallace, W. T. (1987). *Rhyme and reason: Integral properties of words.* Unpublished manuscript.

Rumelhart, D. E., McClelland, J. L., & the PDP Research Group. (1986). *Parallel distributed processing: Explorations in the microstructure of cognition. Vol. 1: Foundations.* Cambridge, MA: MIT Press.

Rybczynski, W. (1986). *Home: A short history of an idea.* New York: Viking.

Sanders, A. F. (1980). Stage analysis of reaction processes. In G. E. Stelmach & J. Requin (Eds.), *Tutorials in motor behavior.* Amsterdam: North-Holland.

Schank, R. C. (1982). *Dynamic memory.* New York: Cambridge University Press.

Schank, R. C., & Abelson, R. P. (1977). *Scripts, plans, goals, and understanding.* Hillsdale, NJ: Erlbaum Associates.

Seligman, M. E. P. (1975). *Helplessness: On depression, development, and death.* San Francisco: W. H. Freeman.

Seminara, J. L., Gonzales, W. R., & Parsons, S. O. (1977, March). *Human factors review of nuclear power plant control room design* (Technical report EPRI NP-309 [Research project 501]). Prepared by Lockheed Missiles & Space Co., Inc. (Sunnyvale, CA) for the Electric Power Research Institute (Palo Alto, CA).

Shneiderman, B. (1974, February). A computer graphics system for polynomials. *The Mathematics Teacher,* pp. 111–113.

Shneiderman, B. (1983). Direct manipulation: A step beyond programming languages. *IEEE Computer, 16*(8), 57–69.

Shneiderman, B. (1987). *Designing the user interface: Strategies for effective human-computer interaction.* Reading, MA: Addison-Wesley.

Simon, H. A. (1981). *The sciences of the artificial* (2nd ed.). Cambridge, MA: MIT Press.

Smith, D. C., Irby, C., Kimball, R., Verplank, W., & Harslem, E. (1982). Designing the Star user interface. *Byte, 7*(4), 242–282.

Sommer, R. (1983). *Social design: Creating buildings with people in mind.* Englewood Cliffs, NJ: Prentice-Hall.

Spanish Ministry of Transport and Communications. (1978). *Report of collision between PAA B-747 and KLM B-7747 at Tenerife, March 27, 1977.* Translation published in *Aviation Week and Space Technology,* November 20 and 27, 1978.

Suchman, L. (1987). *Plans and situated actions: The problem of human-machine communication.* New York: Cambridge University Press.

Turkle, S. (1984). *The second self: Computers and the human spirit.* New York: Simon & Schuster.

Tversky, A., & Kahneman, D. (1973). Availability: A heuristic for judging frequency and probability. *Cognitive Psychology, 4,* 207–232. Reprinted in K. Kahneman, P. Slovic, & A. Tversky (Eds.). (1982). *Judgment under uncertainty: Heuristics and biases.* Cambridge, England: Cambridge University Press.

Weiner, E. L. (1980). Mid-air collisions: The accidents, the systems and the realpolitik. *Human Factors, 22,* 521–533. Reprinted in R. Hurst & L. R. Hurst (Eds.). (1982). *Pilot error: The human factor.* New York: Jason Aronson.

Weiner, E. L. (1986). Fallible humans and vulnerable systems: Lessons learned from aviation. Unpublished manuscript. (To be published in *Information Systems: Failure Analysis.* Proceedings of a NATO Advanced Research Workshop on Failure Analysis of Information Systems.)

Weiner, E. L., & Curry, R. E. (1980). Flight-deck automation: Promises and problems. *Ergonomics, 23,* 995–1011. Reprinted in R. Hurst & L. R. Hurst (Eds.). (1982). *Pilot error: The human factor.* New York: Jason Aronson.

White, B. Y., & Horwitz, P. (1987). *ThinkerTools: Enabling children to understand physical laws* (Report No. 6470). Cambridge, MA: BBN Laboratories.

Winograd, E., & Soloway, R. M. (1986). On forgetting the locations of things stored in special places. *Journal of Experimental Psychology: General, 115,* 366–372.

Winograd, T., & Flores, F. (1986). *Understanding computers and cognition: A new foundation for design.* Norwood, NJ: Ablex.

Wolfe, T. (1981). *From Bauhaus to our house.* New York: Washington Square Press (Pocket Books).

INDEX

Controls: ease of use and number of, 175, 208–9; making to look and feel different, 95; placement of, 22–23
Cooper, J. K., 150, 230
Copying machines, 157
Cultural: constraints, 55, 62, 202; standards, natural mappings and, 23
Curry, R. E., 197, 232
Cypher, A., 224

Decision tree: deep and narrow, 123; wide and deep, 120; wide and shallow, 122
Deep structures, 119–25
Default value, 116
Depression, 42
Derby, S., 128, 227
Descriptions, as aid in discriminating between objects, 60
Design: aesthetics as priority in, 151–55; car radio, 94; deliberately difficult, 202, 205–7; of doors, 2, 11; of Dungeons and Dragons game, 207–8; for error, 131–38, 197, 228–29; evolutionary, forces working against, 142–45; false causality and, 11; faucet as case history, 166–72; forcing functions, 132–38; lessons from the study of slips, 112–14; of light switches, 96; mappings and, 5; model, 16, 189–90; of multiple function clock radio, 31–33; natural, 4, 141–43; of objects for special people, 161–64; poor, 2, 5–6, 94, 96; principles for understandability and usability, 13–33; problems, posed by safety systems, 207; process, complexity of, 158–61; seven stages of action 53; society and, 209–10; subtle-

ties, 144; of telephone, 18–21; of thermostat, 39; tradeoffs, 195; typewriter as case history, 145–51; user-centered, 140, 188–217; user frustration and, 79; why designers go astray, 151–58; see also Designers
Designers: clients may not be users, 157–58; creeping featurism, 172–74; two deadly temptations, 172–77; are not typical users, 155–57; worship of false images, 172–77; see also Design
Dimensions, additive and substitutive, 23
Direct manipulation, 184–85
Display: auditory, 27; importance of, 101–2
Door(s): affordances and, 10, 87–88, 91; constraints and, 87–88, 91; deliberately difficult, 202; interlocks and, 135
Draper, S. W., 70, 139, 180, 223–24, 229, 231
Dreyfuss, H., 238

Edmunds, W. W., 130, 227
Engelbart, D., 180, 231
Ergonomics, 78, 1–217
Error(s): associative activation, 107–9; capture, 107–8; categories of, 105, 109; causes of, 131; correction of, 112, 131; data-driven, 107–9; description, 107–9; designing for, 36, 131–38, 200, 220; explaining away, 127–29; feedback on, 191; loss-of-activation, 107–10, mistakes, 105–6, 114; mode, 110, 113; slips, 105–114; social pressure and, 129–31
Execution: of action, 13, 46, 48, 208–9; gulf of, 50–51, 99–100,

structure, 17; understanding and, 70; of the world, 47–50

Irby, C., 182, 231, 240

Ishikawa, S., 141, 229, 238

James, W., 108

Johnson, H. F., 151

Johnson-Laird, P. N., 70, 223

Jones, J. C., 141, 229, 239

Kahneman, D., 119, 226

Karis, D., 150, 230

Kay, A., 180, 231

Keeney, R., 128, 227

Kempton, W., 39, 220

Keyboard, 145–51, 161–62

Kimball, R., 182, 231, 240

King, M., 21, 155, 219, 230

Kinner, J., 123, 226

Knowledge: declarative, 57; external, 72; faulty nature of, 54; in the head and in the world, 54–80, 187; imprecision of, 54–56; inaccessible to conscious inspection, 117; internal, 67; procedural, 57–58; transfer of from old to new object, 82; of what to do, 81–104

Koenig, W., 150, 230

Kontis, T. C., 54, 221

Kurktchi, D., 204, 234

Landauer, T. K., 66, 223

Lane, E. W., 63, 222

Laurel, B., 181, 231–32

Learning: accuracy of, 55; of arbitrary codes, 68; assimilation of everyday objects and, 12; of digital watch, 31; of poetry, 60–61; rote, 68; simplification through

mental models, 70; telephone systems, 27

Levy, S., 28, 220

Lewis, C., 140, 229

Lichtenstein, S., 128, 227

Lockins, 135

Lockouts, 135–37

Loewy, R., 238

Long-term memory, 67, 189

Lord, A. B., 61, 222

Loudspeakers, natural mappings and, 25–26

Lunenfeld, H., 124, 226

Lynch, K., 196, 232, 238

MacLean, J., 127, 227

Malone, T. W., 58, 208, 221, 234

Manuals, role of, 156, 190–91

Mapping(s): arbitrary, 22, 216; buses and, 25; cars and, 25; computers and, 179; definition of, 5, 23, 75–77; faucets and, 166; intentions of actions and, 5, 9; natural, 23, 25–26, 75–78, 188, 198–99; principle of, 23, 26–27; relation of to visibility, 8; seven stages of action and, 53; telephones and, 22–24; unnatural, design and, 207; user-centered design and, 199; visibility and, 12, 25

Mares, G. C., 140, 144, 229

Materials, psychology of, 9

Math anxiety, 42–43

Mayall, W. H., 9, 219

McClelland, J. L., 116, 226

McCloskey, M., 38, 220

McGurrin, F., 147

Meisler, S., 59, 221

Memory: for arbitrary things, 67; associative nature of, 116; capacity, 67; computer, 180; conspiracy against, 63–66; critical,

Memory *(continued)*
72; decisions based upon, 115; through explanation, 67, 70–72; faulty nature of, 54; frame theory of, 115–16; improvement, 65; as knowledge in the head, 62–66; as knowledge in the world, 72–74; load, reduction of, 193; long-term, 66–67, 191; as maintenance of experiences, 66–67; for meaningful relationships, 67, 68–70; multiple exposure theory of, 118; overgeneralization and, 115; overloading of, 63–66; propositional encoding theory of, 115; retrieval, 67; schema theory of, 115–16; semantic networks theory of, 115; short-term, 66–67, 126–27, 191; thought and, 115

Mental model: definition of, 17; design model as, 189–90; to explain the observable, 39; power of, 69–72; system image, 189–90; taught helplessness and, 42–43; user's model as, 189–90

Miller, D. T., 226
Miller, G. A., 48, 119, 221
Miller, J., 185, 232
Miller, J. G., 219
Miyata, Y., 224
Mnemonics, 65
Modularization, 172
Moran, T., 180, 221, 231
Morris, N. M., 59, 223
Motorcycle(s): Lego, 82–84, 86, 200; memory for meaningful relationships and, 69–70
Multiple exposure theory, 118
Mycielska, K., 107, 225

Naive psychology, 154; naive physics and, 36–38
Narrow structures, 121–24

National Transportation Safety Board, 44
Nelson, T., 212, 234, 240
Newell, A., 178, 221, 231
Newton, I., 36
Nickerson, R. S., 54, 221
Norm theory, 119, 226
Norman, D. A., 51, 60, 65, 69–70, 80, 107, 116, 139, 147, 180, 185, 221–35

Odyssey (Homer), 61
Off the leash (cartoon), 187
Olsen, K., 1
Oral tradition, rhyming constraints and, 60–61
Outline processors, 211
Oven(s): 214; mental model of, 38–39; microwave, 1, 103, 135

Panati, C., 238
Papanek, V., 239
Paradox, of technology, 29–33
Parallel distributed processing, 116
Park, W. B., 187
Parker, S., 208, 234
Patterson, R., 132, 228
Perception: direct, 52; principles of, 23; of the world, 47–48
Perrow, C., 35, 220, 227, 239
Petroski, H., 239
Pew, R. W., 158, 231
Physics, naive, 36–38
Poetry, rhyming constraints and, 60–61
Postal codes, memory overload and, 63
Pribram, K., 48, 221
Prizes, 151–54, 169, 183, 217
Projector(s): gulf of execution and, 51; Leitz, 5; seven stages of action

and, 181; creating, 17–18, 22–23; design aesthetics and, 100; design and, 4, 6–7; feedback and, 99–100; gulf of evaluation and, 197–98; gulf of execution and, 197–98; technology and, 190–91; telephones and, 6, 7, 17–22; use of sound for, 102–4